Critics and Readers Re

DARK TO MORTAL EYES (2004)
"Wilson nimbly sprinkles clue throughout . . . A fresh voice"
Publishers Weekly

EXPIRATION DATE (2005)
"Intelligent and ambitious . . . as thought-provoking as it is riveting"
Alafair Burke, bestselling author of *Long Gone* and *If You Were Here*

THE BEST OF EVIL (2006)
"His writing sizzles; his characters grab you and won't let go"
Robert Liparulo, bestselling author of *Deadfall* and *The Judgment Stone*

A SHRED OF TRUTH (2007)
"A page-turner, with contemporary, likable characters"
Library Journal

FIREPROOF (2008)
"Eric has a knack for capturing what's on screen and making it richer"
Deena Peterson, at *TitleTrakk*

JERUSALEM'S UNDEAD TRILOGY (2008-2010)
"I continually admire . . . his unique ability to make a character truly come off the page"
James Byron Huggins, author of *The Reckoning, Cain,* and *Rora*

ONE STEP AWAY (2011)
"Intense themes, profound insight into the human condition"
Michelle Sutton, author of *Decision to Love*

TWO SECONDS LATE (2012)
"A multilayered story and an insightful exploration into human nature"
Steven James, author of *The King* and *Story Trumps Structure*

OCTOBER BABY (2012)
"A great story full of quirky characters"
J.S. Bailey, author of *Rage's Echo* and *Vapors*

TAMING THE BEAST

THE UNTOLD STORY OF MIKE TYSON

Mike Tyson was the beast.
Rory Holloway was his handler.
Their lives in the spotlight were a zoo.

Rory Holloway

with

Eric Wilson

Printed by: Rough House LLC, 4300 Jog Road, #540966, Greenacres, FL 33454
Distributed by: Bookmasters, 30 Amberwood Pkwy., Ashland, OH 44805

For permission requests, please contact:
Rough House LLC, Attention: Permissions Coordinator, 4300 Jog Road, #540966, Greenacres, FL 33454   or   info@ttbbook.com

For ordering information or bulk purchases, please contact:
Bookmasters, Attention: Sales Office, 30 Amberwood Parkway, Ashland, OH 44805; (800) 537-6727
Sales Office Hours: Monday-Friday, 8:00 a.m.-5:00 p.m. EST

Softcover ISBN-13: 978-1503025707
        ISBN-10: 1503025705

Holloway, Rory, 1962/Wilson, Eric, 1966- authors.
    Taming the beast : the untold story of Team Tyson /
    Rory Holloway; with Eric Wilson.
    p. ; cm.
    Includes bibliographical references.
    ISBN 978-1-940401-84-3 (hardcover)
    ISBN 978-1-940401-83-6 (trade paper)
    ISBN 978-1-940401-82-9 (ebook)

    1. Tyson, Mike, 1966- 2. Holloway, Rory, 1962-
    3. Boxers (Sports)--United States--Biography.
    I. Holloway, Rory, 1962- author. II. Title.

    GV1132.T97W55 2014   796.83092'2
                        QBI14-600133

Scripture quotations are taken from the Holy Bible. New Living Translation copyright ©1996, 2004, 2007, 2013 by Tyndale House Foundation. Used by permission of Tyndale House Publishers Inc., Carol Stream, Illinois 60188. All rights reserved.

Printed in the United States of America

First Edition

"If you refuse to do what is right, watch out!
Sin is crouching at the door, eager to control you.
But you must subdue it and be its master."

Genesis 4:7

TABLE OF CONTENTS

TALE OF THE TAPE
Michael Gerard Tyson

1986 & 1988:	*Ring* Magazine's Fighter of the Year
1986-1990:	WBC Champion
1996:	WBC Champion
1986:	Age 20, Youngest Heavyweight Champion
1987-1990:	Undisputed World Heavyweight Champion
1996:	WBA Champion

Amateur Record:	24 Wins, 3 Losses
Professional Record:	50 Wins (44 by knockout)
	6 Losses
	2 No Contests

Weight:	217-222 lbs.
Height:	5 feet, 10 inches
Reach:	71 inches
Chest:	43-45 inches
Neck:	19 inches
Biceps:	16 inches
Forearm:	14 inches
Wrist:	8 inches
Fist:	13 inches
Waist:	34 inches
Calf:	18 inches
Ankle:	11 inches

INTRODUCTION

THE LEECH

With the stories of top-dollar athletes and sports scandals breaking weekly in the news, the topics in *Taming the Beast* are more timely than ever, and the untold story of Mike Tyson is incomplete without answering pointed questions that still hover over his career:

Who should have held Mike's reins?

Were Mike's women after his money?

When did thugs take over Mike's career?

How did Mike's millions disappear?

Will Mike make peace with his past?

This book's five sections explore these questions through the co-author's extensive research and through unprecedented firsthand accounts from Rory Holloway, Mike's longtime friend and team manager. In doing so, some of the sections overlap chronologically as they build toward a present-day conclusion.

Although Mike often sidesteps the subject of his relationship with Mr. Holloway, when asked by a reporter whom he would call if he were stranded on an island, he answered quickly: "Rory Holloway." It seems a strange response, considering that sportswriters have described Mr. Holloway as the "leech," the "idiot manager," the "thug who stole Mike's riches."

What was Rory Holloway's actual role in the downfall of a sports icon?

That is left for readers to decide.

PART ONE

WHO SHOULD HAVE HELD MIKE'S REINS?

"If you reject discipline,
you only harm yourself;
but if you listen to correction,
you grow in understanding."

Proverbs 15:32

CHAPTER ONE

THE BEAST

I t was a time of myth and legend, of monster and beast. In the 1980s, heavyweight boxing champs were treated as immortals, and few dominated the world's attention like Mike Tyson. He overcame a fatherless upbringing in the Brooklyn projects and won his first nineteen pro bouts by knockout. He threw punches aimed through opponents' skulls, leaving them on the mat as he strode away, a predatory animal bored by the efforts of his prey. Was there a man alive who could defeat him?

Kid Dynamite.

Iron Mike.

The Baddest Man on the Planet.

At age twenty, he earned his first championship belt, the youngest ever to do so, and though his potential was limitless, he still had excesses to overcome. A boxing god beset by personal demons, he turned to others for guidance. If they could only corral him for the next decade or so, surely he would take his place in the pantheon of the sport's all-time greats.

Was taming such a creature even possible, though?

From his childhood to the present, Mike has had a number of managers, everyone from Cus D'Amato to Rory Holloway to Magic Johnson. To understand the challenges they faced, one would need to identify the type of animal they were dealing with. A panda would be one thing. A raccoon another.

But a tiger . . .

In that case, they had a real beast on their hands.

Consider these statements Mike made while under the nervous eyes of his managers:

"I don't want to be a tycoon. I just want to conquer people and their souls."

"I think I'll take a bath in his blood."

"My defense is impregnable, and I'm just ferocious . . . I want to eat his children. Praise be to Allah!"

"I was spoiled, like a brat. I had anything I wanted . . . I've never had a job in my life. What I know how to do is hurt big, tough men—on the street and off."

"I'm just a . . . dark shadowy figure from the bowels of iniquity."

"I guess I'm gonna fade into Bolivian."

Before Mike rose to stardom and later faded, as he so infamously predicted, he considered Rory Holloway a pal and confidant. Before they made millions together, before the tribal tattoo that now claws at the champ's face, Mike and Rory were best friends. Simple as that. The tiger was once a cub, and life was less complicated then.

Who knows this better than Mr. Holloway?

Rory, when did you and Mike first cross paths? Did you sense an immediate connection?

RORY: I guess it all started, in some ways, 'cause of my own bad decisions.

It was 1982. I'd just graduated from Albany High and signed up at Schenectady Community College, taking culinary arts—to this day, cooking's a passion of mine. I remember I got a student loan for $2700, and I thought that shit was a million dollars. Forget schoolbooks. I went and bought a Hatchback, put these big speakers in it.

Stupid me, I wasn't really there for an education. Schenectady was a small school, and I joined the basketball team. I figured I gonna score sixty points a game on these cats, so I skipped practice. Told the coach my grandma was in the hospital.

But the coach was one of these really religious guys. Next time I show up at practice, he calls us into a circle and gives this speech with Bible verses. Then he looks right at me and says, "One amongst us has lied." He tells me he called, and there's no members of my family at Albany Medical Center. I try making some excuse about my car, and he says, "Leave." Just like that. "Leave. We don't want you on our team."

I was devastated. I definitely didn't want to go to school if I couldn't play ball. That ball was my life. I thought I'd be playing at Syracuse and then in the NBA. Now I'm back home at my parents' place, over the family store on Clinton Avenue.

For the next week, I'm in and out of the Army recruiter's, in and out, trying to decide what to do. Then I run into a guy we called Handsome, and he tells me about a job at Berkshire Farms Division for Youth. "They don't pay much," he explains, "but you can stay up there in one of their cottages and work with the kids."

I loved it. Kids, they know who cares about them and who don't, and I just clicked with them. That wasn't work to me. I'd do that for free. I loved being a mentor and I got more outta that than anything, like it was part of my nature, a gift God gave me. I'd be at Berkshire four days straight, then drive eighty minutes back to Albany.

At the same time, Mike had got to be friends with my brother and started camping out at our house. Mike, he was barely a teenager, but he'd already been locked up as a juvenile offender. Mugging. Armed robbery. Boxing was what got him out of that life in Brooklyn and Brownsville, and now he was living and training in Catskill, small town south of us. He hated it 'cause it was so boring. Albany was the closest thing to Brooklyn he could find. Which was fine with us, since Mom took in all the neighborhood strays—that's just the way she is, a real nurturing type.

One morning, Mike's asleep on our floor. In his underwear. Drunk. My dad didn't know who the hell this kid was. Neither did I, really. Dad tells him, "You never drink in this damn house. We don't do that here. I don't mind you staying, but you don't come in here drunk."

"Hey," I say to Mike. "Come hang out with me."

We drove around. He was a shy, reserved, freakin' guy, but right away we had this bond. He'd find me no matter where I was. He didn't know how to talk to girls. I'm like, "Yo, this is my man, Mike." We didn't talk about boxing or none of that. Just good times. Mike and me, having some fun. I'd sneak stuff out of my dad's store, potato chips and snacks, and pass them on to him. One day my pops caught us, standing right there as I'm slipping food to Mike. He was livid.

Later, I needed new wheels. I bought my dad's old Lincoln Continental from the junkyard. Henry Blunt was the guy the whole neighborhood went to if they needed a car fixed, and he got it running for me. It had all these electrical issues. The cops'd think we were blinking our lights at them, even when we weren't touching a thing. Eventually, the Lincoln broke down, so we rented this car with holes in the floorboards big enough to put your feet through, like we the fuckin' Flintstones or something. Wintertime, man, we'd be freezing our asses off.

Mike and me, we was tight. It was an all-natural, organic, special, childhood bond. I knew him better than anyone, and I didn't have to brown-nose—as we say in the neighborhood—or nothing like that. He was just my boy. I treated him no different than I would any of my friends, and that was true when we had no money and when we had all the money in the fuckin' world. Friendship is friendship.

I got some of my best qualities from Mike. There's no fanfare with him. He's humble. He's loyal. He's got a heart of gold. And he's one of the funniest cats you'll ever meet, except he's serious when these ridiculous things come outta his mouth. That makes it even funnier.

I was wearing a different hat then, just being Mike's friend. My quest every day was making sure he showed up at the gym, because that's what he do. He box. Since I had the car and gas, that was my duty. It was a forty-minute drive each way. He got mad when I made him go train. "Mike, if you don't train, we can't hang out," that's what I used to say. From the beginning, he was a fighter-in-training, and not one day of our lives together did I see him use no drugs. He thought people who did that stuff were weak. He drank, though. He'd take the hardest liquor and just turn it up. He'd put the cup down, and it was empty, like a little kid trying to do big-boy things.

When I was younger, I never drank, never smoked. Maybe because of him, 'cause I had to watch his back. I'd say to him privately, like, "Listen, you gotta watch that guy over there . . . boom, boom, boom," or "That girl, you gotta be careful . . . boom, boom, boom."

He'd say, "You're too fuckin' worried, Ro. Man, you worry too much."

This was before I ever thought of being Mike's manager. We didn't know he'd be champ one day. Albany had other promising boxers. Critics said Mike's arms were too short. No fanfare. We'd go to a local fight, he'd take care of business, then we'd be right back in the club.

Wasn't till years later, I see this billboard at the Vegas Hilton: "Tyson vs. Berbick for the Heavyweight Championship of the World." I'm like, "Holy shit!"

That's when it hit me how big all this was.

Mike Tyson is a complex guy. By that, I mean, the Mike you get at nine a.m., that's not the Mike you get at three p.m. or eleven p.m. He can be rational one moment, and do something completely insane the next. You just never know with Mike.

His survivor, con-artist mentality, he never got rid of that from when he was a kid. I say he pulled off the greatest con in sports, making people feel sorry for him. He'd play up the "Mike, the dumb boxer" act, and it worked. That became his game. In a short period, he got to be one of the most powerful cats on the planet in sports, and he had no real teaching how to handle all this.

When I got to be his manager, I tried to coach him for interviews, for his public image, and he'd nod. Okay, okay. Then he'd say whatever the hell he wanted. He'd say how he a barbarian, how he gonna take the pussy. He told a female journalist that he usually didn't interview with a woman unless he could fornicate with her. Can you imagine an athlete saying that today? He'd be crucified.

His biggest gift is how he retains the information he reads. "Yo, that quote is nice. Let me use that." Next, he's quoting Mao Tse-Tung, Arthur Ashe, whoever. People think, "Man, this guy is deep." Fuck that. Sometimes he be in the mirror laughing at himself, that's just him.

Underneath the bravado, the slang, and all this shit, Mike is a good guy. Even today. But understand, we were dealing with a guy who was mentally ill. Every morning was an adventure.

CHAPTER TWO

THE BEAR

O ver the years, sports writers and fans have asserted that if Cus D'Amato were still alive, everything would be different. Mike Tyson would not only have held onto his heavyweight crown for a long and glorious reign, he would have topped Rocky Marciano's undefeated record and proved himself the greatest of all time.

Who was Cus?

Mike's first manager, Constantine "Cus" D'Amato, was everything his name implies, an ornery cuss, an irritable old bear, whose gravelly voice delivered stern commands. He was no-nonsense. No bullshit. He came by it honestly, having been raised in the Bronx by a hard-nosed father, and having seen his older brother shot and killed while mouthing off at a police officer.

During the late 1940s, Cus opened Gramercy Gym. In this third-floor, Manhattan sweat-box, he trained boxers and discovered a shy African-American boy named Floyd Patterson. Floyd was from Brooklyn and wanted to learn how to defend himself. Cus became his manager, guiding him through the amateur ranks to Olympic gold in 1952. When Cus arranged Floyd's first title fight in '56, the boxer shocked the world by becoming the youngest heavyweight champion of his day.

Cus D'Amato was a genius. He could do no wrong.

Soon, though, the struggles of stardom set in. Without unified boxing associations or regulatory commissions, the sport has long been riddled with corruption. Other managers and even Mafia dons wanted in on Floyd's budding career, and sowed seeds of distrust in the young fellow's mind. When Floyd decided to let Cus go, Cus slipped away with his Ukrainian love interest, Camille

Ewald, to her large Victorian home on the banks of the Hudson River.

Located in upstate New York, the Catskill Mountains were the setting for the tale of Rip Van Winkle. There, Cus seemed to fall into a similar decades-long sleep, dreaming of the day he would find and shape another raw boxing talent; not that there was much chance of that in the bygone town of Catskill.

But Cus was resilient. Like Washington Irving's fabled character, he "preferred making friends among the rising generation, with whom he soon grew into great favor," and he opened another gym. It was a small, dusty affair over the Catskill Police Department, an unlikely spot for the fruition of his dream.

In 1980, he got a phone call that changed everything.

Bobby Stewart, a former Golden Gloves champ, was a counselor at nearby Tryon Residential Center. Behind the state facility's 16-foot barbed-wire fence he'd found a kid with the legs and chest of a grown man. During this delinquent's upbringing on the hard streets of Brooklyn, he'd been bullied before turning to violence and crime.

His name: Michael Gerard Tyson.

Cus took note. Brooklyn, huh? Same as Floyd.

He arranged a tryout at his gym, and had trainer Teddy Atlas join him ringside while Bobby Stewart sparred with the thirteen-year-old kid. When Mike threw some hard shots, Bobby threw back, landing a punishing right to Mike's nose in the second round.

"That's enough," Teddy said, at the sight of the kid's bloodied face.

"One more," Mike insisted. "We always go three rounds."

The old man was impressed. By the time that third round was over, he'd found his next world champion.

Cus took Mike under his wing as a ward of the state, providing lodging in his and Camille's home, and managing him at the gym. Though Mike excelled in the ring, he struggled in the classroom, and was kicked out of the local school for his groping of female classmates. Cus had his eyes on the prize, and he wasn't going to let this impede Mike's trajectory. He simply shifted the young man's focus from academics to full-time boxing.

In the short-term, the gamble paid off. When Mike won his first gold medal in the U.S. Junior Olympics, diehard boxing fans took notice. When he repeated the feat by setting a record for the fastest knockout—eight seconds from the opening bell—reporters predicted the kid might have a decent, profitable career should he choose to turn Pro.

Decent? Profitable?

Never had the media got it so right—and so wrong.

When you met Mike, he was living in Catskill with Cus and Camille. Did you know Cus personally? Did you get to see his management skills in action?

RORY: Cus was a good guy. When I took Mike to the gym in Catskill, some days I'd just sleep in the car. Other times his team of guys'd let me watch him train. Cus wasn't crazy about me, but he wasn't crazy about nobody around his fighter. He was protective. Of course, if I didn't do what I do, Mike wouldn't even show up.

Pretty soon, I was an extended part of the family. I'd be at the dinner table at Cus and Camille's. Camille, she was a nice lady, a strong lady, and she'd rub my head the way she did Mike's. Mike introduced her as his mom. Cus was different, though. It took him a minute to warm up to me. Mike would tell me, "Get in the car, get in the car. Man, Cus hate your guts." Still, Mike stuck to me like glue, 'cause he knew I was a good cat.

It didn't matter to me. I knew I wasn't that cat Cus probably perceived me to be. See, my situation wasn't like Mike's. I came from a good family, didn't drink or do drugs. I played sports in school. Give her credit, Mom made sure me and my brothers were always signed up, whether it was football, basketball, whatever. We did it all, even ice-skating. Dad coached Pop Warner football, and Mom worked the concession stands. Weekdays, she worked at the family store and closed up late, so she left us at the Boys Club, where we'd be shooting hoops and playing Ping-Pong till ten at night.

At that time, I had pimples on my face and was very conscious of that, so I didn't talk to girls. My world was on the basketball court or football field. Guys on the team bragged, like, "I had Betty last night" or "I had Julie last night," but I wasn't like that. That wasn't me. Man, Cus didn't know that, so I don't blame him.

Cus was an absolute master at what he did. He excelled at teaching the mental aspect, not so much what to expect outside the ring but what to expect in it. He taught Mike the anatomy of a man, how to break him down. I was privy to the whole thing.

Mike loves the reek of chaos. He functions best in chaos. Can't be nothing smooth, can't be quiet for too long, or he's gotta start some shit. Maybe that's why he was so good when going toe-to-toe with another fighter. Cus taught him how to use that fear and control his emotions. When punches were coming at Mike, he was at his calmest. His vision would get real focused and shrink so he could see everything. He was a master at it.

Cus was a great man. Make no bones about it, he had an agenda for Mike Tyson, like he had with the other fighters around Camille's table. It wasn't a bad agenda, but if any of those guys had been as good as Mike, do we really think it would've been all about Mike?

No, Mike just happened to be the cream that rose to the top. He was Cus's prized possession, his chance to leave his mark. Ain't nothing wrong with that.

When Cus died in '85, Mike was only nineteen, and he was tore up, for real.

Cus was a "student of Zen," according to author Norman Mailer. If Cus were still around, could he have saved Mike from his self-destructive behavior? Did he have that sort of influence?

RORY: What I say is, as great as Cus was on the one end, he was not so great on the other. He's the one who taught Mike you can have the women and the cars, you can do this and you can do that. You can do whatever you want to do once you became champ. Basically telling Mike he'd be invincible, he wouldn't have to answer to nobody.

Mike wanted that invincibility, like the hardcore fighters of the past. Mike is a great imitator. He's a historian. He'd study film and read about Sugar Ray Robinson, Jack Johnson. We was young, and we'd watch old James Cagney movies. Mike'd be mimicking these guys, how tough they looked and acted. He'd wear the gangster hats and trench coats, thinking, "Yeah, we be cool, we be fly." He'd take on that persona.

It's a persona him and Cus practiced and talked about. Half the time if you'd see Mike acting rough and tough, that was Sonny Liston. Next time, it might be Marciano. He portrayed what he saw in the old fighters.

As great as Cus was, he didn't discipline Mike. You know, it's like giving one of these young kids in the NBA a max contract. You start putting money in their hands so fast, and they don't know what to do with it. As a manager, Cus let stuff slide that happened outside the ring, and that led to problems. It fed the monster.

For example, Mike was going to school in Catskill, but he's this cat from Brooklyn who didn't really fit there. The school accused him of messing around with one of the female students, and what's Cus do? He pulls Mike out. He wasn't worried about Mike's education, he was protecting his fighter. Well, Teddy Atlas didn't like that. Teddy the one in the gym carrying out Cus's instructions, telling Mike the stuff to work on, and he thought Cus was giving Mike the wrong idea by not making him take responsibility.

Next time Mike got in trouble, it was with Teddy's eleven-year-old niece. That was it. Teddy pulled a gun on Mike, put it to his fuckin' head. They portrayed that scene in the HBO movie, *Tyson*, and got that part pretty accurate. But even with Teddy wanting to kill him, there still wasn't no accountability for Mike. Cus told Teddy he was done being Mike's trainer. He had to go. You know, like, "You're messing with my meal ticket."

Teddy's an analyst now on ESPN. In spite of what Teddy says about me, and he don't really know me, I think he was a good trainer. He would've been good for Mike, his philosophy and what he gives fighters and stuff, but that wasn't my call. I was just Mike's friend at the time, watching all this go down. It was an education, no doubt.

The ones then acting as Mike's management team, that was Bill Cayton and Jim Jacobs, putting his contracts together and calling in a new trainer for him.

At the time, Mike and me didn't know the shit they were doing.

Man, it wasn't till years later we found out what was really going on.

CHAPTER THREE

THE HAWK AND THE DOVE

It is hard to blame Cus D'Amato for any financial improprieties. He was a stand-up guy who took on his era's seedy boxing establishment, even when it meant using some heavy-handed methods of his own. By all accounts, he was never driven by money, yet it was this inattention to the dollar bill that sometimes hurt his own athletes. At one point, for example, he signed a letter of agreement that granted Floyd Patterson a fee of only $1 for his part in a syndicated TV program put together by Jim Jacobs. That situation drove a wedge between Floyd and Cus.

Despite any shortcomings, Cus was all about his fighters. Since he didn't travel, he didn't attend most fights. Instead, he sat in musty gyms and barked instructions over the rhythmic knocking of leather speed bags, molding men into warriors of body, mind, and spirit. His headstone bears a quote from his own lips:

A boy comes to me with a spark of interest.
I feed that spark and it becomes a flame.
I feed the flame and it becomes a fire.
I feed the fire and it becomes a roaring blaze.

Cus fed that fire, but when it came to a fighter's contract, he relied on the legal and financial services of Bill Cayton and Jim Jacobs.

Bill Cayton was a wily businessman, with sharp features and hawk-like eyes. He started an advertising firm, got involved early on in television programming, and helped Cus manage fighters such as Jose Torres. Through his company, Big Fights, Cayton gathered, restored, and aired boxing films dating back to the 19th century, and eventually sold the collection to the Walt Disney Company for a small fortune. Soon after his death in 2003, he was inducted into the International Boxing Hall of Fame.

If Cayton was the hawk, Jim Jacobs was the dove. Despite his mild nature, he had an impressive resume. He was a six-time national handball champion. He too collected boxing films, which he sold for tens of millions to ESPN, and owned over a half-million comic books. In 1959, he became friends and roommates with Cus. Until his untimely death in 1988, he and Cayton managed boxers such as Wilfred Benitez and Mike Tyson. Jim is in the International Boxing Hall of Fame, as well as in the U.S. Handball Hall of Fame.

In many ways, the partnership between Jim, Cayton, and Cus was based on outdated views of fighters and their worth. Heavyweights of their day, especially those with African-American heritage, were not signing big-dollar contracts or endorsement deals. If a black kid from an impoverished neighborhood got a shot at something better, well, wasn't that reward enough?

Rory, you knew Bill Cayton and Jim Jacobs. What sort of relationship did they have with Mike? How do you think they viewed you?

RORY: I liked Jim. Jim Jacobs was a classy guy, real gentle, real sweet. He knew Mike and me were closer than brothers. I had no troubles with Jim, and I think he had good intentions for Mike. He was a peaceful guy.

Since Jim was an athlete, he and Mike got along. I seen them hug and laugh. They had a closeness through their love of boxing, I think. Jim was a boxing historian with a huge collection of fight films, and he'd ship them up to Mike, who would watch them on a projector in his room, sometimes twenty-four hours a day, to the point that I'd be downstairs, like, "Would you come on, Mike? Let's go."

Now Cayton, I never had a relationship with him. He didn't really talk to me. He was just one of those guys, grouchy and stoic. Greedy. He's smiling in those pictures when he signed the management deal with Mike, but it was all business with him.

I remember Cus bought Mike a car when he turned sixteen, this white Cadillac Seville with a blue cloth-top. Cayton wasn't happy about that. I guess he thought Mike'd just drive off and disappear. Ask anyone who knows him, Mike's a horrible driver. How he got his license, I have no idea. He drove Cus one time, and Cus swore he'd never have to take his laxatives again. And parking? No way. Mike'd just stop in the middle of the street and say, "Park the car, park the car." He sure as hell couldn't do it.

Later, Mike and I had an apartment in Albany, and we're hanging out on the couch, nice afternoon. Mike'd left training, but I didn't know that. We get a call. I pick it up. "Don't say a word," Jim Jacobs tells me. "I know Mike's with you. Listen, if he doesn't get to Vegas now, the promoters are gonna sue him for his cars and everything. They're gonna take it all away." I shake Mike and tell him this. He just laughs, like it the funniest shit in the world. I don't like to fly, but he tells me he won't go unless I go with him. When we land in Vegas, Jim and Steve Lott sweep in, picking Mike up, leaving me on the curb. I got no money on me. I'm just standing there in shock.

Steve was an assistant to Jim and them, and he had a doctor friend who lived close by. That's where they were keeping Mike under lock and key, getting him ready for his fight. Eventually, Mike got me into the house, and I had to tiptoe around 'cause Steve didn't like me being there. I'm a young, single guy, black, and they're blaming me for Mike's indiscretions at the time. That was their perspective.

Both Jim and Cayton, they were very protective of Mike. And you can see why now. They was scared he gonna go back to Brooklyn and fall into his old ways. They didn't want Mike around no black guys, didn't like me hanging around the gym, but I didn't take that personal. I wasn't raised to buy into all that race-card bullshit.

Mike never had much interaction with Cayton, but like I said, Mike loved Jim. I'll never forget the day Jim died. Mike and me were hanging out on Clinton Avenue, right in front of my family's grocery store, which was like a meet 'n greet, everybody having fun and gathered round. Mike got a call and ran to the car. I always had my eye on him, and said, "What's up, man?"

"Jim," he said. "Something happened to Jim."

You could see the pain in his face. He'd already lost Cus, who was a father-figure, and now Jim, who was more like a big brother or something. He was hurting bad.

Listen, what people don't understand is that Mike was in a bubble when he was with Cus and with Jim and Cayton. There were still mischievous things he was doing—the girl at the school, Teddy's niece, and all that—but when they had him, he was a kid. He hadn't yet become that grown man who had all the money in the world and could make his own decisions. They had him on the reins a little bit.

By the time John and me got him, Mike was like an animal on the loose. "I'm doing what I want, I got my own money, and fuck it, this is how I gotta do things." That's how he was when we got him, thinking only about today, not long-term. I seen the difference, since I was with him on both sides of it. It's the same as with a lotta these young guys who get into the NFL. It's called Not For Long for a reason.

Early on, I had no concept how big things was gonna be. Mike was my boy, that's all. The love between two men, that bond, it's stronger than between a man and a woman. There's no lust or emotion or nothing, just pure friendship. Nothing else, right? That's deep, and I took that seriously. Didn't matter if we had no money or lots of it, I knew when we was old we'd still be hanging out, barbecuing in the backyard, our grand-kids running around our feet.

I believed that to the core of my being. I didn't think anyone could come between that, even with Cayton and Jim trying to run me off.

A lot of accusations have been leveled at you and John Horne for mismanaging Mike's money, while not much is said about his original managers. What led to Mike firing them?

RORY: The contracts Mike signed with Cayton and Jim were for seven years. We didn't realize at the time how they taking advantage of him. See, in boxing, a manager gets thirty-three percent of a fighter's earnings. It's not etched in stone, but that's typical. What they were doing, they were both getting that amount from Mike, so he was getting double-dipped. I'd have to get in Jim's head to know how he justified it.

Mike was oblivious. He didn't know his own business, never wanted to hear about that stuff, so he didn't ask those kinda questions. He was just proud to have official management. Thing is, he couldn't even access his own money. He wins his first heavyweight belt in '86, he's the fuckin' champion of the world, and when he walk into the bank he can't get one penny of his earnings without a signature from Jim or Cayton. I'm not the most educated guy, but I had sense enough to know that ain't right.

In '88, Jim summoned Mike to his hospital room. He was dying of leukemia, but he played it off like it was nothing and talked Mike into signing over their contract to Jim's wife. Jim was just looking out for his family, but it was restricting for Mike.

During that time, Cayton and Jim were using Don King as a promoter on a fight-by-fight basis. Smarter that way. Those guys, they didn't trust Don—everybody knew he was a snake—and it gave them power to negotiate the best deals with other promoters on the block. Man, soon as they let Don get close, he started sniffing around Mike.

By then, Mike had married Robin Givens. You gotta understand, Robin is a smart girl, very smart. She ordered the books, since she had the legal authority to see what was going on. Oh, that burned Cayton up. She and her mother, they brought in a lawyer and accountants, and they found things that were inappropriate. She talked to me about it. We saw how Mike was getting raked by his contract, and we brought it to his attention.

Man, all hell broke loose. I think it was the Spinks fight when Robin filed the lawsuits. Mike fired Cayton, which meant Steve Lott and cut-man, Matt Baranksy—both nice guys—were also gone, collateral damage. The courts decided Mike still had to pay Cayton twenty, twenty-five percent till the end of their contract in '92. What could we do?

Me and John Horne stepped in and started building a new team behind the scenes. Did we make mistakes? Sure we did, I'm not gonna say we didn't, but I always had Mike's best interests in mind. We had lotsa decisions to make. At the time, Kevin Rooney was still Mike's trainer, and we was good with that. We figured why change it.

In fact, Kevin would still be working with Mike if he would've just kept his damn mouth closed.

CHAPTER FOUR

THE MULE

Kevin Rooney, a native of Staten Island, was a thin white guy with a mustache and an attitude. He looked more like an extra from that old TV show, *Starsky and Hutch*, than a former New York Golden Gloves champ and winner of over twenty professional welterweight bouts.

Kevin fit right in at Cus D'Amato's gym, where he trained fighters for many years. Under Kevin's tutelage, Mike perfected Cus's trademark "peek-a-boo" style, keeping his gloves up to protect both sides of his head while weaving, bobbing, and peeking out for the right time to strike. Iron Mike is remembered for his jaw-dropping and jaw-breaking power, but those who study his earlier fights find masterful displays of defense.

Much of the credit goes to Kevin, for his ability to pass on Cus's style. He was the one who traveled with Mike to each bout, even after the old man was gone, and he could recite their mentor's words as though they were his own:

"Nobody is born the best. You have to practice and train to become the best."

"Boxing is entertainment, so to be successful a fighter must not only win, but he must win in an exciting manner. He must throw punches with bad intentions."

"Pain is just nature's way of preparing you to fight."

When everything hit the fan and Bill Cayton was fired, someone had to take care of Mike's career. Rory and John filled that role, ushering in the modern era of Team Tyson, but when Kevin got the boot, the media blamed Rory and John. Fans were furious.

Who the hell were these ignorant upstarts, Rory Holloway and John Horne?

Why would they get rid of a skilled trainer, particularly one who'd walked his fighter through numerous battles and a recent world championship?

And what was Mike thinking, letting his wife come in and shake things up?

There's nothing sports junkies like better than a tale of resurrection, and the mythical rise of Mike Tyson had revived the sport. He was "entertaining and exciting" as Cus D'Amato had prescribed, keeping us glued to our seats and TV sets each time he stalked into the ring. As for all these changes to his team? The public wanted an explanation. Like the 1980s launch of New Coke, why mess with a winning formula?

What factored into the firing of Kevin Rooney? News reports claimed that you, John, and Don King got rid of him. What led to that decision, and in hindsight do you regret it?

RORY: Kevin Rooney was another one of these guys living with Cus and Camille, just one of the gym assistants while Teddy was training Mike. After the gun incident between Teddy and Mike, Kevin was put in as the trainer. No paperwork or nothing, just plugged in by Jim Jacobs and Bill Cayton to fill the spot.

Let me tell you, Kevin was the best trainer for Mike. In my opinion, he was the only trainer for Mike. Kevin knew Cus's style of fighting, and Mike was at his best when he was doing that style. It's like someone other than Phil Jackson trying to run the triangle offense. It may look like the triangle offense, may be a version of the triangle offense, but it's not the triangle offense.

For whatever reason, I don't know, Kevin had a real issue with me. To me, it felt more racist than anything, a deep-seated hatred. He'd make disparaging remarks, trying to degrade me. He was just an uneducated country guy. I don't wanna say backwoods, 'cause that sounds too hickey. Just small-town Catskill.

Things got worse when Mike and Robin got married. She went after Bill Cayton about the contracts, and that didn't sit well with Kevin. He thought, "Oh, now Mike's gonna be with this broad, and she's gonna be telling us what to do and how to do it."

He didn't respect the fact that Mike was a married man. It's one thing beforehand, I can go to another man and say, "I don't know if this woman's right for you, whatever . . . boom, boom, boom." Once he tells me he's married, though, I back off. If he tells me he loves her, I love her. I'm not gonna give him no suggestions about his wife. I reserve that to myself. He's married now, and I gotta respect that.

Not Kevin. He was a big-mouthed guy who had no filter. He was making comments about Mike Tyson and Robin Givens for the world to hear. He was talking with a slur, like Popeye and shit, and just couldn't keep quiet. Every time a reporter put a microphone in his face, he'd use the opportunity to make another bad remark about the wife of the guy he's training. I mean, who does that?

Mike went to him like a man. He says, "Hey, hey, Kevin. Hey, this is my wife now. You may not like it, but you gotta keep her name outta your mouth."

All Kevin had to say was, "Man, I understand. Don't worry about it." End of story.

Instead he says, "Fuck you. I'm gonna say what I wanna say."

That was Kevin, just stubborn as a mule, and he forced Mike's hand. Mike was done with Kevin. I told Mike we should stop and think about that. To me, business is business. I was trying to be rational and consider the betterment of Mike and the team. You don't have to like someone to work with them. You got a job to get done.

But Mike gives me this look. "I told you, I don't fuckin' want him."

After Kevin got fired, the whole world blamed it on me and John Horne. Must be our fault. Or Don King's. It's true, we was working with Don as a promoter, but none of that had a thing to do with Mike firing Kevin. We didn't encourage it. We didn't influence it. Mike made the decision completely on his own.

Man, Kevin was furious. It just exacerbated the hate he had, believing he was going through this shit because of Rory Holloway, John Horne, Don King, and Robin Givens. He never took into account it was because he opened his own mouth. Mike asked him to shut up, and instead he kept right on talking. He could've gone behind closed doors and said anything to Mike, right? Mike ain't that kinda guy who's going to fire you because you stand up to him. You don't challenge him in the open 'cause then his pride's involved, but in private, no problem. Thing is, Kevin said this stuff publicly.

Who did you hire as Mike's new trainers? When you saw signs that Mike's skills were slipping, did you consider any other options?

RORY: Listen, at that point Mike thought he was so good that anybody could train him and he'd still knock guys out.

Don King knew about this kid, Aaron Snowell, who used to hang around Tim Witherspoon's gym in Pennsylvania. So we brought Aaron in, and the news ran wild with it. The *Los Angeles Times* reported that Snowell was a Don King flunkie and that being black must be a prerequisite for the job, which was ridiculous. That's not the way I was raised to think, but it's just the sorta thing the media likes to twist around.

I mean, look, we also hired Jay Bright, this heavyset white guy. He was another one of Cus's students. He'd lived in the house with Mike, and I'm telling you, he was clean as a board of health, couldn't get him to go to a fuckin' juice bar. He knew that Cus style, next in line after Teddy Atlas and Kevin Rooney, so we brung him in. Everybody hated him 'cause he got Kevin's job, but he the nicest guy you ever wanna meet. He was a softie, that was the only thing. He sounded like a third-grade teacher, and he trying to train the Baddest Man on the Planet.

Jay really cared about Mike and considered him as a brother. And Mike cared about him. Before all these women messed with Mike's head, Mike wasn't like that, he didn't just throw nobody to the wolves. He gave Jay a great opportunity, Jay made a lot of money, and Stacy McKinley was part of it too. Stacy was a good guy too, but he quiet as a pool table and twice as green.

We just kept the train moving. Interchangeable parts.

After a coupla sloppy fights, I knew we had to get Mike back on track. I'm smarter than people give me credit for, and I knew what Kevin Rooney could do for us.

This one day, I took my friend Gordy and we drove down to Catskill. We rolled past Kevin's house like ten times, a modest home. Kevin had a gambling habit, and I knew he'd lost all kinds of money. Honestly, I was a bit nervous about approaching him.

Gordy and me sat in the Burger King up the street, deciding what to do, pondering what to say. All these thoughts were going through my head. Would Kevin shoot me at the door? I didn't know. To me, the guy was a redneck racist. To me. But you know what, he was still the best trainer for Mike. In spite of what I thought or letting my emotions get in the way, I went there to salvage something.

Me and Gordy finally walked up to the door, and Kevin let us in. His place was a mess, empty beer cans and pizza boxes all over. I said, "Kevin, listen, man, you need to drop this lawsuit against Mike. He needs you. You're the best trainer for the job."

"You gonna pay me $8,000,000?"

"What? Listen, man, I'm trying to be reasonable here."

"Eight million." He just glared at me. "Or get the fuck outta my house."

And with Gordy Keelen as my witness, that was it. Kevin just couldn't get past working for some black guys. He'd rather starve.

It's funny, because that *Times* piece didn't think we'd ever bring in a seasoned white trainer like Richie Giachetti, and that's exactly what we done. In that article, the writer admitted that "boxing writers are the most cynical people on earth," and that tells you what we were dealing with. Right or wrong, this handful of cynical journalists was shaping the public's perception of Team Tyson. So Richie came into training camp for the second Holyfield fight. He'd been Larry Holmes's trainer, and he was this tough guy, smoking cigars, a scar on his face. He brought that edge.

But nobody, and I mean nobody, knew what Mike was gonna do in that ring to Holyfield. That was not a part of the script.

You mentioned that Kevin Rooney filed a lawsuit against Mike? What was that about?

RORY: What the average person doesn't understand is that the fighter is the boss. The promoter goes and finds locations, opponents, and money for the fights, basically answering to the manager. The manager pools the best promoters, trainers, team, and assistants, arranging everything from contracts to transportation to training camp, whatever. The trainer, he's the one in the fighter's ear, the one getting him ready to risk his life in that ring, so he has to be a good fit or it won't work. And Kevin was a good fit for Mike. Ultimately, though, all these people are working for the fighter.

Mike Tyson, he was our boss, not the other way around.

Kevin had that flipped in his head. Years earlier, when Jim Jacobs told him he was Mike's trainer, he took that to mean his trainer for life. Like Mike had no say in the matter. So after Kevin got fired, he sued Mike for future earnings.

It was a hometown drama. The trial was right in Albany, while our team's training for the first Holyfield fight. I felt bad, man. How'd Kevin think he was gonna win based on an oral agreement with a man who was now dead? And we heard testimony from people saying that years earlier Cus'd wanted to replace Rooney anyway.

So there's Kevin up on the stand. They ask him, "Did Mike ever say you were his trainer for life?"

He says, "No."

"Did you ever sign a contract saying Mike would be your trainer for life?"

He says, "No."

"Why, then, do you believe you should be his trainer for life?"

Kevin says, "Because Jim told me so, and Mike never had the right to fire me."

And the all-white jury agreed. Not because Mike ever signed anything or agreed to anything, but because he'd been handed off like a piece of property. Crazy.

It was upheld in appeals, and Kevin Rooney was awarded $4,400,000.

People wanna know where Mike's money went? There's one example, and that barely scratches the surface. The bigger you get, the bigger the target you got painted on your back. Every crackpot, asshole, whore, all these third cousins and distant relatives you never knew about, they all come slithering up from the cesspool.

CHAPTER FIVE

THE COCKROACH

Around every cesspool, you'll find critters and cockroaches and when it comes to cockroaches, few are bigger than Don King.

Does that sound harsh? Wait until you hear how others describe him.

Don King's name is synonymous with boxing. He patterned himself after Paddy Carroll—the man who promoted African-American champ, Jack Johnson, in the early 1900s—and he helped stir interest in the sport like never before. Don has the look of a mad scientist, with tufts of white hair rising like smoke from an overactive brain, and few have matched his marketing genius. In his heyday, he was a ubiquitous figure, the mastermind behind two of history's most-viewed heavyweight fights, the "Rumble in the Jungle" and the "Thrilla in Manila." When Ali or Holyfield or Duran stepped into the ring, Don was often there in the spotlight, dressed in immaculate if not eccentric clothing to offset his wide but crooked smile.

All this by a man from Cleveland, Ohio, whose early run-ins with the law included charges of illegal bookmaking and second-degree murder.

Hey, rumor is that a cockroach could survive a nuclear war.

By the early 1980s, though, the house that King had built started crumbling. No longer was he commanding the same purses for his prizefighters. No longer were the Pay-Per-View crowds forking over money as they did for Ali in his foot-shuffling prime.

Like Cus D'Amato, Don was in danger of becoming a washed-up, middle-aged has-been. He needed a new product, a fresh fighter who could excite the masses.

Enter: Mike Tyson.

The problem was that Mike was in Cus's fold. Cus was a wily veteran, flanking his boys with crafty managers named Bill Cayton and Jim Jacobs, and they knew Don's game. Although they worked with Don on occasion, they were careful that he didn't dig his hooks too deeply into their fighters, especially their rising star, Kid Dynamite.

Don King hung around the edges, rubbing shoulders, patting backs.

Waiting for an entry point.

In 1988, the passing of Jim Jacobs and the arrival of Robin Givens cracked open the door, and Don darted in to gather up any crumbs. He had others to contend with—Donald Trump, for example—but trusted his animal instincts as he skittered after Rory Holloway and John Horne, knowing they had ties to Mike.

It seems obvious where this is headed, right? If a nuclear blast cannot destroy a cockroach, Kid Dynamite had no hope.

Over the years Mr. King has been sued numerous times, and boxing greats are some of his most vocal accusers: Muhammad Ali, Larry Holmes, Tim Witherspoon, Mike Tyson, and Lennox Lewis. He earned the moniker, Teflon Don, by showing an uncanny ability to keep legal and criminal charges from sticking to him. He flashed those teeth, pulled out wads of cash, and watched the accusations slip-slide away. Coincidentally, perhaps, he has been a generous donor to the campaigns of politicians such as George W. Bush and Barack Obama.

Don King Productions still chugs along today from its Florida headquarters, though Don is now a widower in his eighties. That has not stopped Mike from going on record and calling Don a "wretched, slimy, reptilian motherfucker."

"Cockroach" no longer sounds so harsh.

Knowing Don's reputation, why didn't you advise Mike against using him as a promoter?

RORY: You know, people have blamed us all these years for letting Don King get involved, but in his own book, Mike puts that on Bill Cayton and Jim Jacobs.

Just goes to show, fans believe what they want to believe.

But we did meet with Don King, that's true. He was lurking around Robin's house, and I mumbled to him that Mike needed some help. John Horne made it seem like he was part of the package, so he set up a meeting. Don came slithering into Albany, all of six-foot-five, hair sticking out to here. Me and Mike, we met him in the Omni Hotel.

People wanna know why we got involved with him. Well, it wasn't based on his looks, right? It wasn't based on his hair. It was the fact that he the best at what he do, the Mt. Rushmore of boxing promotion. Show me someone better, and we would've gone with him. I just think that's a smart approach in business, period. You ain't gotta like the person you're sitting across from. If we're making millions of dollars, I don't have to go to your house, be your best friend. If you're the best at what you do, we good.

Robin was suing Cayton at the time, telling Mike he was being taken advantage of. And Kevin Rooney had just won his suit against Mike. It all led to a perfect storm.

Don got in Mike's ear. "Kevin can't do that to you, Champ. It's like willing a nigga"—pardon the expression—"like willing a nigga to the white man."

To this day, I have no idea how Kevin won that suit, but Mike sure as hell didn't need this black-power shit. That was a favorite tactic of Don's, telling young black men, "We're brothas, we got to stick together. Look at me. I've got the bling, bling, bling."

What you have to understand is—and this goes for white kids, too—you gotta be smart and play the part.

You wanna be relaxed and be yourself, that's fine, but you'll be judged by the way you look. You fill your mouth with gold, wear baggy pants with your ass hanging out, got tattoos past your sleeves or coming up your neck, you're gonna be perceived as a thug. You're gonna look like a damn fool. That's just the way it is. If I'm going to a meeting at the bank, I don't take five black guys in with me. Five black guys walk in, and the bank's gonna think there's a problem, right? You gotta use your head. I don't care who you are, there's nothing wrong with saying, "Yes, sir," "Yes, ma'am," "Please," and "Thank you." That's how you get respect. It don't just come to you.

When Don spoke all that racial stuff around me, it went in one ear and out the other. He's an old-school gangster who gonna tell you what you wanna hear. John was in tight with him, probably thought he'd be his successor, but I knew he wasn't my friend. Don King was never my friend.

Don figured I was his best chance at getting through to Mike. Not like that was any secret. Each time Mike put his arm around me, he was telling the world, "This here's my boy, this is my point man," and I became a bigger target. Don wasn't the only one trying to get in on the action. Mike's name was becoming global, with CEOs, supermodels, street thugs, all sorts of people circling round.

Even the Donald, Donald Trump, was involved. He was talking with Robin and her mother, offering his services as an adviser or some shit. He was a big name in Atlantic City then, and it was in his casino where Mike knocked out Michael Spinks, with all these celebrities there in the crowd—Madonna and Sean Penn, Muhammad Ali, Matthew Broderick, Sugar Ray Leonard, Jack Nicholson. Everybody, man. Actors always wanna be boxers, and boxers wanna be actors. Nowadays, you see Justin Bieber up there in the ring next to some fighter. It's the craziest thing.

So why didn't we work with Trump? 'Cause he wasn't as good as Don King, that simple. He was Mr. Atlantic City, but he didn't know the fight game, how to negotiate purses, TV deals. His thing was real estate. A few years later he filed for bankruptcy, but give him credit, he bounced back. Trump, man, he's as cold and cutthroat as Don King. They're two sides of the same coin. And you know, they both have some crazy hair.

Trump would invite Mike and Robin out on his yacht, and he once had me watching after his drunk wife at a party. He was cool. People accuse him of being racist, but I never saw that. He loved to check out the sistas, that's what he told me. Then a rumor started that Robin had screwed the Donald, and that got Mike's blood boiling. Was it true? I don't think so. But we sure as hell weren't working with Trump after that.

So we're there in the Omni, and Don tells Mike he oughta be paying me a salary. "Listen, Champ, Rory here doing all this work for you. How many years he been with you, huh? That's your main man, and you're giving him crumbs. Let him stand on his own two feet."

And Mike's like, "You're right, man. You're right."

That made me proud. It wasn't about the money, it was about our friendship.

Don't think I didn't see what Don was up to, though. It was strictly business to him. Did that mean I gonna pass up good money to keep working with Mike? Hell, no. I didn't care about an amount, that's not why I was in it, but neither of us wanted the ride to end. We was still having fun. And staying close to Mike, I could watch his back.

I pulled in $250,000 a year as Mike's manager, which was plenty more than my checks before. Under typical management terms, I could've made even more, but most of that was going to Cayton and Jim's wife till '92. Since Cayton was still the official guy on the books, people dubbed me as a "quarter-million-dollar friend," getting money for nothing. That wasn't the case. I was doing managerial duties. I was doing a job.

One sports-industry executive said, "Horne and Holloway were ill-equipped for new roles as managers . . . to call them naïve is an upgrade." What's your response to that?

RORY: Cus used to say, "People who are born round don't die square." Well, Don King definitely wasn't no square, and we knew that going in. Shit, Don was an octagon, or a fuckin' trapezoid, or something.

Listen, it didn't matter what we did. If we hadn't talked with Don, people would've criticized us for that, too. We couldn't win.

You just have to have thick skin. People were saying all kindsa stuff—we was "yes" men, we was hired guns. It's frustrating knowing that's not who you are. Your wife, your parents, your brothers and sisters, they have to endure this stuff, all the talk about you in the papers, the barbershops, the stores. The perception was that we were Don King's cronies, but that was so far from the truth it's not even funny. Don had to watch what he said around me, 'cause I was challenging him all the time.

Thing is, Don King is tenacious. He once rode a donkey up some mountain trail in Mexico—this towering black man in a big sombrero, his ashy feet dragging on the ground—to fetch Julio César Chavez for a fight. That's just Don. He's a greedy, greedy guy, a manipulator, but he's also a brilliant promoter who's turned more kids of impoverished backgrounds into millionaires than anyone I know.

You gonna ignore a guy like that 'cause of what you heard about him?

You think Ali, or Duran, or Holmes didn't know his reputation before they worked with him? They knew. But I'm telling you, he's the best.

Were we naive? If John Horne was naive, it was for thinking Don would have his back no matter what. He figured he was like Don's son—not that Don was some model father to his own kids or nothing. And for me, it was for believing that when this train reached the end of the line, Mike and me'd still be together. Old fighters, they're always running out of money or getting into tax trouble, so I didn't expect it would be no different with Mike. But rich or poor, we'd be together.

I'm loyal to a fault, that's just me, sometimes even to the wrong guy. And Mike was my guy. He was this newlywed in his early twenties, still just a big kid really, at the top of the boxing world, and all these forces were bearing down on him. What he needed from me was my loyalty. Part of that meant putting together a team for him. I didn't have no college education, but I'll say this, sometimes the smartest guy in the room is the one who can plug the right people into the right spots. It takes a group effort. Nobody's so brilliant he don't need the help of others around him.

Did you consider Don King a member of Team Tyson?

RORY: Did Don play a part in what we did? Absolutely. But a team member? Absolutely not. When he waved his little American flags and said all this stuff about Mike being a hero sent from God, the whole time I saw Don as a man just doing a job for us.

Maybe John saw it as something more. John's his own breed.

CHAPTER SIX

THE CHAMELEON

With his tall frame and athletic build, John Horne had dreams of making it in Hollywood. In the mid-1980s he moved from Albany, New York to the palm-lined streets of L.A. He did stand-up comedy in the clubs, played small parts in movies, and produced a small-budget film. Anytime cameras were rolling, he wanted to be nearby.

John was also a basketball fan, a high-school friend of NBA player Sam Perkins. Through that connection, he organized a 1986 charity slam-dunk contest between Larry Nance and Spud Webb. The event was being held in Las Vegas, and Mike Tyson was in town training for his next fight. On a whim, John invited Mike to be a guest judge.

That was a pivotal time in American culture. Michael Jackson was the king of pop, Eddie Murphy was the box-office king, and break-dancing and rap were merging into the mainstream.

During the charity event, John recognized that Mike's appeal might bridge two worlds and serve as an inspiration to the urban community. Here was a kid from the projects about to fight for his first world title, a rags-to-riches story blending *Rocky* and *Boyz 'N the Hood*.

Tinsel Town could not script it any better.

From that day forward, John had a working relationship with Mike and played a role in bringing together Mike, Rory, and Don King. John aimed to be a sharp-dressed, well-spoken front man, and was the most vocal of the crew during press conferences. Together, they would all make millions of dollars as they took over the boxing world for the next fifteen years.

So where did things go wrong? These days, John and Mike do not even talk on a regular basis. What made Mike go so far as to call John an "arrogant guy"?

Rory, how did you get to know John Horne? Do you agree with Mike's assessment of him?

RORY: John and me, we were just kids who went to school together in Albany. We didn't run in the same circles. He was a year ahead of me, I think, so he was more friends with my older brother. John came from a family of athletes, had that lean sports body. He probably didn't work out a day in his life, just had that gene. His family was like *The Cosby Show*, these decent, hardworking people. His mother was a crossing guard for like forty years, and I always admired his father. He was the big chief.

When John set up the slam-dunk contest in Vegas, Mike was already there in town, training at Johnny Tocco's. John didn't know Mike from Adam, so he called me in Albany, and I set it up so he could get into the locked gym. I thought it'd be good for Mike. At that time, people knew about Evander Holyfield and Tyrell Biggs—they were the pretty boys, young Olympians with all the connections—but there wasn't much talk about Mike yet. He was new on the scene.

After the contest, John was stuck to us like glue. Even when we tried to get rid of him, we couldn't shake him. Mike treated him awful, but the man was glue, for real.

John's a very ambitious guy, and he always had a knack for wheedling his way in with athletes and actors. He was a chameleon, always trying to blend in. He used to be friends with Eddie Murphy and with Jerry Buss, the owner of the Lakers. They played poker together. That's just John, always trying to hook his wagon onto someone.

So he started painting the picture like he the man. "I can get you to Mike Tyson," that kinda thing. That's how that all came about. He wasn't tricking me, though. He was no threat to me, so I didn't care.

36

John believes he did a lot for Mike financially, and he was right for feeling hurt by the way things went down. I respect John as a businessman. But I seen it coming, 'cause he the type of guy who didn't respect Mike, didn't know who Mike was. He acted like he bigger than Mike.

You gotta know how Mike works. He feels like he's the big ticket—and he should feel that way, particularly in public. A Rottweiler's okay as long as you don't look him in his eyes. He sees that as challenge. The only beefs me and Mike ever had was in private. He's my friend, he's my boss. I never challenged him in the open, or even on the phone, 'cause Mike's the kinda guy who calls and puts you on loudspeaker so he can feel big in front of a roomful of women. John didn't get that. He'd be like, "Who the fuck you think you're talking to, Mike?" Acting like he Mike's boss.

Was John Horne arrogant? He's incredibly arrogant. It's a universal consensus that he's an asshole. A prima donna. But part of it was him just doing his job, right? He was in the same position as I was, just not as close to Mike as me. We wasn't two peas in a pod, but he was protecting our interests. Not everybody gonna like you for that.

John's not the greatest person at being politically correct, so he has this knack of rubbing people the wrong way. He said some things, especially to the commission after the Holyfield rematch, that were totally wrong at the time. He was fighting for his fighter, but it's the way he went about it. When you deal with people, you gotta understand that it's not just what you do, it's how you do it.

Some of the team around Mike complained that John talked down at them, instead of to them. I was in agreement with that. He could be an arrogant SOB. But I'd tell them, "You gotta look at the big picture. You can't be so small-minded. We might have different interests or motives, but we're all trying to get to the same place."

Listen, when John moved to L.A., that was right up his alley. Even in school he was the guy who wanted to be on the cover of the yearbook, the best-dressed, all that. Always trying to be something he's not.

He tried all sortsa stuff. He was a B-rated actor and a less-than-conspicuous comedian. He says he gave up his Hollywood career for Mike. Really? What career? Back in the '80s, me and Mike went to see John at the Comedy Club, and he was getting heckled and booed. Even Mike was heckling. John was no good. I'm not saying he couldn't get better, 'cause everyone's gotta start somewhere. A career, though?

Years later, he gave it another shot, acting and producing in a small-budget film. I took my wife to see it, figuring we'd support John. We're in the popcorn line, it's a busy evening, and I'm rushing her. "C'mon, we gotta get in there and find a seat. It's starting in a few minutes." Man, we walk into the theater, and there's not one person in the damn place. We could have any two seats we wanted. It was tragic. And then we see John up on the screen, playing a detective or something, and he's coming at someone with a pipe, his knees bent like he's some kung fu master. It was funny as hell.

Once John hooked his wagon to Mike Tyson, it's true he didn't have much time left for that Hollywood shit. That's because handling Mike was a full-time job. I hate to use that word for another human being, but that's the truth. Mike needed handling. If we weren't there to corral him, he'd be running the streets and getting into trouble.

A beast needs a handler. Mike needed a handler.

And we were those guys.

John cuddled up to Don King during that time. I really think John saw Mike as the short-range horse, the one who wouldn't last. Most fighters stay in their primes for just this short window of time. Don was the long-range horse, the thoroughbred. John's a gambling man, so that's where he was placing his bets.

Don's smart, and he played on that. Hell, he treated John better than his own son. But I knew what Don was. I seen him walk into a ring with one fighter, and when that guy loses, walk out with the other. Still, John believed it went deeper than business. He probably thought he had the same bond with Don that I thought I had with Mike.

Listen, John was good at what he did, from a business perspective. It was just all about the job and what benefited him. I wasn't tripping about that. He conveyed that attitude to the team, though. He didn't hang out at training camps or get his hands dirty. Not that it's part of the manager's job to do those things, so he wasn't obligated. That's fine. But the guys on the team, they saw me as a manager who was in the trenches with them. They knew that John was home sipping his wine, acting like a big shot, while me and Mike was in the mud, getting ready for war.

For me, it was never about some career I gave up. It was about my friendship with Mike. When Mike was done, Rory Holloway done. Simple as that.

CHAPTER SEVEN

THE DOG

Those old enough to drink Hi-C in the 1990s knew who Mike Tyson was. And those old enough to listen to Tupac in his heyday knew all about the ineptitude of Mike's crew, Team Tyson. Mike had the skills to become the greatest heavyweight of all time, and instead, as reporters explained to us, his potential was stripped away by a group of wannabe managers.

Rory Holloway and John Horne, what a pair of douchebags.

That was the consensus on the streets.

Who was this Mr. Holloway, though? What could archived documents, articles, and film clips reveal about his character? What was he like before and after the diamonds and Ferraris? How did those closest to him describe him?

Rory's upbringing was nothing like Mike's. He was born in Hartford, Connecticut, one of the wealthier cities on the eastern seaboard, where his mother served in rich white folks' homes and earned a reputation as hardworking and trustworthy. When she fell for a charismatic fellow from North Carolina, they started a family together, and eventually landed in Albany, New York.

Albany sits on the west banks of the Hudson, nearly 140 miles north of New York City and 40 miles north of Catskill. The working-class community of less than 100,000 people serves as the capital of the State of New York, and is one of the oldest remaining settlements from the thirteen original colonies. Friday night football games and the annual Tulip Festival are big events here. A far cry from crime-ridden Brooklyn.

While Mike was running with his gang through Brownsville's alleyways, Rory was in Albany's Lincoln Park running hills for Rudy Kelly, a hard-ass football coach.

While Mike was mugging old ladies, Rory was clipping his sports jerseys and All Saints choirboy robes to the clotheslines. While Mike was brooding in Juvie, Rory was living under one roof with his father and mother, his three brothers, and children his mom adopted out of abusive situations.

By all accounts, the Holloway home was a haven for many in the neighborhood. Bev Holloway, Rory's mom, explained it to me like this: "I had to do something. The world is selfish, and no one's thinking of the kids. They're raising themselves."

She knew all about being a victim, and ignoring the helpless was not an option.

More on that in chapters to come.

Despite the apparent model family, Rory and his father were never close. Willy Holloway was loved by the community as a Pop Warner coach and as owner of the local store, where customers lined up around the corner for the renowned fish fries, but his charm disguised a cruel side that taught Rory to keep his head down and avoid confrontation. Instead, Rory found two father-figures in the Albany public-school system, two white men who taught him about self-discipline and respect. One was Eddie Pierce, a middle-school basketball coach. The other was Jerry Spicer, a high-school teacher and coach who later became a principle.

What made these two men so important to you during your childhood? What did you learn that you were able to use later in managing Mike Tyson?

RORY: Man, Coach Pierce was this young, skinny guy, flat butt, chest all puffed out, and he had this blond hairpiece. Just a cool cat. He took coaching real serious, like he running a college team instead of a buncha middle-schoolers. He was big on passing the ball and playing as a team. In practice, he'd put these tin lids on the baskets so we couldn't even shoot. Just pass, pass the ball. I used to hate that. And he'd make us play defense with our hands behind our backs, teaching us to move our feet and stay low. He put this confidence into us, you know, pushing us, expecting the best from us. Game-time, Coach marched up and down the sidelines in polyester bell-bottoms, whistle hanging from his neck, and man, he be the chalkboard king. I don't know why he never got to the high-school level in Albany, must've been political or something, 'cause he was a great coach. I know he wanted it, too. With him, our team went undefeated for a number of seasons. I hardly knew what it meant to lose.

And Jerry Spicer, he was a mentor to me. He this gentle man, never raised his voice. He made me feel like he really cared, like it was more than just his job. I'd go to his office and talk about stuff I was dealing with. He'd listen and nod. Give advice, if I wanted it. He just loved his students, and I felt that from him, man. I felt loved. That shit, that can make all the difference in a young kid's life. You never know what he's dealing with at home, if his girlfriend just broke up with him, whatever. Just knowing someone cares, that's deep. Those're things we valued on Team Tyson, that loyalty and love.

Mr. Spicer, it turns out, is still involved in education in the Albany area, and he was asked for his recollections of young Rory. Here was Mr. Spicer's emailed response:

Rory was polite, kind, and gentle for as long as I knew him. His father taught him how to compete on the court and on the football field. I was a teacher and young coach, and loved the Holloway family. They were easy to like. When Rory met Mike Tyson, I believed Mike was the lucky one. I remember telling Rory not to quit his job and go with Mike. Wow! What'd I know?

Wait. He called Mike the lucky one?

Based on the way the news portrayed the end of the Tyson era, one would assume that Mike was lucky for getting away from his douche-bag managers. Could Mr. Spicer be describing the same man that legendary reporter George Plimpton labeled an "unsavory character"?

The picture seemed incomplete.

Rory, Mr. Spicer says he advised you not to quit your job to go with Mike. What other jobs did you hold before taking the reins of Team Tyson?

RORY: As a kid, I did all sortsa odds-and-ends jobs, and I guess all of them prepared me in some way, right?

First job I remember, this van used to come around, pick kids up, and take us out to the suburbs in Loudonville, these rich, fancy mansions. These people were living large—nice lawns, yards, sprinklers. I was just gazing, like, this is ridiculous. I never seen sprinklers in my life. In the van were these boxes of cookies, and they'd assign you one. "Rory, you got a box." They dropped you off at one location, and you gotta go house to house, ringing the doorbells, trying to sell the cookies. My older brother, Cameron, he'd come home with bank-roll. But I was the shy guy. I was quiet. I be out there all day, like nine hours, and I couldn't sell jack. Other guys, they had the gift of gab and they'd sell their whole box. That didn't work out for me.

In the summers, when I was maybe twelve or thirteen, my mother used to send us down south, loading us on the Greyhound with chicken wrapped in tinfoil. We looked forward to it. Don't forget, my father had a buncha relatives in New Bern, North Carolina. He had twenty-one, twenty-two siblings, and they all had kids. We had a hundred cousins, easy. Every other house was someone we was related to.

While we down there, how we'd earn money was we'd get on this bus, all packed in tight, and go to the tobacco and blueberry fields. That was the hardest freakin' work. Listen, you had to work your ass off to get a couple dollars. You'd be hot. These old ladies, they got babies on their backs, and they're picking more than you. And picking the cotton, that was even worse. When I seen that movie, *12 Years a Slave*, man, I known firsthand how hard that work was. My hands were bloody. I'm telling you, that was the real Southern experience, like you stepped back a hundred years or something.

When I learned how to drive, I drove my father down south one time. I was keeping it at probably forty miles an hour, showing him how safe I was, hoping he'd let me take the car. That's when his Lincoln was brand-new, and I be getting a bucket, washing it for him each day. He'd say, "Why the hell you keep cleaning my car?" Man, I envisioned owning that thing someday. I wanted to keep it in shape. I'd get mad 'cause he be putting toilets and water tanks in there, hauling junk around. He fixed up old apartments and buildings, made me and Cameron help him, and then he wouldn't pay us. "You got a roof over your head, dontcha? You got food to eat, dontcha?"

It was the same at the store in Albany. The whole family, we was all part of the daily operations, running the cash register, stocking, slicing up the blue fish into strips, brushing on the tartar sauce. You couldn't be in that store without smelling like damn fish, but people, they come from all over for those fish fries. It was the hang-out spot, guys and girls, even hours after the sun go down. You think we got paid? No way. You a Holloway, you gonna pull your weight. That's just the way it was. How could I complain when I seen my mom working sometimes seventeen hours a day? Her feet, they be swollen, her ankles like watermelons. And my father, he was playing the big shot the whole time. He'd pull money outta the register and throw dice with the guys or be gone for hours with the ladies. Meanwhile, Mom's busting her ass. That tore me up, man.

The job I loved was at Berkshire Farms Division for Youth. That's when I knew I could do something that mattered. I seen my mom always helping kids, just this big heart, you know. And I guess I got some of that from her, 'cause I had this way of working with the boys and girls there. Made me feel good. We had these other cats come in with their knowledge and degrees, but they couldn't figure out how I got through to these kids when they couldn't. "How do you do it, Rory?" Plain and simple, I cared. Same as what Mr. Spicer showed me. These kids, you can't smoke-and-mirror them.

Cus D'Amato never went to college, yet he was a self-taught student of human nature. Do you believe you were adequately prepared for managing the Baddest Man on the Planet?

RORY: Man, nothing could prepare you for that. I'd be lying if I said different. Mike Tyson and Michael Jordan, these were the two most recognizable sports figures in the world at that time. Boxing's even bigger than basketball in a lot of countries. You got fighters from all over—Mexico, England, Russia, the Philippines, Jamaica. It's a global sport. It crosses all demographics, race-lines, backgrounds. And in the middle of all that, here was my boy, Mike, this international star. We never, and I mean never, saw that happening. Hell, you can't predict or prepare for that.

But was I the right man for the job? Absolutely.

You remember Chuck Daly, coach of the Detroit Pistons? When they hired him, he didn't have a single winning season in the NBA, but he led them bad boys to back-to-back championships. Bill Gates, he dropped outta college, right? It's not always about your qualifications on paper. A degree's a good thing. I encouraged both my kids to go to college. But when a fighter steps into the ring, he's going to war, and he needs a band of brothers. It takes heart. Takes chemistry. A team's mettle gets tested in the trenches, that's where you form that deep bond, not in some classroom. Like Mike says, I was his point man. Loyal as a dog. I took pride in that, protecting my guy. That was my passion, my fuckin' life, and I knew we needed a team he could trust.

Day of the Berbick fight, in Vegas, I wasn't Mike's manager yet, just his friend, and he wanted to talk. He was crying, going through pre-fight ritual, saying how he don't deserve this. Man, that was like a badge of honor, him coming to me. That was sacred.

Next day, he'd done it. He was heavyweight champ, the youngest ever at just twenty years old. He saw me in the hotel lobby, two raggedy suitcases in my hand. He asked where I was going.

"The airport," I said, "so I can get back to my job at Berkshire."

"You don't got to work no more, man," he tells me. "It's me and you. We champions. We ate bologna together, now we eat steak together."

I'll never forget that moment. From that day on, if he won in the ring, I won in the ring. If he lost, I lost. If he fucked up, I fucked up. I took it just as hard. Wasn't no one else who could go to war with him like I could, not with that same intense loyalty.

CHAPTER EIGHT

THE LIONS AND THE LAMB

War. That is how Rory describes the battle in the ring. Since Cain's murder of his brother Abel, fists have served as . . . well, as handy weapons. Each time a boxer answers the bell, he takes part in that symbolic struggle of man vs. man and man vs. himself. He leaves the comforts of home and squares off against his foe. The fans roar, cheering not just for blood but for glory. They join vicariously in their warrior's struggle as he overcomes pain, doubt, and fear, to grasp victory in both hands and raise it high.

Pugilism—the fancy word for it—was first recognized as a sport in 688 B.C., when ancient Greeks included it in the Olympic Games. The Romans later injected new brutality to such showdowns, with contestants wrapping their hands in leather straps studded with bits of metal. These bloody affairs often ended in *klimax*, when the men each took turns throwing a punch at a time until one delivered the crushing blow.

Talk about some ruthless bastards.

Then came the gladiators, facing each other in battles to the death with various forms of armament and weaponry. It seems flesh-on-flesh blows just were not entertaining enough.

Many sportswriters and athletes consider boxing the world's most demanding sport. In the 1700s, it returned to vogue, taking root amongst the cultured peoples of Great Britain, where a bare-fisted Englishman, Jack Broughton, racked up a list of wins and earned his resting place in Westminster Abbey. He was forever linked to tragedy, though, because of his opponent who died after their forty-five-minute duel. In 1743, the Broughton Rules tried to mitigate boxing's risks.

Even so, it was still a bare-knuckled spectacle, and encountered another setback when a three-hour-long heavyweight bout between James "The Deaf 'Un" Burke and Simon Byrne led to Byrne's death from injuries sustained. This prompted further safeguards, and in 1838, the London Prize Ring Rules were implemented, banning biting, butting, kicking, and gouging.

Under these stricter guidelines, a sturdy bricklayer named Tom Sayers became the new champ, but clergymen and politicians still protested, and London was in an uproar when American champ, John Hennan, arrived to take on Sayers in 1860. Charles Dickens and William Thackeray were among those who ignored the heavy police presence, joining the throng to watch these "ruffians of the ring."

It wasn't until 1867 that a shrewd Cambridge athletics organizer drafted changes which would silence most reasonable objections. Dubbed the Queensberry Rules, they required boxing gloves, three-minute rounds with one-minute breaks, and a ten-second knockout count during which the downed man could not be assisted. These rules stand largely unchanged to this day and are credited for the preservation and legalization of the sport.

Pierce Egan, a British journalist, once called boxing "the sweet science of bruising," and few have defined it better. It requires a mastery of one's own breathing, musculature, and emotion, as well as an understanding of an opponent's physical and psychological vulnerabilities.

The goal: breaking your opponent down, piece by piece.

By all accounts, Cus was ahead of his time, teaching Mike how to break a man's body and will. How dangerous is the sport of boxing? Were you ever worried about Mike's physical well-being?

RORY: Every time he went into the gym, for real.

Thing is, Mike was a boxing historian and enthusiast. His knowledge helped him a lot in the ring, so the fight was like slow-motion to him. When punches were coming, he was calm. Cus had him well-prepared, like a well-oiled machine. He taught Mike everything he knew, the good and bad of what to expect when he got hit, and how to hit the other guy in certain places. What to feel and what not to feel. These other guys, the trainers like Teddy, Kevin, Jay, they were doing maintenance, an extension of Cus, keeping the machine running. Cus already built the machine. Mike was the machine.

My responsibilities were helping Mike outside the ring, but for over fifteen years I was there watching what he went through. The trainers kept the machine oiled, but if the trainers were gone, I could step in and do the job. I wasn't part of Cus's school of boxing, but I was in the gym with Mike every day. He didn't even wanna start sparring till I was there. He'd always be asking me, "Was my feet right? Did I drop my hand?" I'd tell him, "You missed a jab. You gotta move after each punch." It's stuff I caught inherently. If he off his game, I knew he off.

Boxing's dangerous not just during the fight but during all the sparring sessions. A fighter takes thousands of blows in his career, tens of thousands. The headgear, that protects you from getting cut, that's all. You still feel the impact. I seen guys who had concussions from a few rounds with a sparring partner. You ask him for the salt at the dinner table, and he passes you a bottle of ketchup.

See, Mike wasn't just a piece of meat to me. Most of these managers, they have ten, fifteen guys in their stable. One of their guys gets knocked out, gets brain damage, gets his head beat in, they put in the next one. You're just a commodity. With me, I didn't have a love of boxing beyond my relationship with Mike. He's what mattered.

This sport, along with mixed martial arts, has gotta be one of the deadliest in the world. In MMA, you get kicked in the face, shinbone on your skull, you could die, right? Boxing, every blow is the equivalent of someone taking a bat and smacking you upside the head. A guy don't always have his hands up. He's gonna get hit quite a few times. It's almost kamikaze, 'cause you don't know when your time's up. One punch, and it's over. Roy Jones. Invincible. He was knocking cats out. Then he gets knocked out once, and it starts happening to him all the time. He was done.

I give credit and respect to all fighters, whether you in the amateurs or in the pros or making millions or no money at all. To get in that ring and put your gloves up, to go toe-to-toe and put your life on the line, that takes a special kinda athlete to do that. You gotta be a little bit off maybe, a little something gotta be missing. It's very barbaric, since the beginning of time.

Mr. Holloway makes a point. Even the Queensberry Rules cannot disguise the sport's brutality. Statistically, auto racing, scuba diving, mountain climbing, horseback riding, and skydiving are all deadlier than "the sweet science," yet critics of boxing point to its list of victims.

Who doesn't cringe when they hear of the November 2013 brawl, fought at Madison Square Garden, during which Russian fighter Magomed Abdusalamova endured life-threatening injuries from hundreds of punches? He stayed on his feet until the final bell, caught his own cab to the hospital—after officials failed to arrange for an ambulance—and still lies in a bed dealing with permanent neurological damage. Despite a stellar professional record, his career is over.

Who hasn't witnessed Muhammad Ali's slurred speech and jittery movements and wondered about the sheer volume of punches he absorbed over the years? His symptoms, we are told, are related to Parkinson's disease, but other fighters do suffer from Punch Drunk Syndrome, *dementia pugilistica*, brought on by cumulative cerebral damage.

Who can read about the 1962 match between Emile Griffith and Benny Paret and not feel some empathy for them and their loved ones? Caught in the ropes, Paret was pummeled and defeated. He then slipped into a coma and died ten days later. The referee never presided over another bout. Griffith was horrified, and though he kept boxing, he was never the same. It was only in old age that Griffith met Paret's son, who embraced him and told him he was forgiven.

Should more safeguards be implemented?

Or should boxing be banned altogether?

The only way to regulate danger completely out of existence is to limit the very things that make humans feel alive. It's a challenge every parent, coach, and boxing manager faces, finding that balance between protecting those they love and allowing them to do the things they choose.

Do you think boxing needs more oversight? Did Mike experience long-term damage? What measures are in place currently to take care of fighters, financially, medically, and so on?

RORY: Most of these fighters come from abject poverty. Even the parents aren't usually educated enough to deal with the promoters. These fighters are like sheep in a den of lions, just so happy for a few dollars, and promoters take advantage of that. Before Team Tyson revolutionized the economic scale for a boxer's pay, these fighters didn't know what they were worth. They didn't even know what to ask for. Listen, you get in there and risk your life, that's priceless.

Floyd Mayweather, before he was known like he is today, he used to sit with me in my mom's restaurant in

Vegas, around '97, and we'd talk for hours about the finances of the sport. I saw it in his eyes, how he soaking it all in. Floyd was sharp and charismatic, even then, but still fighting in hotel ballrooms. I'd hear him on the radio, repeating stuff we talked about. I'm happy he made it. He's a true professional.

With Mike, it was in that first Holyfield fight he experienced extreme damage from head-butts. He was concussioned. Holyfield had a very unique way of doing it, even on tape where it looked like a motion of his punch or something, coming up with the crown of his head. In the second fight, we wanted a referee who'd watch for that. We wanted to prevent that. But Holyfield caught him again, and it was like a razor sliced Mike's head wide open.

The danger is always lurking. These fighters are really warriors. The referees are trained to look for medical concerns, but there ain't no insurance policies, no pensions, nothing. Once in a blue moon, you find a manager or promoter who cares, but most of these fighters don't get shit. I'm happy we're in a day and age where guys're earning some real money, but it ain't enough. That Russian fighter who got hospitalized after the fight last year, he had nothing to cover his ass financially, and that's a travesty. His team put together a trust for him. It shouldn't have come to that.

You ask me what I think? I think there should be a universal commission put in place, universal health insurance for these guys. As soon as these fighters sign with a promoter, the promoter should say, "Listen, man, I got this insurance package set up for you." The promoter, that's the one getting the whole cash pie from each fight. He takes a percentage for himself and divvies up the rest to lotsa people, the venues, the security, the fighters. After the fighter gets his due, the manager typically gets a third of that. These promoters are benefiting the most, so they should step up, making sure these kids who're bringing in all this money are taken care of.

Listen, the fans are the ones who get hurt. We don't get to see that match we wanna see between two fighters because one promoter doesn't wanna let the other fighter's promoter have any of that cash pie. He says, "You come fight under contract with me or we don't have a deal." It's bullshit, man.

I seen Mike's own words about it. He says, "Everyone in boxing probably makes out well except for the fighter. He's the only one that's on Skid Row most of the time. He's the only one that everybody just leaves when he loses his mind."

Now to me, Mike lost his mind and left me, but he's got a point, right? The way it's set up now, the fighters are the ones who get screwed. I wanna see something put in place that looks after their welfare too, some regulation. The NFL, the NBA, all these other sports are operated that way, even the UFC. The football players, they took the league to task about all these concussions and stuff, and they got a settlement.

But boxing? Man, it's so corrupt it's not even funny. You got these sheep. They be thinking they're something fierce, but they have no idea what they're walking into.

And Mike? He was the littlest lamb of all. We had him in position to be the first billion-dollar athlete, but it wasn't just lions he was facing. Since Day One, women have been a serious problem for Mike, and his trouble, it all started and ended with the foxes, cougars, and chicks. They were the ones holding his reins.

You ask Mike, he thinks he's the hunter.

But he is the one being hunted.

PART TWO

WERE MIKE'S WOMEN
AFTER HIS MONEY?

"Stay away from her!
Don't go near the door of her house!
If you do, you will lose your honor
and will lose to merciless people
all you have achieved."

Proverbs 5:8-9

CHAPTER NINE

THE CHICKS

E**very** generation of boys has its own lingo for cute girls. In the 1970s, Farrah Fawcett and Pam Grier were "foxy chicks." Brooke Shields and Grace Jones were among the "babes" of the 1980s, and Cindy Crawford and Halle Berry led the pack of 1990s "hotties."

As for Mike Tyson, he was never hung up on the lingo.

Woman . . . That's all he needed to know.

He dated many of them, from actress Robin Givens to supermodel Naomi Campbell, and he is remembered for his womanizing almost as much as for his achievements in the boxing ring. Some idolize and others demonize him for that fact.

No matter which way they are viewed, his relationships with the opposite sex were complicated from an early age. Mike grew up with his mother, older brother, and older sister in Brownsville, New York. They lived in a cramped, hotbox tenement on Amboy Street. Even into his teens, Mike slept in the same bed with his mom. Lorna Tyson collected welfare checks, but they didn't cover her drug habit, and in her apartment she sometimes had sex with men for a few bucks despite the presence of her children. Mike's father lived his own life out on the streets, visiting on very rare occasions.

Sickly and overweight, Mike suffered at the hands of local bullies and the schoolgirls who stole his glasses and called him names. Unable to find his place in a classroom setting, he fell in with a rough crowd called the Jolly Stompers, and shuffled in and out of juvenile detention. Authorities grew frustrated and shipped him north to Tryon Residential Center.

Lorna did not even fight it. She had already given up hope, maybe on herself. After Mike was moved from the state system into Cus D'Amato's care, she had infrequent contact with him. He was a tender sixteen years of age, just starting his climb to athletic greatness, when she died.

Cus took over as Mike's legal guardian. "He's my boy," Cus said. "I have a very deep affection for him." Camille became the steadfast mother-figure who fixed Mike hot chocolate and cradled his big head against her chest—that is, when he was not picking her up and twirling her around. Mike loved the shocked look on the faces of his Brooklyn friends when he introduced this elderly white couple as his father and mother.

Then, less than three years later, Cus succumbed to pneumonia.

Mike was devastated. The projects had already taken the lives of many acquaintances and his mom, and now even the sleepy backwaters of Catskill could not fend off the ogre of death. Mike joined other trainers and fighters as a pallbearer at the funeral, his movements like those of someone suffering shell-shock. He felt vulnerable and alone. He was only nineteen.

Flash forward twelve months. Las Vegas, Nevada. Mike Tyson vs. Trevor Berbick.

Mike is about to fight for his first world title, and he has two goals. One: avenge Muhammad Ali, who will be sitting ringside and who lost the last fight of his career against Berbick. Two: heft that belt for Cus, the man who always said this day would come.

There was a problem, though. Mike needs penicillin injected into his buttock to offset the gonorrhea burning through his loins. He blames it on a visit with a hooker, whom he labels a "brash girl." Really? With all that was on the line—his future in the sport, the years of training, and Cus's legacy—he could not keep it in his pants another week or two?

It was a sign of things to come.

Rory, did you ever meet Mike's mother? Were you aware of his visits to prostitutes?

RORY: I wasn't privy to the interactions between him and his mother. She just wasn't around much, you know, and Mike didn't really talk about her. His brother Rodney was a cool cat, and I knew his sister Denise. He loved her. Man, she was the sweetest girl in the whole world. She was quiet, overweight. It's a sad thing. She eventually died of obesity.

I can't really pinpoint why Mike got into all kinds of behavior, but once he got money, I can tell you from being another young black man, he was just looking for love. Did he visit prostitutes? Yeah, I'm sure he did, 'cause he was looking in all the wrong places. Looking for something to share. Something special. Something to hold him down. The fire inside him was burning wildly out of control.

With Mike, it's not about money or houses or cars. That stuff don't mean shit to him. It never has. What he really wanted was something pure. The tigers and the pigeons, the way he loved having them as pets, that was part of it. Wanting something simple and sacred.

Mike once said he would watch women like a tiger and want to devour them. Did you ever hear him say things that concerned you? Did you address them?

RORY: One thing about Mike is he speaks the truth. He tells people this kinda stuff and they don't believe him. But there it is. He told you, so why you so shocked?

People underestimate him, though. They think he's just this big, aggressive animal. No, Mike cares. He's thoughtful. He closes his eyes and processes things, just like you and I, right? He may not react the same as you and I, but if he loves something, he's there. He's in it. It's all or nothing with him, man.

I feel sorry that he didn't have what I had growing up. He didn't have that inside him. I always wanted that for him, 'cause he's done so much for so many people. Maybe he's done it in awful ways, in his own weird ways, but he means well. It still don't make it right, but he means well.

Mike was a strong guy. I never seen him back down from another man, not in the ring, on the street, nowhere. But he's always had this weakness. It's the women he cannot fight. They call the shots.

Both Mike and me, we were shy at first. Mike's this goofy guy, and I'm the quiet guy. Mike's first girlfriend was in Catskill. Holly Robertson, I think. We double-dated in my old Lincoln, took the girls to the drive-in movies. After that ended, we spent nights riding around Albany, before the championship or anything, and girls everywhere just ignored us. We didn't know what to say, didn't have no rap. We had no game. We just turned up the music—that was Mike's only requirement for a car, a good system—and scoped out these chicks on the corners, dreaming of the day.

It all changed, man, when we rolled up in the fancy cars. We went from having no girls to we couldn't get rid of them. Suddenly, we're the hottest cats in Albany, Troy, Schenectady. Girls're leaving notes on our windshields and shit.

Mike was just Mike, never really changed, but now he had ways to magnify that crazy side of his. Plus, he got more and more people watching his every move. I'm surprised, though, that this one incident never hit the tabloids. If we had the paparazzi around back then, you would've seen Mike's picture on the front pages. You'd still be able to pull it up on the Internet and laugh about it yourself.

Well, this happened at the Bone Center, in Albany. This was the place where all the action started happening—with the girls, I mean. Mike wasn't married. I wasn't married. We had this opportunity, and we took it.

Get this, Mike called me Pony Boy, and I called him Stallion.

One sunny Saturday afternoon, I'm watching TV and still exhausted from the night before 'cause I'd had my fun. All of a sudden, I hear this horn blowing. It's just blowing, blowing. I poke my head out the window, and Mike's down there in his new BMW. He was in Catskill, so he must've just drove all that way to get here. He's looking up at me through the sunroof.

"Who you got up there, Pony Boy?" he asks me.

I'm like, "Nobody. Come on up."

"Yo, you come on down, and bring a towel."

"A what? Whatcha talking about?"

"Just do it, Ro. You'll see in a minute."

So I go down, he opens the car door, and the heavyweight champ of the world's sitting there in a pair of damn undies.

What the hell?

I'm like, "What're you doing with no clothes on, Stallion?"

"Man, I was in a hurry," he says.

I say, "How'd you get past the toll booths? You had to go through two just to get here."

"Just give me the towel, give me the towel."

There was some funny times at the Bone Center. We had ourselves more fun than should be legal, if you know what I'm saying.

CHAPTER TEN

THE COUGAR AND THE RATS

In 1987, Mike was the new world champion, Rory was his best friend, and they were bachelors in their early twenties with cars, money, and women gathered around. They rented an apartment on Albany's Lancaster Street, and did not worry much about furnishing the living room or stocking the fridge. Most of the action happened in the bedrooms, which was how the place became known as the Bone Center—not real classy, perhaps, but at least they were straightforward about their intentions. Mike kept a growing list of available girls in his tightly guarded Black Book.

With plenty to keep them occupied, the pair of young men did not dabble into drugs. Mike believed in taking care of the machine that Cus had built, and Rory was a fellow athlete who had seen enough substance abuse by friends and relatives to know that was not for him.

Plus, all of these willing females? They were intoxicating enough.

Some of the girls were known on the streets as hood rats. Mike had a thing for them. They were his sort of girls, coming from nothing, trying to survive, holding nothing back. If they wanted sex, they let that be known through their clothing—or lack of it—and through their speech. No guessing games. No romantic pretenses. They were all there for the same thing, and if you expected a relationship with more substance, loyalty, or commitment . . . well, the Bone Center was not the place for you. Thank you, ladies. Don't bother coming again.

Rory was a few years older than Mike, fully committed to working long-term in the ring with his friend—from bologna to steak. But hey, if this new-found desirability was part of the deal, who was he to complain?

Are the legends of that apartment true, or have they grown larger with time and retelling?

RORY: We were caught up in our fun, no doubt about it. Just pure fun. Wasn't no drugs involved. We were having a ball.

The only qualifications for the Bone Center were, there were no qualifications. Man, sometimes we had like seven girls in our place. I'd pull up to the club around closing time, sporting a brand-new Rolls-Royce. Everyone's coming out, and I be having silk pajamas on. I'd lean out the window. "Come here, come here. How you doing? What you having for breakfast? We have breakfast at the house." Then Mike and me, we coordinating over the phone. He's at the Bone Center, asking me how many girls I got, and he telling me how many he got. "I got three, Ro. Three." I tell him, "I'm not superhuman," and he's like, "No, no, bring whoever's there with you. We make it work."

I admit, I made my mistakes. I'm not gonna sit here and tell you otherwise. Some days, though, I watched the way my boy was with these women, into one room, into the next, more than one in a room, whatever. He liked it all. Listen, no woman was safe from his womanizing. He was self-serving and maniacal. He just had these inhuman testosterone levels.

Listen, I was no angel. I was doing my thing too, but I knew how to turn it off. Mike, he took it into the stratosphere.

The AIDS epidemic was nightly news in the '80s. Mike had dealt already with a sexually-transmitted disease. Did those issues worry you?

RORY: You're right. Back then, everyone was worried. Couple years later Magic Johnson even went public about how he was HIV-positive, this basketball god, this guy we looked up to. That was scary as hell. I seen pictures of people wasting away in hospitals, and I sure didn't want that being me or Mike. Of course, we was young, not really thinking. I know for a fact Mike passed things along to some women, and even that didn't stop him. I figured, hey, if Mike don't got AIDS by now then that shit don't exist.

And hey, these girls were in on this too. Lots of times they got well-compensated. Mike was incredibly generous, even giving money to Holly in Catskill, back before he had money to give. It was that way even later. Whether it was $5 or $500,000, he was giving it to anyone with a sob story. He might never have built a monument or a Boys' Club, but he took care of family and friends, paid mortgages, rent, doctor bills. And he taught me to be that way too. That's why it's ridiculous to think I ever stole from him, 'cause if I wanted something all I had to do was ask. Whatever was in his pocket was mine. That's how we rolled.

For the first time, though, Mike had real cash, and he was buying these project girls jewels, cars, fur coats. He'd take them shopping at Gucci and Versace, and man, some of them, they'd get back to the ghetto worried about getting robbed. They just wanted the money. Few days later, they're in Versace returning the clothes for cash.

I was waiting to see a woman who had some moral fiber, some gumption. I wanted to hear one say, "To hell with that, Mike, you can't run off for two or three days and come back with another girl rolled up in your pocket. No, I'm better than that."

These women had a price, though. And Mike knew it. In his mind, everybody has a price. Listen, when I seen a lady who could stand up to that, I knew there was a good woman. A rare find.

We bounced around back in the day, and Mike always caused a buzz. We had our crew at the time, this cast of characters like the Brat Pack. There was Geno, a cop from Colonie, the next town over. He was cool with us. And this white guy, Charlie Curto, he was part of our crew. This other white guy, Don McGavin, we called him "Donkey Don." He was short and skinny, but the girls said he was hung. This scrawny kid, right? We thought that was funny as hell. Donkey had the juice since he with us, he had his ghetto pass. I'm still friends with him to this day. He owns a big sporting goods store now, has a daughter of his own. Then there was my younger brother, Todd, he was the life of the party. People thought he was fuckin' crazy 'cause he'd say and do anything, and he wasn't afraid of nobody. Everyone loved Todd.

So we were hanging out in the clubs, and some cats had a problem with us. Albany had a lot of good fighters then—Benjamin Goldstein, Tony Marshall, guys who could've gone somewhere—but it was Elijah Tillery who was supposed to be the next Ali. Built like a Greek god. And he was a bully, every weekend getting into street fights. He's shuffling and dancing like Ali, knocking dudes out, holding his hands up. He'd always take his shirt off. Could be the middle of fuckin' winter, and off comes his shirt. Everybody was scared of this guy, except for Todd. Elijah left Todd alone.

Word got around that Elijah was coming for Mike. I tried keeping them apart, diverting Mike to another club, down a different street. I didn't want Mike getting in trouble, but you got these two titans in the same town, and a clash was inevitable, right?

Mike, he's this Brooklyn cat, and he don't give a fuck about nothing. One night at this club, we hear Elijah's outside, sitting on Mike's car. That was our pimp-mobile, and Mike storms out there, ready to mess him up. A crowd gathers round. Mike tells Elijah to get the fuck off his car, and they both stare each other down. Finally, Elijah stands and tries to play it off, but the bully knew not to mess with Mike. The territory opened up again after that, jack.

Some of the best times were at Sal's. Sal DiCarlo. One night everything was shut down, and Mike and me was desperate for someplace to go. We crossed over the tracks into Colonie and saw this little place. We walked in, and it was all country music, country folks. The music stopped. Everyone looked at us like, "What the hell you doing here?" We were probably the first two black guys ever stepped in them doors. Next thing, our friends start going there with us, and Sal converts it into this disco place, hip-hop and R&B, no more country music. His place became our home away from home, our paradise. We were sneaking in bottles of Cristal champagne. The whole 'hood was up in that joint, and Sal's business went through the roof. Even years later, we dropped in and said hi to Sal, right up till he died. He and his wife were good to us.

When did Mike first take notice of Robin Givens? Was she the first celebrity he fixated upon?

RORY: Robin wasn't the first, no. Back then, one of the hot ebony models was Beverly Johnson, tall, incredibly gorgeous. My mom always wanted to meet this lady, right?

One time Mike was gone for a coupla days, then he calls me. "Ro, pick me up at the airport."

I go out to the airport, and into the car slides Mike and Beverly Johnson. She's sitting right there in the backseat. I'm like, "Oh, shit."

Mike's all dressed up, showing me that he's the man and this his woman. Guess they met in New York City. She was really, really nice. She was a lot older than Mike, on her last days in terms of competing with girls like Naomi Campbell and Tyra Banks, but still good-looking. I'm tripping out. I mean, Mike was a roughneck cat, we been catching girls from the 'hood, and now he's stepped his game up. Way up. How'm I gonna beat this one?

He tells me to drive them to Albany. I'm still stunned. We pull up at my family's grocery store, where my mom's working these sixteen, seventeen-hour days. Mom's name is Bev, so maybe that's why she had this interest in Beverly Johnson. She turns and gets to meet this woman, and all day long Mom has this smile on her face that she can't wipe off. She just can't believe it. What's Ms. Johnson doing here with Mike?

Mike and Beverly's fling didn't last long. They hung out and messed around some. My mom never forgot that, though. That was the first celebrity we saw him with.

Eventually, Mike dated all kindsa models and stars— Miss USA, Kenya Moore, and Miss America, Suzette Charles—but he was a strange guy, and his preference was the average hood rat. He'd buy her diamonds and stuff, dress her up. That's who he liked, even when it got to the point he could date any girl in the world, and I mean anyone. I guess they all wanted the bad boy. And Mike, he was the baddest.

Thing is, when he'd get with these celebrities, he was just who he is. He didn't change. These girls were living in this high-class world, parents hoping they get with a doctor or lawyer. Instead, here's Mike. He's so far from that, you can forget that shit.

The one he fell real hard for was Robin Givens. Head over heels. I'm telling you, when he saw her, all we could do was hold on for the ride.

CHAPTER ELEVEN

THE HONEYBEES

Robin Givens. For many, her name stirs strong reactions to this day.

In 1987, *People* magazine said there was "no ceiling on her talent," yet three years later *Ebony* described her as "the most hated woman in America." She posed nude for *Playboy* in the early 1990s, and later made appearances—fully clothed, of course—on the TV program, *Praise the Lord*. She is not an easy woman to categorize.

Born in New York City, Robin is a year and a half older than Mike. Like Mike, she was very young when her father left, and she and her sister were raised by a mother who worked hard and did anything to survive. Robin attended a private school in New Rochelle, New York, and graduated from Sarah Lawrence College in 1984. Harvard Medical School records show that she took one class there before a call from Bill Cosby ended her postgraduate work. She was sassy, smart, and cute, and he encouraged her to pursue acting. She made appearances on *The Cosby Show* and *Different Strokes*, then landed a regular role as snooty Darlene on *Head of the Class*.

When the show debuted in 1986, she had no idea Mike Tyson would become a fan. She had already been linked romantically with stars such as Eddie Murphy and Michael Jordan, but they treated her as a fling. If the newly crowned heavyweight champ had money, he had a shot at getting her attention. Robin's mother, Ruth, also had a penchant for wealthy men, and once filed suit against a Yankees baseball player for giving her a venereal disease.

Robin and Ruth. Two busy little honeybees. And for them, making lots of money—uh, honey—meant they had to collect a lot of pollen.

How did Mike and Robin meet? Was there genuine chemistry between them, or did you suspect that Robin was after something more than a relationship?

RORY: It all started with Mike. He'd been seeing different girls, and really liked this one named Gloria. He met her and her sisters at a club in Manhattan, got to be friends with the family, and their father was a big fight fan. "These Dominicans, they beautiful," he told me. "Ro, I gotta introduce you to the oldest sister." I wasn't ready for nothing serious yet, living it up at the Bone Center. I knew that much about myself.

But then Mike, man, one day I walked into our place, and his eyes were glued to the TV. It was that show, *Head of the Class.* Robin was on, pretty and petite, and he was just sitting in the dark, staring. I said, "What's wrong with you?"

His tone was really serious. "I gotta have her." He knew what he wanted, and sure enough, he thought of a way to get it. "What's that guy's name?" he asked me. "John Horne, right? He's out in Los Angeles. Call him, and see if he can get us in touch with this girl. Do it, Ro. C'mon."

Mike Tyson was the biggest thing in boxing, and that was all John needed. He had his way in. He called Robin's publicist, dropped the champ's name, and they set up this meeting in March of '88. It was much anticipated. Mike was taking a bath every day for almost a week beforehand. He was practicing in the mirror what he gonna say. He and I flew into LAX and checked into this huge suite at the Beverly Wilshire. Once we got settled, Mike was ready and on his best behavior.

This whole group of us converged on LeDome, a restaurant on Sunset Blvd., like it was a damn business meeting or something. John, Mike, and me, we were looking good, and we introduced ourselves to Ruth,

Robin, and Robin's sister, Stephanie. Robin had Mike's full attention in her black velvet dress, real stylish, clinging to every curve. And he looked fly in a blue Armani suit. She seemed impressed.

Mike got them laughing at the table, and Robin said later that he was easy to talk to and even her mother was surprised at how comfortable he made her feel. He had that ability—his voice, his humble act, and him being this tough guy. I seen it a thousand times. That's his game, and the girls eat it up. Well, Robin and Ruth had their game too, and he was into it deep. When I say into it, this fool was giving Robin his heart and soul.

The rest of the year, the two of them dated off and on, skiing, movies, fancy dinners, trying to keep the romance going even though both had their own careers. Now that Robin was linked with the champ, her name was blowing up in the news and tabloids. She was a household name. And Mike, well, he was his usual self, sending her all these gifts—a dog, a diamond necklace, a low-cut red-leather suit, whatever.

I had mixed feelings about Robin. She was nice and had this classy thing about her, so I tried not to prejudge her. My problem was, she wasn't controlling the show. It was Ruth at the helm, almost like the Kardashians pimping out their daughters for the social blitz. To me, Ruth was just Ruthless, 'cause she was so freakin' determined. Mike was a way to help her and her daughter advance their careers, to get on that level with the famous people, the Donald Trumps and all. That's just the way I saw it. Their actions and some conversations confirmed it for me. It wasn't about Mike. It was about them.

Did Mike and Robin love each other? I know he really loved her, but I can't get inside her head. I'm not sure if she ever loved him, but she tried, I'll say that much. Without Ruth around, it may have worked. Then again, I don't think a Robin Givens would like a Mike Tyson under different circumstances. Robin didn't go for average guys, guys with Mike's background. She was high society, and he was very uncouth. Was that what she really wanted? That was my question for a lot of these females he dealt with. Was he the guy they'd be with if he wasn't filthy rich? If he wasn't the most successful athlete in the world? Listen, good-looking men walk down the street every day, and they don't have girls flocking after them. So why Mike?

Mike and Robin got married without telling anyone. As his best friend, what was your reaction?

RORY: I knew Mike wasn't ready for marriage, but his life was feeling fragile. The Dominican girl, Gloria, he heard she was in a fatal accident coming home from Jersey, and that shook him up. A sweet, young girl, so full of energy. You never know when someone gonna be taken from you, right?

So the deal with Robin, he did it impulsively. He didn't sit back and let it all come together organically. He was overwhelmed by this TV beauty, and it's like he was searching for something to call his own family. With the Dominicans, he seen a glimpse, and he was yearning for that. So my man's falling in love, falling hard, and I was helpless. You ever tried talking a person outta love? That shit don't work.

Robin started wearing a ring around, showing it off to Joan Rivers on *The Tonight Show*, but there wasn't no date set. Then in February of '88, I heard how she and Mike was getting all cozy at the NBA All-Star game in Chicago. They went that same afternoon, get Father Clements to read them their vows, and later made it official at the courthouse. It happened in a blur, you know, like Mike afraid we gonna talk him out of it. He snuck and did it, didn't even include his friends.

After that, it bugged him that I was all alone now. He tried again to hook me up with Gloria's oldest sister, but I knew Mike needed me at that time. Did he see what was going on? I don't know. But I could tell, this man was wading into some deep waters.

I'm sure you heard what the media was saying about the marriage. Did you agree with their portrayal of Robin as a gold-digger?

RORY: Here's what I think. Robin was an opportunist, and her mom was all in. When I say "all in," I mean Ruthless was stuck to her daughter like your big toe's stuck to your foot. She right there calling all the shots, whispering in Robin's dainty little ear, rubbing Mike's big head. "Oh, baby, we your family now." And he was buying into this shit.

Robin got a joint bank account with Mike, and started looking through all his finances. That's when everything hit the fan with Bill Cayton and Jim Jacobs. Barely married, and she's suing Mike's managers and turning his team upside down. She had a point, though. I'll give her that. Mike's contracts weren't good for him in the long run, but I guarantee you Ruthless was back there pulling strings.

Having access to Mike's money through Robin, Ruth went and bought this house in Bernardsville, New Jersey. A fuckin' mansion, over $4,000,000. Except this wasn't a house you'd see Mike in. It was more like a castle, all this old furniture, these antiques, the type of place where Ruth could throw her tea parties and invite Oprah over. First time I went in and sat on the couch, Ruth told me, "No, you can't sit on that." I moved to a chair. "You can't sit there . . . You can't sit there . . . You can't sit there."

Finally, I'm like, "Where the fuck can I sit?" That made Mike laugh.

The little demands started piling up. One time we're all riding in the limo, and Mike was wanting to get a nice place for his sister Denise. Ruthless said, "She doesn't need to live in a new place like that. It's too good for her." And Mike didn't even defend it. I was looking at him like, "You kidding me, Mike? You gonna let her talk that way about your sister?" That was my first glimpse that he had no balls around women.

Ruthless looked at me next. "What're we going to do with you?"

I'm like, "What you gonna do with me? What you talking about?" I was on the books, but not making anything close to six figures yet.

Ruth said, "You're making too much."

And Mike just sat there, didn't say a freakin' word.

He was easy pickings. I can only imagine what Ruth and Robin were talking about behind closed doors. Man, I tried warning him, but that was a mistake 'cause the man has no filter. He's that guy you want at the party, and you don't want at the party. The most entertaining guy in the world, but you never know what he gonna say. You for damn sure don't tell him something if you want it kept secret.

So we at dinner one night, and he looks across the table and tells Robin and Ruth, "Here's what my man said about you guys. He thinks you're trying to rob me." My butt-cheeks clench. My hands turn sweaty. It gets quiet, but Mike, he's just brutally honest. He turns to me. "Go on, Ro, tell these bitches what you said."

A lot of the time this was his way of saying what he's feeling, except he put it on you. Later, in that high voice, he pulled me aside and said, "I'm sorry, man. I'm sorry."

During the infamous 1989 Barbara Walters interview, Robin accused Mike of physical abuse. Did you consider him capable of that?

RORY: Absolutely, unequivocally not. When Robin talked that shit to Barbara Walters, she was trying to set Mike up, plain and simple. She and her mother wanted to make it seem like he was mentally unfit. It was a calculated plan. They'd called in doctors to examine him, counselors and psychiatrists who declared him clinically depressed. They started giving him antidepressants. Now they got him on national television, all drugged up like a zombie. He's practically drooling, dressed in this ugly-ass sweater like he's fuckin' Chucky's son, while his wife says this stuff about him in front of the whole world.

I was at the apartment up in Albany, and I'm watching this on TV. I can't stop from laughing, but it's sad as hell. I'm thinking that this cat's newly married and already he got everything swirling around him. The man can't hardly enjoy his own wife, not with her mother attached to her hip 24/7, and now these two women're plotting a takeover—his cars, house, bank accounts, estate. What a nightmare.

Robin and Ruth, they had a way of making sure the press was always around. Especially when Mike fucked up. He's a horrible driver, ask anyone who knows him, and he likes to drink. He drove into a tree on Camille's property, this winding driveway, and Robin and Ruth rushed to see him at the hospital, dragging the reporters in with them. You tell me, is that what a normal, caring family do? The news speculated that Mike was suicidal, but that came from Robin. Mike denied it, saying. "I have too much to live for."

Where Robin came up with this stuff, I don't know. Mike, he might get mentally or verbally abusive, that could be, but he would never hit a woman. I never seen that in all my years with him. Can you imagine Mike Tyson, this guy who knocks out grown men in the ring, hitting hundred-pound Robin? It's ridiculous, right? She'd crumple like a rag-doll. I once seen her haul off and hit him like an MMA fighter, right in front of his friends. Spit flew out of his mouth, and he didn't do nothing. He ain't that kinda guy. He was like a tiger with a cub swatting at it. He just sat there, calm. Sometimes he might've pawed at her and pushed her away, but he never hit her. Never happened.

That's not saying he was faithful. Listen, Mike was always on the prowl, his wandering eyes never stopped. Robin claimed she once caught him with lipstick smeared in places lipstick shouldn't be, and found condoms in his pocket after he been out late on his own. The way she tells it, Mike said, "Who you love don't have nothing to do with who you . . ." And then he shut up.

One time, they in his Bentley arguing about him being with some other girl, and it turned into this physical tug-of-war. He crashed the damn thing, and when the police showed up, he told them they could just have it. A $180,000 car? They probably thought they hit the jackpot. When their supervisors found out, these guys were put on leave.

Not long after the Walters interview, I got this call and raced down to the house in Bernardsville. The police were fanned out in front. Robin had told them her husband was on the roof about to jump. Who's not gonna believe her? She already planted the seeds. When I pulled up, the cops said, "Mike threw something at one of our officers. You better go in there and get your man, or we're gonna have a problem." I figured Robin would be traumatized, but I found her and her mom giggling in a bedroom.

I looked frantically for Mike. Later, I found out he took off through the woods behind the house and headed for Manhattan. He was chillin' with the Dominican family, sitting in their hi-rise apartment in a pair of raggedy shorts he grabbed while making his escape.

"I had to get out," he said. "Robin and Ruth, they were driving me fuckin' crazy."

In the long run, I think them ladies bit off more than they could chew. They thought Mike was the big dumb boxer, easy prey, but it backfired. Mike got the marriage annulled after only eight months. Robin kept the clothes and the jewelry, but didn't get the house, didn't get no divorce settlement. He rushed to the bank the next morning before the doors opened. He got a cashier's check for $9,000,000 and put it in my name, in case they tried to stop him cashing it later. Robin and Ruth, they raced to his other bank, and before we could stop them they pulled out $1,000,000. It was insane.

In Robin's book, she says, "Rory had wisdom beyond his years . . . he has insight and perception . . . an old soul in the body of a young person." Does that surprise you?

RORY: You know, I never had a personal issue with Robin. It was mostly her mother. When I seen my man hurting, though, I had to defend him. That's who I am.

Couple years ago, Robin was in a production called *Gold-Digger.* She must have a sense of humor, right? Papa J, a very close friend of mine, he got us tickets. We were sitting near the front in the Beacon Theater, and the whole time I was afraid she'd stop and point at me from the stage, give me that hard look. After the play, she was signing books, and I tried to duck past.

"Rory," she called out. She hurried over, wrapped me in this big hug. It was nice. I could see that she'd changed and matured.

After her breakup with Mike, she hooked up with Brad Pitt—he was just getting started in acting, not like he is today—and then she remarried and divorced again. She's had her hard times, but she's religious now and straightened around. Good for her, you know. I have no ill-will. That's how life is, right? We all learn and we grow.

But Mike, he was tore up after everything happened. The relationship with Robin, that was his first real hope, his shot at having a normal family for the first time in his life. When that crumbled, he was a mess. I never seen him like that, crying in the dark, me just holding him against my shoulder. I'm telling you, those were dark moments.

Then Don King, he slinks in and wants to advise us on how to handle matters now that Robin's blown up the management team and caused all this turmoil. He tries to make Mike feel better, bros before hoes, and all that. "Those nasty, skanky, low-down bitches," Don says, hair waving back and forth.

Mike squirms in his chair and finally explodes. "Stop it! Stop it, I can't take it anymore! I loved her, man. That was my wife."

Don sits back, eyes wide, and just shakes his head. "Lord Jesus, Champ."

Everything was falling apart for Mike, and watching what he went through, hearing his pain, it was rough. You'd think that would scare me off any serious relationships, right? But Mike finally introduced me to the girl in Manhattan, the older Dominican sister. We took the elevator up to her parents' hi-rise apartment and knocked on the door, playing it cool, even though the whole time I was sweating it. I mean, girls in the five boroughs don't pay no attention to us guys from upstate.

Then she opened the door. Sheila Carrasco.

Whoa, she was hot.

Mike's good at picking out the right thing for other people, and he hit this one outta the park. Best gift ever. She was hot, but it was an innocent hot—very little make-up, nails well done, quiet, real attentive to her mother, cooking, setting the table.

All reason went out the window. After watching Mike suffer, I should've known better, but this girl was everything I dreamed of. I jumped in with both feet.

CHAPTER TWELVE

THE BIRD OF PARADISE

The Dominican Republic is a Caribbean paradise, alive with greenery, beaches, and wildlife. Its national flag is quartered with blue and red squares, held together by a white cross, and stamped in the center with a Bible on a coat of arms—the world's only national flag to bear a Bible. The motto is *Dias, Patria, Libertad,* which means, "God, Fatherland, Freedom."

The Carrascos were a traditional Dominican family, close-knit, Catholic, and fiercely loyal. Grandfather Carrasco led the migration to New York City decades ago, gaining U.S. citizenship. Like fellow countrymen Oscar de la Renta (fashion designer) and Albert Pujols (baseball star), he sought new opportunities on American soil. His daughter married another Dominican, and they established roots as a couple at 108th Street, in a Manhattan apartment. She birthed and raised three daughters—Sheila, Gloria, and Alba—while crafting grand draperies which she sold from her living room. Her husband worked in a coat factory, providing for his girls.

As youngsters, Sheila and her sisters endured the "horrific" uniforms and strict guidelines of nearby Catholic schools. They were three birds of paradise, fluttering about Manhattan with high cheekbones, wide dark eyes, and light coffee skin. Their parents encouraged church attendance, but focused more on believing in God and never hurting or offending anyone. They epitomized their national motto, and instilled those values in their daughters.

Like many Dominicans, the Carrascos were baseball and boxing fans. When they moved to a different hi-rise, they never expected this new place would one day serve as a home away from home for Mike Tyson and for his right-hand man, Rory Holloway.

Rory, you were in your mid-twenties, with all the freedoms of bachelorhood. When you met Sheila, what made you think you were ready to settle down with one woman?

RORY: Those were interesting times for me. Mike and Robin had got married so I had the Bone Center to myself, but it just wasn't the same without my boy around. I was used to us guys hanging out, cracking up. I knew Mike missed our times, too—but that wasn't all he be missing. He called sometimes, wanting to sneak over. One time I told him, "You're married now. You can't be doing that shit."

He said, "C'mon, Ro, who you got there?"

"Nobody."

"C'mon, I hear a girl's voice."

"That's the people next door," I lied.

Coupla nights later, he came over anyway. His head was low, like he dragging a ball and chain. Probably hoped I'd give him a pass or something.

"Listen," I said, "you gotta give me the Black Book." He didn't say nothing. "Mike, you can't be fuckin' around no more. Give me the book."

"Man, why you always such a downer, Ro? I hate you." He looked like he was in agony, but he handed the book to me.

It was the changing of the guard, like he passed me the secret key, the king's magic wand. I'm not gonna sit here and say I didn't use it. The list was right there.

One girl in particular, I wanted her bad. Anastasia or something. German. Long legs. Mike called her for me, pulling off this whole act about how he was married now and his friend Rory feeling low. "This guy, he's my best friend in the whole world. He has money, and he'll take care of you. He'll treat you right." Well, she ended up at my place, which tells you the kinda girl she was. We

80

rolled around under the covers, and I thought this was the beautiful life. It tortured Mike knowing how he was missing out.

After my romp with Anastasia, I was done. To be honest, I was losing respect for a lotta these girls. Some of the things I seen them do to get with Mike and his money, I started thinking all girls was like that. Didn't they have no moral compass? You know, you just start wanting something deeper, more meaningful.

Listen, you come from the 'hood, you don't talk about this stuff. People thought the Holloways was this great family—and it was good, I'm not saying that—but I seen the way my father treated my mom. I seen the way he jumped on her, the way he dragged her down the street. That does something to you as a kid. That shit stuck with me for years. He had no boundaries, just this slick hustler mentality, hanging out with these other women right in front of us. It made my stomach turn.

My youngest brother, Chris, he wasn't privy to that. Todd, he was the one my dad bragged about, the phenomenal athlete. And Cameron, he took the brunt of it, even got whipped once with a brown extension cord, but he never broke. Me, I was the observer, taking it all in. It's painful, and to this day my mother don't ever talk about it.

In his own ways my father was a good cat, teaching us about life and hard work. That humbled me, made me thankful. Cameron and me had to work for every penny we got. Thing is, even when we earned it, we didn't get it. My mother knew and felt bad about that, but she was under the thumb of a tyrant. Easters, she tried to sneak us new clothes. She worked long store hours so we didn't have to be in there, so we could play ball and be kids. It was like my dad thought we was all put on this earth to serve him.

We should all be reexamining ourselves and learning from what went on. You think that gonna happen? Everything you do as a parent, it shapes your kids later. You spew pain and poison, that hurts them. I wasn't perfect, but for damn sure I knew I didn't want to be that kinda man who make his family fear him. I'd rather be respected than feared. Respect lasts forever. It ain't about muscles or money or even the words that come outta my mouth, but my actions and my deeds. I wanted to find a woman who we could raise children together, show them we love them and love each other.

That was pivotal. That's what I wanted.

Did that even exist? Were there women like that out there?

Then I met Sheila, and she showed me something new. She was nice and very cordial, but she wouldn't even flirt 'cause she'd been seeing this guy for a year or two. That depth of loyalty impressed me. Man, it made me want her even more.

But if there was any mutual attraction, she sure hid it well. I'd call. "How you doing, Sheila?"

"I'm fine. How are you?"

"I'm fine . . . boom, boom, boom." And that was it. Sheila seen my car, fine clothes, my bank-roll, and she still wouldn't budge. I just had to be patient, 'cause I knew more than ever she was one of them rare finds.

Sheila, what can you let readers about Rory? What're your memories of meeting him and Mike? What did your father think of it all?

SHEILA: I actually knew Mike before I ever met Rory. My sisters and I bumped into Mike one night as we were leaving this club. He was coming in with his entourage, and he just stopped, said hi to us, and invited us back inside. Rory wasn't there. I found out later that

Rory was more laid-back, not really a big party guy. Well, we had a fun evening in the club, hanging out with Mike in the VIP area, but we didn't expect to ever see him again. I mean, Mike Tyson was a big star, so we were surprised a few days later when he stopped by our place to visit Gloria. He came up, sat on the couch, and he barely took his eyes off my sister. It was cute. We told my father, "Hey, Papi, come meet Mike Tyson." He thought we were making this up. He walked out, shirt hanging out of his shorts, and his eyes bulged when he saw Mike right there in our living room.

After that, Mike was like our big brother. We had friends and neighbors in and out all the time, all our Dominican girlfriends, and Mike was just another part of the family. He loved it. He made us laugh. When things cooled off with him and Gloria, he still came by sometimes. Then Gloria had her accident, just a tragic thing, you know, coming home from this popular skating rink over in Jersey. That was so hard on my dad and mom. Really hard. Mike was at her funeral, and then he disappeared for a while. The next thing we know, the news was reporting his surprise wedding to Robin Givens.

At that time, I was seeing a guy. He was decent, hardworking, but things got a little weird anytime he saw Mike's limo outside our building. He felt threatened by that. When Mike stopped coming around, things were better, and then one day Mike asked if he could stop by with his friend named Rory. Sure. Why not?

Rory was polite. He just sat there in our apartment, this quiet demeanor. I caught him glancing over, checking me out, never realizing he was interested. Mike gave him my number, and Rory and I started talking on the phone. We got together a couple times with Mike's entourage, all hanging out, and then Mike called and asked if he could come over and we'd have lunch. Instead, Rory showed up. Was it something they planned out? I wasn't sure what to think. Rory told me, "Well, Mike got caught up out there, and I just decided to come. We can still go get something to eat, right?" So we did. We had a great lunch and got to know a lot more about each other.

After that's when the first kiss happened. It wasn't forced. It felt really nice, really natural. It brought up all this confusion, since I was still kind of seeing the other guy, and I shared with Rory how I felt uncomfortable about it. He was really sweet. He said there was nothing to worry about, his feelings for me were honest, and we'd take our time. Even though neither of us wanted to stop, he wasn't pushy. I loved that about him.

Later, I learned about some of the abuse that went on in his own home, and I was so thankful that wasn't the way it was with me. I considered myself blessed to have both my dad and mom, since being raised with both parents was kind of rare in our community. They were so great together, and even from a young age I idolized them and wanted that too. They were poor, hardworking people, but they made us feel rich. My mom could make a meal of black beans and rice seem like a feast. She was so creative. My parents spoiled us in a lot of ways.

My father passed in 2009. He was seventy-nine, and loved by so many people. I still look up to my mom. She was a stay-at-home mother, a very strong woman, and I pray I can be half the woman she is, especially with the losses she's gone through—her daughter Gloria, and a son who only lived a few days. We just celebrated her eightieth birthday, and it made me so happy to see her dancing the *salsa*, smiling, and having fun. She is still full of life.

Rory, how did you win Sheila over? What happened to her previous boyfriend?

RORY: Man, I tried everything. I pulled out the big guns. Mike would dress me up in furs and rings, and I'd go to Sheila's apartment looking like a clown. She wasn't impressed by all that. Eventually, we kissed and things started heating up. She broke up with her boyfriend, but he was angry. He still called. He wouldn't go away, right? It got worse and worse, till he was leaving messages like, "Wait till I see you" and "Blood will be spilled." She was scared, and this was my girl now. That shit wasn't funny.

Mike had a fight coming up, maybe the Bruno fight in Vegas. Sheila was hanging out with us by then, and even got to sit ringside with Whitney Houston. I mentioned to Don King how Sheila's ex was threatening her, saying something gonna go down at the fight.

Don just listened, nodded, real serious. "Lord Jesus," he said. "That ain't right." He told me not to worry, he look into it.

I don't know what kinda buttons he pushed or levers he pulled, but we never heard from Sheila's ex again. It wasn't like he disappeared, you know, permanently. It wasn't nothing like that. Nothing physical. We found out her ex was on probation or something, and Don had the powers-that-be apply some pressure.

It's rumored, Sheila, that Rory proposed to you in an unusual way. Did his money influence your decision to marry him? Is it true that Donald Trump was in attendance at your wedding?

SHEILA: When Rory and I first started dating, he had friends who told him I was just after his money. I wasn't raised that way. My family wasn't like that. Even with Mike, we never ever asked for one dollar. We never saw him as a meal ticket. My family genuinely cared about him. I was hearing things on my end too. Some of my friends and cousins, coming from a Hispanic culture, had their opinions about me being with an African-American man. Nothing ever said to my face, just whispers here and there.

For the Bruno fight, Rory arranged for me and some close family and friends to fly out to Vegas. He had it all covered for us. He was so thoughtful, and by that time we were pretty serious about our relationship. It was a fun trip.

Well, one day at the Hilton, I'm up in the room taking a shower. We were going to a show that night, I think. Next thing I know, here's Rory stepping into the shower with me. Except he's dressed to a T, looking very gallant in this tailored suit and tie. He gets down on one knee right there in the water, still wearing his polished shoes, and pulls out a jewelry box. It was so romantic. He asks me if I'll spend the rest of my life with him, and I'm just so surprised, I'm like, "Oh, my God. Yes. Yes, of course." That was it. We never did make it to that night's show.

We had our wedding in Bernardsville, in the summer of '89. Mike still had the house Ruth had bought, and it was a perfect setting. We hired a friend who was a wedding planner. She was so great at throwing functions together, and she made this place look absolutely beautiful. She knew who to call. The food was amazing. I was getting stressed out, though. All my friends wanted to be in the wedding, and I didn't know how to turn them down. It kept getting bigger and bigger, and I was overwhelmed by all the preparations. Rory was with Mike at training camp in Vegas, and many times I would call him in tears. It was a bittersweet time for Mike, but he'd get on the phone. "No, Sheila, you got nothing to worry about. I got it. Do it, do it up." He contributed a lot.

Even now, people remember that day. A lot of guests even hooked up and met their partners there. Donald Trump was there, Don King, Father Clements. Lots of celebrities, close friends, family. It was big. Rory and I never had a honeymoon, though. In those days, Rory was managing Mike, and he believed in being there with his guy through camp and everything. The Carl Williams fight was next, and Rory was gone weeks at a time. He was very committed, and I respected that.

We got pregnant, and I carried our first child the full nine months. I ran a high fever, which affected the baby's development. Royce Sharaud was born January 14, 1990, but he had some issues with his lungs. I held him. Rory was there, and we both held our child. We prayed for our child. We were hopeful Royce would come out of this, and it didn't turn out. He was with us only a day and a half. Rory was just devastated. Through all that, my family was there for me—my mom, my sister Alba—but I felt like I was less of a woman. I felt guilty somehow. Rory stood by me, so sweet, telling me we'd try again and it would be okay. We called my dad to prepare a burial in the same plot where my sister Gloria rests. We bought a little casket. To this day, it still triggers something in me. It's just something that never leaves you.

It was a really rough time. Rory wanted to be at my side, but he had to set up camp in Japan, preparing for the Douglas fight. His heart was so heavy, and even with all the support, a deep depression came over me. Before the fight, Rory flew me out to Tokyo with him so that I could have a change of scenery.

Of course, the newspapers jumped all over Rory and Team Tyson after the fight. It was ugly. They had no idea what we were going through. They didn't know the loss we'd just suffered. And then Mike's loss in the ring on top of that? We felt like the whole world was caving in on us.

It's funny how things work out, though. On April ninth of the following year, this blessing came to us when Michael Paris was born. Three years later, I gave birth to Gloria Nia. My mother has helped so much with our babies. They call her "Lela," which is their version of *abuela*, the Spanish word for "grandmother." Both kids are fully grown now, two beautiful adults, and they still love their Lela.

In many ways, my mother was instrumental in us staying together. She knew the career Rory had, traveling and facing temptations, so she watched our children and let me go put in time with my husband, flying with him to the camps and fights. Rory always made me feel secure and comfortable. We were best friends. He avoided the after-parties, to him that was opening the door to the devil. He just never gave me a reason to suspect him of anything. His attention was on me. We're now celebrating our twenty-fifth anniversary, and I wouldn't be with him if he were anything less than honorable.

RORY: Let me tell you, Sheila is the most incredible woman. Mike introducing us, that was his best gift to me. Even with all the cars and houses, Sheila and I hardly had time to enjoy it. We were on this wild ride, 24/7, just nonstop work. People can say what they want, but they don't know. When the rug was pulled out from under us, she stayed right by me. She never doubted me. She didn't let nobody strip me of my manship. She never changed. She's just a special, special woman.

CHAPTER THIRTEEN

THE PANTHER

Mike was a wounded animal. As Rory and Sheila worked on the foundations of a lifelong marriage, Mike mourned his breakup with Robin. In a span of five years he had lost many people close to him—Cus, Jim Jacobs, his mother Lorna, his sister Denise, Sheila's sister, Gloria—and he was not yet twenty-five years old. Certain species in the wild slink away to nurse their wounds, while others become more aggressive and unpredictable, and he was of the latter group. Bearing his claws, he went on a sexual rampage.

One of the first creatures to wander across Mike's path was unlike any he had ever encountered. She came at him with slender, shapely legs, a narrow torso, and a radiant set of teeth to offset silky ebony skin.

Her name was Naomi Campbell.

Naomi was born in London, England, and studied ballet as a young girl in Italy. At age 15, she appeared on the cover of *Elle* magazine, and she was the first black model featured on the big September issue of American *Vogue*. Though she represented numerous designers, appeared in hundreds of magazines, and walked countless runways, she insisted that she was not getting paid the same as her blond-haired, blue-eyed peers. Other top models stood by her, refusing to work unless she was given fair treatment.

And hey, the girl deserved credit for practicing what she preached. She was all about racial equality, even in the bedroom—where she is known to have slept with men ranging from Robert De Niro (actor) to Adam Clayton (U2's bass player) to Mike Tyson (yeah, you know the guy).

Naomi's fiery temperament did not always sit well with others. In 1987, Elite Model Management accused her of abusive and manipulative behavior toward the staff, yet it was that very fierceness which lunged from her photos and captured the fashion world. Soon, she was picked up by another agency and by the time she was twenty, she was listed as one of the world's original supermodels, along with Cindy Crawford, Linda Evangelista, Claudia Schiffer, and Christy Turlington.

Would such an exotic creature stop there? Not even close.

Like Mike, Naomi thrived on chaos and controversy. She perpetuated her bad-girl image with appearances in Madonna's *Sex* book and in racy music videos, and added to that image each time she was named in another assault case, whether against assistants, associates, or a pair of police officers at London Heathrow airport. British Airways even banned her for life. When she later admitted she was dealing with cocaine addiction, her run of erratic behavior seemed more comprehensible. She checked herself into rehab and tried to put things back together.

These days, Naomi continues her involvement in fashion, and channels much of her passion through various charity efforts. She is still fierce, always one picture away from being the face of the next fashion campaign—or the subject of the next tabloid issue.

As a model, Naomi's been "shot" thousands of times by photographers, but she has never been easy prey. Far from it. When Mike, the mighty hunter, tried to shoot down this panther for his own pleasure, he had no idea what he was dealing with.

In the process, he discovered something he and close friends never thought possible.

Is it true that Mike sought advice from a famous pimp after his breakup with Robin?

RORY: You gotta understand, Mike was messed up in his head at that time. His image had taken a hit during the stuff with Robin, and he was losing endorsements left and right—Kodak, Diet Pepsi, beer, batteries, you name it. He was just coming apart. Not that he could ever follow orders long enough to be in a damn commercial anyway.

So he hears about this guy, Iceberg Slim. In the 'hood, this cat was like the king of pimps, and Mike takes me and Don King to see him in this rundown apartment. He in there like he holding class, all this psychological stuff. Pimpology 101. Of course, Mike's paying him for this stuff, just soaking it all in.

He starts running his mouth about Robin. "Man, this bitch, she got me fucked up, but I'm running the show now."

And Iceberg, he's just real calm, and he says, "Mike, you're not well. You're not well, son. You can't face women right now."

He was right. You'd think Mike been with Robin twenty-five years, the way he was going through it. He was weeping like a baby. Drinking. Eating. Gaining weight, up to almost three hundred pounds. All that weight was in his ass, so he looked like a damn rhino. We had a fight coming up and we had to get that weight off him fast. I had him working out in Hefty bags, covered in Albolene. Man, whatever it took.

Crazy thing is, Mike was never faithful a day in his life, not even with Robin. It wasn't like I didn't want him to be married, to be happy, but I knew he wouldn't be true to one girl. And he was so sloppy about it. Here, he's this famous guy, the New York media following him all over, cameras everywhere, and he thinks he not gonna get caught? He was always more concerned about earning street cred than about covering his tracks.

One day back in Vegas, Mike calls me from the Hilton. "Get over here," he says. "Get over here." I don't know what the hell he wants, so I go over to the hotel. I walk into the room, see him lying in the bed. He throws back the sheets, and it's Robin Givens laying there. Mike says, "See? Fuck this bitch. C'mon." And he walks out. That was his way of dissing her, saying it was over. He was never the same.

Leading up to Mike's first loss as a pro boxer, did he seem distracted? Were there signs that his anger and womanizing were getting worse?

RORY: Sure there were, but the way he showed it was almost funny sometimes. Sad but funny, if that makes any sense.

This one time, we're in Chicago at this dinner, me, Mike, Don King, and John Horne. Around the table, there's all these guys. Mike Ditka, this hard-nose coach from back in the day. Richard Dent, a linebacker for the Bears, big guy from Brownsville. And Michael Jordan, who at that time was the next big NBA star. Mike Tyson's sitting there with his drink of choice, a Long Island Tea, and when he drinks, his real feelings come out. You never know what you're gonna get. Mike don't know how to drink. Most people sip it, right? He turns it up like a glass of water, and when sets it back down empty.

We're all talking, and Mike's on his third drink. He's getting more loose, more loose. I'm telling the server to water his drinks down 'cause I see where this is going. Mike stares across the table at Michael Jordan. He says, "Hey, man, you think I'm stupid? I know you fucked with my bitch." Jordan looks like he just seen a ghost. "I know you messed with her," Mike says. "You can tell me." Jordan, it's obvious he just wants to get up and run. He wants no part of this. Mike turns to Ditka. "Man, you think somebody scared of you, all that racist shit you been talking?" He says to Dent, "Y'all scared of this damn white man, Richard? He ain't nobody. You gonna let him talk that way?"

It was a circus, for real, that night. Don King trying to change the subject. Me and John trying to hold Mike down. Mike telling everyone he's gonna bust Jordan's ass. Jordan's dressed sharp as always, and he can't get out of there fast enough.

I hate to say it, but Mike's attitude changed after Robin, almost like he went on the warpath. He'd stop the car in the middle of New York City, ask a girl on the sidewalk to see her driver's license. She old enough, it was on. No brakes whatsoever. That got the attention of guys in the business. He was a prime target. They'd spot his Bentley pulled up in the 'hood, and they knew Mike Tyson close by. You got mothers there giving up their daughters. Just some sad, sick shit. All of a sudden it's not just about me keeping my boy in check, but also keeping all these bloodsuckers away.

For a while there, Mike was hanging out with Al B. Sure! You remember him? He worked with Quincy Jones, won some Grammys. He was this smooth R&B cat, had all the ladies drooling over him in the late '80s. Well, he and Mike both loved the ladies, and they were holed up in Mike's mansion in Bernardsville, doing their thing.

Ends up they had one of Bill Cosby's relatives over there, a young woman. They having their fun, but Bill's not too happy about it. He calls up Don King. "Don, we need to talk about this young man you been promoting. He done this to the girl, and he done that to her."

Don was real sympathetic. "Good Lord, Bill." He was shaking his head, his hair waving around. "Good Lord." Then Bill drops a hint that he gonna take some legal action, maybe even file a lawsuit. Don's an old-school gangster, and that changed his attitude real quick. He says, "Now c'mon, Bill, you know she sucked the pee-pee. You know she sucked the pee-pee." Bill was furious, just trying to protect his family. Don says, "C'mon now, cut the shit. You ain't doing nothing to Mike. You leave him alone."

Man, this was the sorta stuff that was always going on. It was grueling. I cared so much about Mike, and I had no life. You think I enjoyed my Rolls-Royce? You think I was out scuba diving in the Bahamas with my new bride? We still never done a vacation like that. You kidding? How could we enjoy this stuff, when I was always on guard, always in protection-mode? Always putting out fires. My head on a swivel. I never knew what the next day gonna hold for me. "What's the next thing? What's the next thing?" That phone ring, and I'd be like, "What now?" It could be the cops or some lawyers or some girl trying to blackmail him. I never knew.

And ultimately, I didn't want to get The Call.

Someone telling me he fuckin' blew his brains out.

It used to kill me, man, seeing this guy hurting. He was hurting so bad. He was in a struggle with himself, and I couldn't help him. He had everything, and had nothing. He'd be in the car mumbling to himself, "Why me?" Partly, it was the deal with Robin, partly he didn't think he deserved all this stuff, the fame and the success and the money. "Why me? Why me?"

He scared me when he talked that way.

When did Naomi Campbell come into the picture? What was that encounter like, and did you think there was anything more than hormones involved in her relationship with Mike?

RORY: It was at a Russell Simmons' party, this big apartment, a buncha celebrities. I was there to keep Mike out of trouble, doing my usual babysitting job, and when I looked over, he was talking to this girl. I had to rub my eyes. I mean, the most exciting thing at that time was

Naomi Campell. She was wild and vivacious, with these legs that went on for days.

I'm stuck holding their drinks 'cause Mike says he gotta use the restroom. Next thing I know, Naomi's following him in there. Holy shit. Guests are walking up. "Bathroom's taken," I'm telling them. Minutes go by, and it's getting uncomfortable. I finally crack open the door. "C'mon, Mike." I see Naomi. She's up on the toilet, heels and long legs spread, skirt hiked up, and Mike's pumping away.

A girl like that, well, I didn't think she'd ever wanna see Mike again, but a week or two later she shows up at his place real early. "Let me in, Michael. It's me, Naomi." She was after him. She'd chase him whenever she got upset, thinking he was supposed to show up somewhere. She go searching for him, yelling in that British accent she had. Mike liked her a lot, but at that point he wasn't sure what he wanted.

As his friend, there were times I said stuff, tried to give some advice. What people forget, though, is that Mike is a complex human being. He's a grown man who gonna do things his way. It's hard enough getting a stubborn little kid to fall in line, right? Imagine dealing with an individual who got all kindsa drives and desires, and who got all the money in the world to go after them things. You get in the way of that, it's like you just tied yourself to the tracks and the locomotive is coming.

My job was to tell Mike the do's and the don'ts, the pros and the cons. That's the only thing I could do. He still do the opposite most of the time. Sometimes I'd start an argument, a big one behind closed doors, and then walk out. He'd come after me like that little kid. "I'm sorry, Ro. I didn't mean to act like that." I had to get in his head, give him some positive reinforcement. You had to say what you wanna say and walk away. You plant the seed and watch it grow. But you couldn't get confrontational and get in his eye. You do that, and you start waking the beast.

When we were out in Vegas for one of Mike's fights, Naomi came to see him, and it was like the fuckin' Ringling Brothers. All these friends of mine were there 'cause I'd bring out ten or fifteen for each fight. We had fun. That would cost me around $100,000 every time— the planes, the food, the rooms, everything on my tab— but I wanted them to be part of this stuff I was experiencing. Then in stormed Naomi, stirring things up. The guys got in arguments with her, and she'd cuss them out in her accent. They'd sit back. "This fuckin' bitch, where she come from?"

Mike was just Mike. Any other guy, he meets a girl like Naomi, he gonna settle down and kiss her feet every day, but Mike wasn't that guy.

One day, she came over to the Vegas Hilton, and we heard he was in the other room messing around with some girls. This is on the twenty-ninth floor. Naomi starts screaming outside the suite, scratching at the door, banging at the door, kicking at the door. So she gets out on the balcony of the next room. One slip and she's dead. I rush out to stop her, and when I look down, I almost pass out. I'm like, "Oh, shit. She's gonna die, and then we're all gonna end up in jail." All I see's those long legs, and she climbs from one balcony to the other balcony, no net underneath, to get into that damn room.

They were both so fiery. No fire and water, just two fires. They had that kind of relationship where it was all or nothing.

Mike would be clubbing and come outside, and she'd be standing in six-inch heels on the hood of his car, putting dents in it and talking shit. Mike would just scratch his head and walk away. Later, he'd grab her and they'd have passionate sex, and it would start all over again. That was Mike and Naomi.

She was different than his hood rats. She was a strong, independent woman. My wife got along with her, and they had fun talking, walking around, shopping along the Strip. You'd see Naomi go into a jewelry store, come out with a ring on her finger, and you knew she bought that rock with her own money. Mike didn't like that. He wanted to be that guy who dress the girls up. I'd tell him, "But those girls just want you for your money," and he'd say, "I know, I know." He didn't care, long as he got what he wanted. The money was a way of controlling them, so a girl like Naomi was a threat to him.

Mike made plenty of bad decisions with women, blinded by the moment, but he knew, he knew deep down, there was no way he could be boyfriend and girlfriend and marry Naomi. She was a cool girl, but they was just two young people outta their minds. You could've made a movie about them. It would've been intense. Listen, there would've been someone drawing chalk lines around a body or something, 'cause she was too fiery, and he knew that.

He pulled me aside once. I'll never forget it. He said, "Ro, I think I met my match." He paused. "Naomi, she scares me."

That made me laugh. We finally found someone even crazier than him.

CHAPTER FOURTEEN

THE PEACOCKS

Crazier than Mike?

Actually, the man's newsmaking antics had just begun, and soon the crazy train named Mike Tyson would come barreling down the tracks like never before.

In 1966, Mike boarded the train in Brownsville. Even as a kid, he loved trains and train sets, and he rode his own express through years of delinquency into early adulthood, then waved his hands out the window as it blew through Atlantic City, Las Vegas, and Toyko from 1985 through 1990. Though he gave the controls briefly to his wife and mother-in-law in 1988, they were off the train now, and he clambered into the engine car to take charge of things himself.

Perhaps he did not know that an engineer must use his head to negotiate a safe and successful journey. Or perhaps he just misunderstood which of his heads to use.

In 1991, the Cayton-Jacobs contract was nearing its end. For nearly three years, Rory Holloway and John Horne had carried out managerial duties with less pay and less options than afforded typical managers, but soon they would have full ability to guide their fighter's career. Never mind those who had bashed them for Kevin Rooney's dismissal and for Mike's diminished pizazz in the ring. This was their time to shine. To prove the critics wrong.

Rory and John arranged a weekend at Mike's mansion in Cleveland, and invited Showtime bigwigs and boxing fat cats to come negotiate a deal. "Will Mike be present?"

"Absolutely," they assured their guests. "You'll meet the man in person, take your picture with him, get an autograph for your kids." Hopefully, some large deals would also be signed.

It is hard to understand how bold and idealistic their goals were. Consider this: going into the 1990s, there was only one African-American CEO on the *Fortune 500* list, and only one who was head coach in the NFL. Ignorance was still visible in the halls of power. As a rule, black athletes were overseen by educated, privileged, Caucasian males.

In July of 1991, with the Showtime meeting only a day away, Mike headed in a different direction. Executives were flying into Cleveland as he headed for Indianapolis, Indiana. Contracts and CEOs be damned. How could he resist the plumage and finery of the Miss Black America Pageant?

All aboard, and full steam ahead!

Mike stoked the engines, driving the train to dangerous speeds as he approached this critical curve in his career.

You had business meetings arranged for Mike. With that in mind, why would you let him wander off into trouble in a neighboring state?

RORY: Mike's own worst enemy was time on his hands. Look at his days back with Cus. Cus had Mike competing in the ring every month. That kept my boy sharp and out of trouble. Thing is, it ain't easy to maintain that schedule, not when you're the top of the food chain. Between fights, I was always worried. I had ulcers. You give Mike that kinda freedom, and it's just a matter of time before things go balls up.

Training camp, that's where we had some control. Mike had a goal and we the guys on his side. So in '91, we out in Ohio, in Amish country, preparing for the first scheduled Holyfield fight. This ranch was far from trouble, with fishing lakes, a track, an indoor pool. I prided myself on running solid, clean camps—no drinking, no fuss, no women, no drugs—'cause when a fighter goes into a ring, it's a life-and-death situation. We was locked down, getting Mike in peak condition. We took this shit seriously.

Mike, though, he still making his connections, working the angles like an addict. He got these people around who called themselves his friends, and they was doing what they could to compromise him and our camp. He had his East Coast pimp and his West Coast pimp, Craig "Boogie" from Mt. Vernon, New York, and Kevin Sawyer from Los Angeles. These guys didn't give a damn about him. They'd roll up in nice cars to women on the streets, sell it like they Mike's confidants, and get Mike whatever he wanted. If these guys anywhere near Mike, they be enabling him. In my opinion, you might just as well light a crack pipe and put it in his mouth. It was the same equivalent. They were killing him.

During camp, Mike ended up tearing some cartilage, and we postponed the Holyfield fight. Now Mike's got time on his hands again. Always bad news. Me and John, we tried to make good from the bad, and we set up the meeting with Don King and Showtime. Mike's coming to the end of his old contracts, finally a free man, and we wanna make sure he gets the Pay-Per-View dollars. Forget HBO. If one or two million people pay to see him fight on TV, shouldn't the man see some of that profit?

So these executives, they show up at Mike's house and they're sitting around. We have a nice luncheon, good food. We've booked these commercials, promo shots, and all kindsa stuff. Everyone's smiley, slapping shoulders, excited to meet the champ himself. We ready to take Mike to the next level. Team Tyson about to go big-time.

And Mike never shows up.

A day before, Mike informed us he was taking a quick trip. Don King was furious about it. Me and John, we told him not to go, he got business here to take care of. We begged him. I didn't even know Mike's plans, but I tried to go with him 'cause that way I still got a chance of keeping him outta trouble, right?

"Fuck y'all," he said. "I'll be back. Already got my tickets and everything . . . boom, boom, boom. Why you always so worried, Ro?"

Think about it. We got guys waiting to sign contracts to help his future, and he just disappears. Our team got blamed for screwing up Mike's career, but that is so far from how this went down. John was working on Mike's behalf. I was working on his behalf. You think I couldn't have used the tools at my fingertips to get Mike whatever he wanted—and I mean anything? Instead I risked my friendship to say, "No, we're not doing none of that." When an athlete today gets caught in a compromising situation, you don't hear no reporters blaming their agents and managers, 'cause we all know these young men are responsible for their own actions. And hell, Mike was the biggest and richest around. So you tell me, how you gonna stop him?

We found out later that Craig "Boogie" and them snuck my boy off to Indiana. And what they got in Indianapolis? The Miss Black America Pageant. Lotsa single, good-looking women. Who even let this man in there? I mean, you got all these girls strutting around, dancing, and there's Mike lurking around the edges, just licking his chops.

Mike said nothing to us about what happened. Not a damn word. After he didn't show in Cleveland, he told us to get the Showtime guys together again and we'd do it in New York. He gonna be there this time. He promised. So me and John, we packed up and headed east. We smoothed things over with these execs, hours and hours on the phone, and put stuff in place. We still got a shot at making this deal work.

We're in New York a little later, just a normal day, and we got Mike in the car. The radio's on, and they say something about a girl accused Mike of rape. I turn and stare at him. "Who's Desiree Washington?" I'd never heard of her. Mike shakes his head. "It's just bullshit." Back then he was in the tabloids a lot, so I figure maybe he's right. Maybe.

But within twenty-four, forty-eight hours, it wasn't bullshit. That shit was spread across every news outlet in the world.

That's how I first heard it, on the news, same as everyone else.

Me and John went into instant damage control, but Mike just takes off in his Porsche to D.C., where he can fuck around with another of his women, Sherry Brown.

Later, we found out how he been at that pageant flirting with all the girls. They showed it on a TV in the courtroom, a video someone filmed while the contestants were rehearsing onstage. There's Mike in fuckin' HD. I can't believe I'm watching this. These girls're like primping peacocks, and he's eying the ones he likes. He points his finger and says, clear as day, "I'm gonna fuck you. And I'm gonna fuck you. And I'm gonna fuck you. And, ooooh, I'm really gonna fuck you." He laughing like it's all some joke.

Except this wasn't no joke. This was something serious.

One of the girls he pointed out was Desiree. She's the one who brung the charges against him, saying he took her on a date and then raped her.

CHAPTER FIFTEEN

THE KITTEN AND THE SHARKS

The first Miss Black America was crowned in 1968. The pageant highlighted the poise, beauty, and talent of young black women, and was a bold step forward in an era during which many African-Americans viewed their dark skin as undesirable and unattractive.

By 1977, the pageant was a prime-time NBC televised event, and in the following years, the social conscience began embracing black as beautiful. The pageant's oath of positivity expressed each contestant's commitment to mental and spiritual strength, self-confidence, and eloquence. Oprah Winfrey and Toni Braxton were former contestants who built solid careers upon that early foundation. In Oprah's own words, the pageant "put a flower in my mind."

In the summer of 1991, the pageant was held in Indianapolis, Indiana. Desiree Washington arrived as an eighteen-year-old flower from Rhode Island. She was a recent high-school graduate, voted "most friendly" and "most talkative" by her class. She still lived with her parents, in a ranch-style home that had a swimming pool off the back deck.

A potential gold-digger? The evidence did not suggest it. She seemed initially more interested in wearing the pageant crown than in chasing after anyone's riches.

As it turned out, though, Mike Tyson chased after her.

He asked her if she would go out with him. She suggested the movies or dinner. He said he wanted to do a lot more. She told him that was pretty forward of him. He admitted that was true, but why be shy about what he wanted? She gave him her number. Although she had scheduled pageant activities the next day, she answered when he called her room at one-thirty a.m. He was a big name, admired by her dad and her grandpa. She must have been flattered. She threw on some clothes and joined him in his limousine outside her hotel.

At that time of night? What was she thinking? Imagine for a moment a kitten entering a tiger's cage. Is the kitten lured by the danger? Or blissfully unaware of it?

Either way, little kitty, that was a pretty dumb move.

After a bit of kissing in Mike's limo, Desiree followed him up to his room at the Canterbury Hotel. She used the bathroom, freshened up. He took that to mean this was "on like Donkey Kong," as we said in the 1990s. She told him no, she should leave. A consensual date did not imply consensual sex. But as far as Mike and his raging libido were concerned, the kitten had entered his domain even after he made his desires clear. If she wanted out, why did she ever get in?

Supposing her intentions were money-driven, Desiree had him right where she wanted. From here on out, it was her word against his. A little blackmail, a quick payday.

Ka-ching.

After all, Mike Tyson was one of the world's highest-paid athletes at the time.

If, however, she was the naive girl she later portrayed on the witness stand, she found herself in a truly terrifying situation. Mike was twice her weight, manipulative and persistent. He had been with plenty of women in the past, oftentimes because they pursued him. He was used to having his pick of the litter, and the word "no" was not in his vocabulary.

Later in the day, after their encounter in Suite 606, Desiree Washington called the Indianapolis police and claimed she had been raped. She made the call after her mother pushed her to do so. Then, despite making allegations, she continued with pageant activities for the next two days, which caused the lifting of some eyebrows. Was that the normal response of a traumatized girl? She later brushed off the question, explaining that she was no quitter.

Only two people will ever know what went on behind those closed doors, but Desiree slipped into the shadows in years to come, even assuming other names to escape the past, while Mike went on to further glory and riches in the ring. He still swears to this day he is innocent.

Is it correct, Rory, that you were present at the trial? What did you think of Mike's defense team?

RORY: I was there in that courtroom every day. Me and John Horne, we wasn't part of the defense, but we showed up to support our man. People called us thugs and lowlifes, lots of accusations, but neither of us have ever been part of no felony. Look it up. Investigate. For me, man, just walking up those courthouse steps, knowing my family's seeing all this, that was one of the most embarrassing things I ever done.

This trial was in early '92, two years before O.J. At the time, it was the biggest spectacle of the decade. Prejudice, bigotry, sexism, you name it, it was all involved, and Mike couldn't have picked a worse place to put himself in a bad situation. Indiana was a known hotbed for racism. Me and my friend, Shorty Black, we learned that while driving up to the jail. We stopped to ask a cop for directions, and he rattled off the names of some roads. "You go right up here, go a mile or so, make a left." He gave us this weird grin. "And then you'll be sitting prettier than two porch monkeys."

Shorty looked at me like, "What the fuck?" We knew then Mike was in deep.

Don King even went out to the cornfields to meet with the head of the local Ku Klux Klan, the fuckin' Grand Puma or Ku Koo Dragon or whatever. Don, a big black man, and he thinking he gonna negotiate with the Klan to get Mike out of this. He had some balls for trying, for real, but they just cussed him out. Think what you want about Don—and yeah, you gotta keep his hand out of the cookie jar—but ain't nobody gonna fight for his fighter like that man.

During the trial, people also blamed Don for the mess-up lawyer he brought in, some tax attorney thrown into the middle of a criminal case. This guy, Vincent J. Fuller, he'd actually been in big cases before, even represented Hinckley Jr., the one who tried to assassinate President Reagan. Fuller knew Mike's record. Every time Mike turn around, some girl was saying he pinched her ass or abused her or did this. Even some of them other pageant girls testified against him. He done all these indiscretions, and all that added up. So you weren't gonna argue that Mike some choirboy, right?

Instead, Fuller made a case of how Mike was a womanizer. He said it just proved that Miss Washington was after Mike's money, 'cause even knowing his reputation, she climbed in that limo and went up to his room. With the civil suits Mike faced in his past, with his history of sexual allegations, how else was Fuller supposed to defend him?

Well, that started the rumors that Don King sabotaged the whole thing. Which made no logical sense. Mike was bringing in lotsa money, so why would Don want his fighter convicted? But the media ran with that, then the streets ran with that. Everyone had a theory. Everyone blaming someone else.

Mike had got himself in a bad situation, and he started grasping at straws. I don't know where he found this voodoo guy, but he looked just like Miles Davis. Said he was a witch doctor. People paid him to make their problems go away. He come over one night, no shoes on, stares out into the woods. He walks out there like he doing something spiritual, comes back and says he talked to the something gods and now everything gonna be alright. "And oh, by the way, I need a check by noon tomorrow." I could see through this shit, but you know, Mike was desperate.

One day, the guy convinced Mike to go into the shower and pour a bucket of milk all over himself, like it supposed to cleanse him or something. Then he tells Mike to write down the names of all the prosecutors and lawyers on a piece of paper. While he's staring at those guys in the courtroom, he supposed to eat the list and swallow it. You see Mike over in his chair, chewing on this damn wad like a madman, staring hard, like it gonna do something. This huckster took tens of thousands of dollars from Mike.

Yeah, and look at how that turned out.

It was always this way with Mike, everyone coming at him for something, skimming what they could. The smell of that money, man, it got the sharks circling.

Special Prosecutor J. Gregory Garrison. Man, that guy was a real piece of work. Arrogant. Posturing for the cameras. He was eating up all this attention, loving every minute of it. The Indiana system had a big fish on the line, and he gonna make damn sure they get this thing in the boat. Hold up Mike Tyson like a trophy.

Garrison had other motives too, but we'll get into that later.

Did you believe Mike was guilty? Or did you suspect Desiree Washington had ulterior motives?

RORY: Desiree said later how this trial traumatized her, how she just wanted it all to be over so she could get back some normalcy. Okay, but the minute Mike was convicted, what she do? She filed a civil suit. She already got justice, her "rapist" behind bars, and now she ended up also getting a $1,000,000 settlement. That's how it went.

My personal opinion, I don't think it started that way. Here's a girl from a strict upbringing, strict parents, and she just got overwhelmed by the fact she with Mike Tyson. She goes into his room, they do what they do, and she breaks curfew. There's no doubt it was a booty call. The pageant had a strict curfew, and she gets caught, so she makes this story up and thinks that be the end of it. Then it gets rolling, and all of a sudden the people around her takes over. It snowballs and gets bigger and bigger. They figure they can teach the champ a lesson. They want skin, they want blood, and they think they can turn blood into money. Mike got caught in the wrong place at the wrong time, and it all spiraled outta Desiree's control. That's how I believe it went down.

Thing is, she had a pattern of this, which wasn't never shown in court. Back in high school in Rhode Island, she once accused a kid of rape. Turns out she thought she was pregnant and was scared how Daddy gonna react when he realized she wasn't a virgin. Later, she dropped the charges. Man, that should've been said at the trial, right?

Do I think Mike raped her? No, I don't believe he did. I think Mike didn't know when to stop, but in his own mind she was a willing partner.

Listen, by no means am I gonna condone anything like that. Rape is a horrible thing, and I don't care if it my brother who done it, that shit is wrong. It's a sensitive subject, people gonna take sides, but I don't think this was one of those situations.

As an observer sitting there in the courtroom you could clearly see they had no physical evidence that Mike did anything. There was this sequin dress that got held up in an evidence bag, the dress she was wearing in the hotel room. The lawyers pulled out the dress, shook it a little bit, and sequins fell off. They asked, "If a man as big and strong as Mike roughed you up, as you allege, why didn't detectives find one sequin in that room?" Then, "Why did you go into the hotel-room bathroom, where there was a lock on the door and a phone on the wall, and not call the cops to report this?" And, "Why did you walk past hotel security and not tell them you'd been assaulted?"

It became her word against his word.

In the end, Mike got himself convicted. No, not 'cause he done something wrong in that room, but 'cause of the way he handled the whole thing—brash, arrogant, not taking it seriously. He thought he was bigger than it all. Like a lotta these athletes, he thought he invincible, thought nothing could touch him. He was just difficult, man.

It was a long, tiring process, and I'm telling you, Mike isn't normal even when his life's depending on it. Camille was in the courtroom, poised as always, saying how she knows he is innocent. That lady deserved all the respect. And Mike's just making a joke of the proceedings. His lawyers, they couldn't sit him down and coach him through this. You think that gonna work? You think my boy was paying any attention? Hell, no.

The prosecutor calls Mike up on the stand, and he starts talking about his sexual escapades, his conquests, all in graphic detail. "They love me. I like to hurt them. I'm well-endowed. When I'm doing it, ooohh . . ." Certain people think this is funny, others just gawk at the floor. Then he tells the judge the details of having fellatio with his accuser. This is in the court record. He figures he can work this, same as always, goofy and likeable Mike, and the judge gonna just lap it up.

It was rough to watch this go down in front of you. It was all like a freakin' game to him. His own words were crucifying him up there.

Judge Patricia Gifford, she was this white-haired woman, glasses, look like she somebody's grandmother. She just watching Mike on the stand like he's an idiot, like she can't believe the words coming out of his mouth. The reporters were jotting it all down. I'm thinking, "Mike, you just put yourself in jail. What's wrong with you?"

Took the jury almost ten hours to come back with their verdict. Guilty.

Then Mike faces the judge for sentencing, and man, he wanna play bravado right to the end. He shows no contrition or nothing. He looks the judge right in her eyes, and says, "Yo, you do what you gotta do." Some shit like that. Real ignorant.

Even then, Judge Gifford showed compassion. After everything she heard from his lips, she gave him every chance. Her initial sentence was ten years for a Class B felony, and my knees buckled, then she suspended it down to six years. And he only had to do half of that, if he could stay on good behavior.

Camille gave Mike a final hug and a kiss. That was sad to watch. As I left the courtroom, it was just this lonely feeling. I was blown away, after everything we worked for, everything we fought for together. Here's Mike being marched away—the first time I ever seen a friend gonna spend time like that in prison—and I'm worried about him behind bars. How my boy gonna deal with that? How he gonna survive being confined?

CHAPTER SIXTEEN

THE LADYBUG

Poor Mike. Iron Mike. Locked away.

The full sentence handed down by Judge Gifford was six years in prison, plus $30,000 in fines, and 100 hours of community service and psychotherapy. When the reports of Mike's guilty conviction came out, the average citizen assumed a man as imposing and powerful as the former heavyweight champ would be shuffled away in chains to a facility as secure as San Quentin or Alcatraz. He would eat unidentifiable slop from a plastic tray, and exorcise his inner demons in the prison yard, pumping weights, growing bigger, stronger, meaner—and beware the beast when he was unleashed once more.

In reality, Mike's incarceration took place in the Indiana Youth Center, a medium-security facility in Plainfield, Indiana. One of over fourteen hundred prisoners, he was Inmate No. 922335. He no longer had to answer to his team and his managers. He had none of the physical and emotional demands of training camp. He did not have Rory Holloway at his side, holding him to a prescribed diet and workout routine. Hell, he felt freer behind bars than he had in ages.

He would later admit in his book: "I really didn't want to leave the prison . . . I enjoyed just being able to chill and get visits from celebrities and TV journalists."

Mike gained weight while gorging on snack cakes. He exercised irregularly, using the excuse that he had no speed bags or boxing ring. He thumbed through books on philosophy and religion, got tattoos of Chairman Mao and Arthur Ashe on opposing shoulders, and welcomed visitors from Spike Lee to Larry King to the inimitable Maya Angelou.

Oh, and he also welcomed gaggles of females. Letters poured in from around the world as well, with offerings of photos, panties, and other tokens of mindless affection. In exchange, he dished out money and gifts like cheap candy.

Poor Mike.

Mike later bragged that he copulated with visiting women in the shade of the prison yard, and even impregnated one of the female guards—though she did not carry the child to term. For a man serving a sentence for rape, he was given a shockingly negligent amount of freedom.

Of course, bribes and payoffs are part of prison life, part of working the system to get what you want—a cigarette, a cellphone, a sexual favor—and prison employees are not above corruption. It was later made public that Mike paid $10,000 for roof repairs to his drug counselor, who in turn offered herself to him. On another front, an employee filed a lawsuit against the penal system, claiming workers and officials had violated regulations by profiting from Mike's stint in the Plainfield, Indiana facility.

And, as always, there were people after his money.

Did he care? Did a man still worth millions give a damn? As long as his lusts were fed, he seemed willing to play the victim in their schemes. For Mike, it was a tried and tested formula.

Clothes + Cash + Cars = Pussy.

In 1995, Mike earned early release for being, according to the prison staff, "a model prisoner." Did the female guard and drug counselor put in a few good words as well? One wonders.

Did you visit Mike while he was in prison? Were you aware of the attention and favors he was getting from within and without?

RORY: While he was in prison, I did every day with him. That's how it felt to me. That was my boy. So of course I was going to visit him whenever I could.

It wasn't easy, though. I was married with two children, living in Guilderland, a section of Albany, at the time. And, man, I hated to fly. So I made that drive more times than I can count, back and forth to Indiana. You gotta give it to John Horne, he made a lot of visits too. We had power-of-attorney while Mike was serving his sentence, and we took that serious. My man had all these things to keep up and maintain—his mansions in Vegas and Cleveland, his cars, properties, pigeons. I don't even like pigeons, but me and Jay Bright helped with them. When Mike got out three years later, he still had all the same stuff, the same gas in his tanks. We had his back. We didn't touch a thing.

I guess he was doing plenty of touching, though. Not like that surprised me. I'd pull up in Indiana after a long drive, and the guards, they'd tell me I couldn't visit till the next day 'cause Mike got women lined up to see him. He getting more punani in there than he was outside. Next thing, I'm stuck sleeping in the damn parking lot, afraid some hooded goon gonna pull me out into the cornfields. It was messed up.

All that stuff in the prison, how Mike pulled that shit off, I don't know. But money talks, right? And Mike's money, it could scream.

As Mike Tyson neared his March 25 release date, he narrowed his affections to a particular female admirer. Her name was Monica Turner, a Georgetown University Medical School student he had met years earlier at an Eddie Murphy party. Monica won him over with regular visits to the Indiana Youth Center, and she was waiting when he earned his freedom.

Another honey trap? Another gold-digger?

It seems Mike would have learned by now, but before the year was out he had bought Monica a multimillion-dollar estate in Bethesda, Maryland, and later, her own Ferrari, Range Rover, and Mercedes Benz. By April of '97, he also gave her a wedding ring.

Not that any of this guaranteed him peace of mind, new monogamous resolve, or firmer trust in females. The cesspool was swirling like never before. He was still rich, still famous, and now an even bigger target of blackmail with his record as a convicted rapist and registered sex offender. He was facing—if you'll pardon the pun—a full-frontal assault.

Considering Mike's history, what measures did you take to protect him from future litigation?

RORY: Listen, this thing took more than three years out of Mike's life. It stripped away a piece of his soul. When he was released, he was a shell of himself, physically, emotionally, and psychologically. He was wary of other people. You'd think he's not gonna be messing with no women now. He's a marked man. Hell, he might give up on them all together, go for men or something.

Well, that ain't how it happened. No, Mike still gonna do what Mike do.

He set up this bedroom in his house in Vegas, this love nest. He concealed these sophisticated video-recording devices so he can record all future sexual encounters, as evidence if he get accused again. He didn't do it for amusement, for some kinda strange fetish. He did it so he got it on tape that this consensual between two adults. Nobody thought this gonna be Studio 54. "Yo, Rory, grab us a beer and we watch the tapes." I wasn't gonna get no excitement from that. No, he making sure his bases is covered.

We also hired security. These guys, I gave them instructions that they not just keep trouble away from Mike, but they keep him from wandering into situations he can't get out of. He in training camp? He want to go into the strip club? No, that wasn't gonna be in our favor. I can't tell you how many times he fired this one guy, Anthony Pitts, 'cause Anthony tried to stop him from going in somewhere. He'd cuss Anthony out, tell him he gonna do what he want, and Anthony don't work for him no more. Like a kid throwing a tantrum. Next morning, I'd smooth things over and hire Anthony back. My ulcers and blood pressure were getting worse by the day, but this shit was just routine.

Then, there was Mike. He worked his own angles. He had his psychotherapist who stayed in close contact, evaluated his well-being, and turned in favorable reports to Judge Gifford. That was part of the sentence. This therapist, Dr. Goldberg, tries to cut a deal with us where he gets a percentage of Mike's earnings. We told him no way, that sure as hell wasn't gonna be how this went down. Next thing, we find out Mike and Dr. Goldberg are off banging girls together, in on it as a team. You believe that?

Listen, if Mike Tyson puts his arm around you, watch out. He after something. He wants your wife, your daughter, or niece. Maybe he want something else, but you damn well know he ain't all of a sudden your best friend, 'cause that ain't how it works.

We used our financial resources over the years calling in preachers, ministers, counselors, anyone to help Mike find some peace and calm. He got baptized, the whole nine yards, all this fanfare—and right after the baptism he's having sex with one of them choir girls. Another guy, preacher named Jerome, he came every day and tried to teach the Word of God—and a week later he's there in the whorehouse with Mike. Mike wasn't sure who to turn to anymore. Who was real? Who was honorable? Who was pure?

In prison, he got into the Koran and converted to Islam. When he came out, he went to the mosque a coupla times. He told the team they gotta throw out any alcohol, and the only women they better be talking to is their wives. It was beautiful. Well, that lasted all of a week or two. He blamed it on the imams and their self-serving interests, using him to draw in donations like he's Islam's new poster-boy. Maybe that was true. Or maybe he just want to do what he wanna do again. That's how my boy works.

I'm telling you, Mike corrupts those around him. He likes it down there with the hood rats, and he like it if you down there with him.

What did you think of Mike's relationship with Monica Turner? When you heard that she filed for divorce in 2003, what was your reaction?

RORY: Me and Monica, we was cool. We never had an argument. She was very nice, a very pleasant girl. Quiet as a ladybug. She was in school to be a doctor, and she just came across as real intelligent. She stayed in her lane, never questioned me—least not until things fell apart. We can get into that later, but I don't hold that against her.

I will say, when Mike married her, it was part of this pattern. When he in training, getting sick of the hard work, he always want to run off and tie the knot. That was his way of doing it. Don't ask me why. And at first the two of them seemed happy, you know. In my opinion, a woman gives a man children, you know she's in it for real. And I think that was the case with Monica. She stuck by Mike for years.

Then he fell back into his old ways. She and Mike, they had this corporate account, and Mike tried to say it was for their kids, but what he do, he would go and stay in a hotel for weeks at a time with some woman he found. Every time he ready to go home, Monica would get a care package. It became habit. He'd say, "John, call my accountant and send her a million dollars." We all knew he was doing it to get back in the house, to smooth things over. Then everything alright.

On top of that, Mike had all these chemical concoctions, a fuckin' treasure chest of venereal-disease medicines, and Monica had to worry about that shit. None of this was in Mike's name 'cause he didn't want the media running with that. It was in my name, Rory Holloway. I didn't care if someone thought bad about me. That was my friend I was protecting. The way I see it, you don't run around telling someone that you their best friend, that you glorious and brave. You show it by your actions.

Don King once told me, "Your problem, Rory, is you fall in love with your fighters," and I guess he was right. I was sadistically loyal.

Listen, I would never say Monica was a bad person, or Robin, or this other girl. Mike makes them bad people. These women get to the point where they're like, "Hey, this fucker's so wild, I better get what I can get. This shit might not be here tomorrow." He puts them in that state of mind. If you married to this man, and he screwing every woman he can find, you don't see no future there.

By the end, Monica got millions from him, but can you blame her? She getting some security for her kids and her. She doing the best she can.

Things might've even worked out between Mike and Monica, except that they let two other females into the mix. I'm telling you, if Robin and Ruthless were the honeybees, these two were the queen bees.

In the end, we all felt their sting.

CHAPTER SEVENTEEN

THE QUEEN BEES

Rich, powerful males have long had a penchant for keeping beautiful women within reach, sometimes an entire harem of them. Isn't that every man's fantasy?

As enticing as it sounds, this apparent luxury has brought down rulers and lords throughout the ages. President Bill Clinton nearly lost his office after rumors went public of a soiled dress and misused cigars. King Solomon, considered one of the world's wisest men, housed hundreds of women for his personal pleasure, but later allowed his kingdom to be divided by his various affections and idolatries.

Samson is history's most famous example of a strong man brought low by the opposite sex. As a boy, he was dedicated to God, and blessed with uncommon strength. Abiding by the stipulations that his lips touch no strong drink and his locks never be cut, the musclebound, long-haired fellow wreaked havoc on Israel's enemies. His feats including killing a lion with his bare hands, and an army of Philistines with a donkey's jawbone.

Talk about a bad-ass. He seemed indestructible.

Enter: Delilah.

Delilah was in league with the enemy. She lured Samson into her bed, then begged her lover-boy to reveal the secret of his strength. Despite toying with her for a while, he eventually caved to her pleading and admitted that his hair was his secret. Cut it off, and he would be reduced to an average man.

The rest of the story is well-known.

Delilah lulled Samson to sleep—after a rowdy session in the sack, no doubt—then let in a gang of Philistines to chop away at that mane. When Samson awoke, he discovered that he had been bound and sheared like a sheep. His captors led him away to Gaza, where they gouged out his eyes and mocked him. Samson the Great, Samson the Strong . . .

Ha! Samson the Pitiful.

Later, they paraded him out at a great banquet as an object of jest. He called upon his God for one last burst of strength. Fumbling blindly, he braced his hands against two pillars—and pushed. His final supernatural heave brought down the entire complex on the heads of the revelers, resulting in hundreds of deaths.

Including his own.

One more man playing victim to his unbridled ego and lust.

Is there a modern-day-Samson equivalent more fitting than Mike Tyson, surrendering his secrets and strength to multiple Delilahs? It remains to be seen whether he will overcome his previous blindness or succumb to more humiliations. While a list of the women involved in his unraveling could fill pages of this book, two of the lesser known were also two of the most ruinous and influential: Shawnee Simms and Jackie Rowe.

Who was Shawnee Simms? How did she get involved in Mike's business affairs?

RORY: Well, she's Shawnee Jackson now, married since 2002 to former NBA-player Jimmy Jackson. I hear Mike walked her up the aisle and gave her away. Good for him. It was never physical between Mike and her, not as far as I know—which makes it even more unbelievable how she wormed her way in with him. She must've done some voodoo magic or some shit, 'cause in five years or six years she did as much damage to Mike's career as anyone else I know.

She first got involved in '97, I think, through Craig "Boogie." Remember, he was Mike's pimp, just this gypsy guy, traveling around, hooking girls up with P. Diddy one day, some other rapper the next. We had this thriving business, helping Mike make millions, and "Boogie" wanted to get his hands on it. Thing is, he wasn't ever gonna get control unless he could get me out of the way. He didn't have that kinda juice. He didn't have Mike's respect for nothing more than his ability to bring him a broad, that's it. When the beast had an appetite, he fed him. Simple as that.

"Boogie" kept watching, waiting, and orchestrating. Somewhere along the way he found Shawnee Simms from down in Atlanta. He said to her, "We be partners. If you listen to me, I'll show you how we get the champ." They were Batman and Catwoman, and they gonna tag-team Mike. "We get Rory out, and the champ is all ours."

The moment Shawnee came into the picture, that was the beginning of the end. Pretty soon she's on the phone with Mike twenty-four hours a day. I known the man for thirty years and I never in my life seen him on the phone like that, like it glued to his damn ear. Shawnee got the gift of gab. She telling him he should be making a hundred million a fight. He needs to ditch his friends from the past. She had his attention, and when I tried saying anything, he got mad at me for questioning her.

She's in his ear, and he starts giving her all this money. She says she need a hip replacement or some operation, and he sends someone to Atlanta on the bus or train or plane so they can deliver thousands of dollars in cash to her. She's pulling the strings.

In a short period of time, she owns Mike. She's got him completely manipulated and castrated. She even convinces Mike's new wife, Monica, that all this is in the best interest of their marriage, their future, and all that. Being a medical student, Monica's smart, but she doesn't know a thing about this shady world of the Shawnees and "Boogies" and Jackie Rowes. All she knows is her husband's money is disappearing and maybe Shawnee's right that his team is at fault. Maybe it's time for a change.

You think Mike had a chance? He was caught between two women. He was outflanked, outsmarted, and outgunned.

Soon, Shawnee sends word through the grapevine that she Mike's new manager. She doing this. She doing that. First order of business, she goes to the WWE, the wrestling guys. Me and John, we'd already set up a deal with Vince McMahon at WWE. Vince came to the house. It was all worked out, this scripted thing that would help promote wrestling. Mike would get a seven-figure appearance fee. Then Shawnee comes in, messes it up, and does a lesser deal. That got "Boogie" upset, 'cause she was cutting him out of the action. He goes after her, claiming she owes him from the wrestling contract. And what's she do? She pulls a power play with Mike, and says, "Craig's trying to extort $200,000 from me from the McMahon deal." Mike gets mad. He goes and knocks "Boogie" around, beats his ass.

None of this got in the papers or nothing, but this is the way it went down. Shawnee was trying to do business fictitiously, fuckin' up Mike's contracts and assets. She supposed to be some entertainment manager or something, but this woman was just bad news all around. Some say she ended up with $5,000,000 or $7,000,000 of Mike's money. I don't know. All I know is she got away with a lot.

And the irreparable damage she done in the process, the damage to his career, that was much worse than any money she stole.

The craziest part is she didn't have to sleep with Mike, didn't even have to deal with him in person. She controlled this shit by phone. He was obsessed with her, and she manipulated it all from Atlanta. You ask me, that makes her the baddest bitch of all.

Yeah, you heard it coming from my mouth, she the baddest bitch of them all.

Shawnee Simms was not the only one who took advantage of Mike's weaknesses. A week after his infamous rematch with Evander Holyfield, he was under intense media scrutiny and his morale was low. Instead of running for cover to one of his lavish mansions, he roared into Brooklyn in a red Ferrari, and slid up to the home of a woman named Jackie Rowe.

Jackie was ready for him. Her table was spread with fried chicken, rice, and collard greens. She had neighbors cheering for him as he arrived.

"You da man, Mike. You da man!"

As the cheers subsided, she waved the crowd away with ring-studded fingers. Each diamond was a memento from Mike, a symbol of their longstanding relationship. She led him into the apartment building, where the aroma of her home-cooked food greeted them. Her teenage son sat beside Mike at the dining table, this respite from the reporters and crowds.

All so cozy. Why, they were just like family.

No, not "like" family. If one was to believe Jackie Rowe, they were family.

Who was Jackie? Was she simply another schemer, or an actual relative of Mike's?

RORY: Jackie's another girl from Brooklyn, a person from the streets. Mike knew her back when they was seven or eight years old, but didn't see her again till he was heavyweight champion of the world. Funny how that works, right? For years since she been pretending to be Mike's sister, even arching her eyebrows the way he does, pretending to do business on his behalf. She's not the first person to claim she's his flesh and blood. These are just the sort of cesspool people he gravitates toward.

Listen, Jackie's no more related to Mike than she is to the Pope. It's just what these women do. Mike's had them come at him with lawyers, take him to court for child support, make all sorts of wild claims. This one girl, Natalie, she got pregnant and told Mike the baby was his. She named it D'Amato, like there's some special connection to Cus. Give her credit for doing her homework, right? Well, it worked, 'cause Mike started handed her money every month. Lots of it. Natalie brung D'Amato around one time, and the kid didn't look at all like Mike to me. "His hands," Natalie said. "Look at them, they're exactly like Mike's. They got the same fists."

You kidding me? Me and Don King, we were skeptical. We finally convinced Mike to take a paternity test, and come to find out the baby ain't even his. What's Mike do? He accuses me and Don of paying the doctor to switch the results. Just his pride, his stupid pride. He didn't wanna admit this girl been robbing him from Day One.

Sometimes we settled in cash to make this stuff go away. It was a distraction for our fighter. With Jackie, though, Mike let her hang around. He knew she ain't his sister and there wasn't no sexual thing between them, but she was like one of his pimps helping him get women. He needed these kinda tentacles of Satan to feed his desires. Everyone knows his weak spot. It ain't no secret. And here's Jackie saying, "I got these bitches under control for you, Mike." She sneaking him weed, winning him over with food, reinforcing that he don't need Rory Holloway around.

At that time, I was the target. I was the one in the way, and that made me the enemy. I knew if Mike followed after Shawnee and Jackie, he gonna lose his

Showtime deal and tens of millions of dollars, maybe even get sued for breach of contract. Their deal with him was ironclad. We'd worked long and hard to build this thing, and it was all about to tumble down. I seen it. It come to me just like Noah's vision that a flood was on its way and people gonna die. Didn't take any special ability to read the signs.

Sure enough, it was the perfect storm after the Holyfield rematch. Mike was vulnerable, wondering who to trust. Up until then, he was an incredible friend to me, always had my best interests, always brutally honest. I knew I could depend on him.

But after the fight, something switched over. He became real distant. He saying things I knew someone else must've put in his head. He got Shawnee and Monica in one ear, Jackie in the other, and they wanted him to end things with Team Tyson. It was all part of Craig "Boogie's" plan for them to separate Mike from his contracts and cut in on future earnings.

It wasn't no peaches and cream, though. Jackie and Shawnee couldn't stand each other—Jackie, the New York queen bee, and Shawnee, the Atlanta queen bee. They both wanted control. How they worked that out, I don't got a clue, but they did.

And they chopped up Mike's career, divvying up the pieces.

I figured after he lost all this money and all these fans, after he went through his divorce with Monica and everything, there wasn't much worse that could happen to him.

Man, was I wrong about that.

CHAPTER EIGHTEEN

THE FILLY

It is said that one of life's greatest tragedies is for a parent to outlive a child.

In May of 2009, Mike was a decade past his boxing heyday and only weeks from reemerging as an actor in the box-office hit, *The Hangover*. He was in Vegas when he received a call that his four-year-old daughter Exodus was on life support in a Phoenix hospital. Her older brother had found her lifeless at home, her neck caught in their treadmill's cable that dangled beneath the console. The girl's mother and Mike's former girlfriend, Sol Xochitl, had tried keeping her alive until paramedics arrived.

Mike rushed back to town, and TV cameras recorded his arrival at St. Joseph's. Prayer vigils were held, while reporters heard stories from neighbors about the little girl's fearless and fun personality.

At noon the next day, she was pronounced dead in her hospital room.

The police made it clear there was no evidence of foul play. The treadmill had not even been plugged in. It was a bizarre and tragic accident, nothing more.

Mike told reporters he did not have words to describe his grief. How could words capture even a fraction of his emotion in that moment? "I took responsibility," he said. "She had to be buried, she had to be taken care of." He added that he did not want to know the specific details of her death. "If I know somebody's to blame for it, there will be a problem."

Rory, did you ever meet Exodus? What did you think when you heard the news of her death?

RORY: It's sad, man. I don't even know Mike's kids, and I regret that. That's a connection I thought we'd always share, two fat-ass old men, talking crap to our kids in the backyard. Not no fancy house, just us telling our children about what we used to do, how fly we was. He was the best man at my wedding. Sheila and me asked him to be the godfather of our son. He said on TV at one of the fights, "Congratulations to my godson, Michael Paris . . . boom, boom, boom." That was a special thing.

Today, he doesn't even know Paris. He could pass him on the damn street and not realize it. That tears me up. That's not how I thought our ending was gonna be.

When I found out Mike's daughter died, it really hurt me. I wanted to be there for him, you know what I'm saying? That bothered me a lot. One of my biggest regrets is that I didn't go to her funeral. I really regret that.

I didn't go to Camille's funeral either. I was mourning, but I was too concerned about people looking at me, thinking I'm that guy they seen on the news who somehow ruined Mike's career. I was too hung up on that. The other thing was, I heard how Mike was doing drugs now, in and out of rehab. I didn't know what situation I'd be walking into. In private, if Mike feels like I done something to him, punch me in my face, kick my ass. But I didn't want to show up and cause a scene during these solemn moments for either Exodus or Camille.

I should have gone, though.

Looking back, man, I know I should've been there for him.

Despite Mike's grief—or perhaps in reaction to it—he applied for his third marriage license less than two weeks after this daughter's passing. He and Lakiha "Kiki" Spicer had dated off and on for years, and he was now more aware than ever that each day was precious. He was forty-two, she thirty-two, and they already had a baby girl and a baby boy together, Milan and Morocco. Why not tie the knot and make it official?

It was a simple ceremony, no family members present. If that seems odd, consider that Mike had very little family left. His biological parents and sister had already passed, as had Cus D'Amato and Camille Ewand. While he still maintained a friendly relationship with his older brother Rodney, it was not close enough to warrant special travel plans.

As for Kiki, her family situation was complicated by the fact her stepfather, an elderly Muslim cleric, had been imprisoned since 2005 for running scams, fraudulent loans, and violating the RICO act. Having worked under him, Kiki and her mother both served short prison terms as well—guilty by association. Kiki was already pregnant with Mike's child when she started her six-month stint at Alderson Federal Prison Camp, the same place Martha Stewart once did time. Naturally, Kiki's family still holds that they are all innocent, victims of religious bias.

The wedding bells rang on June sixth, in a small Vegas chapel, but to most who heard of the event, they sounded more like warning bells. No matter how you sugarcoated it, Mike and Kiki's union was a classic recipe for disaster.

He was a felon, drug addict, and recovering alcoholic. He owed back taxes to the IRS.

She was a felon as well. And the mother of two infants in diapers.

Did they really believe they could live happily ever after? Good luck with that. The tabloids were already sharpening their knives for the next tasty headline.

But Mike and Kiki surprised everyone. In interviews, Mike praised her for turning him back from the brink of rage and depression, and Kiki commented on his respectfulness and his role as a father to their children. He was trying to change, and admitted in an *ESPN* magazine article: "I had a difficult time becoming a human being. I stayed in the animal category a little too long." Such self-revelation was therapeutic, and Kiki was smart enough to recognize that.

While Mike pulled in paychecks for further cameos in *The Hangover* franchise, his wife partnered with Spike Lee on a 2012 Broadway stage show that featured Mike "ad-libbing" from his wife's script. They called it *Undisputed Truth*. It was a hit. Give her credit for completing the project while raising toddlers, and for understanding that Mike's fans loved his brash style.

However, the show's uncensored and crowd-pleasing approach masked the fact that significant chunks of his past were left out.

Call it Kiki Chili . . .

Full of beans and spice, but not a whole lot of meat.

Kiki Spicer was still very young when she met Mike. Did you ever suspect they would get married? Considering her recent endeavors, were you aware that she had any business acumen?

RORY: Kiki's family lived in Philadelphia, and her father was friends with Don King. That's how they got connected to Mike. Kiki's father and mother started bringing her around, almost like they baiting Mike, like they had designs for him and their daughter. That's just the way I saw it. I mean, Kiki was only thirteen or fourteen, very quiet and cute, nice and respectful, with this long pretty face and dark ponytail. A filly from Philly. Definitely not one of Mike's usual project girls. Then over here you got the world champ in his early twenties, with his reputation for womanizing. It was bad news, right? Just asking for trouble.

From Day One, Don didn't like it. He knew it was like waving meat in front of a wolf, so he asked her parents not to bring her around no more. He told Mike, "Leave these people alone. These are not the people to mess with." Far as I know, Kiki didn't see or talk to Mike till years later, when she was of age. The two of them got in touch after he was in prison, they dated some, and I guess that spark just never went out. She ended up being his wife.

Is Kiki good at business? I can't tell you what she know or don't know. They say she went to fashion-design school, was a marketing executive, did some wardrobe stuff for music videos or whatever. In her own words, she "a hustler." Sure, she hooked up this deal with Spike Lee. Well, that ain't hard to do. You representing Mike Tyson. He don't make the millions like he did in the ring, but he still got earning power. There's still a little gas left in that tank.

I don't really know Kiki, but I know her family pedigree. In my opinion, she and these other people are just trying to run the gas all the way out. The little she makes with Mike is a lot more than she gonna make otherwise. She driving a Porsche now. She puts up with his shit—the drinking, the drugs, the rehab—'cause it's the last hurrah. They got taxes to pay, mouths to feed. Whaddya expect?

Listen, at first I didn't think this relationship with Kiki was gonna last. No way. Mike was still Mike. But people mellow out as they get older, and I think him losing his daughter made him step back and reexamine. I seen pictures, and now he and Kiki have these beautiful kids. I hope they make it work. I really want that for him.

I'm telling you, it ain't easy being a parent, and Mike didn't have no dad around to show him how it's done. Mike's father took off when he was young. The man came around a coupla times, and Mike always proud to show him off, but then he disappeared again. So how's Mike supposed to be this loving parent when he ain't never seen the right way? That's a hard question. The closest he had to a father-figure was Cus D'Amato. Cus and Camille, they opened heart and home to not just Mike but a buncha these fighters—Jay Bright, Teddy Atlas, Kevin Rooney, and so on. They're gone now, but you visit that house in Catskill, you stand on that porch, sit on the bench overlooking the river, and there's something about it. You just know, you feel it, that mostly good things came from a place like that. Mike's got that in his favor.

Mike has a lot of qualities I admire. He's a sensitive guy. He loyal. Honest. He knows the way he treated women ain't right, and it cost him.

For a long time he just wanted to be like actors Errol Flynn and James Cagney, or boxers Jack Johnson and Jack Dempsey. Those were cats Mike admired, who bragged about their conquests. Even Ali said how early on he chased women all the time. Mike admitted in that *Tyson* documentary that conquering so many women took more from him than it gave to him. He finally realized that. My boy, he processes stuff.

"What I done in the past is history," he said. "What I do in the future is a mystery."

Well, that's true for all of us, right? But I think Mike's past is still a mystery in his own head. If he can get over the blind-Samson bit, if he really look at the ones closest to him, he'll see how the team we put together wasn't what robbed him. All these women he let in, they sucked more than just head, they sucked his money and his life and his blood. Me, our team, we weren't the thugs. We was Mike's family.

Cus and Camille's home in Catskill, NY where Mike once lived.

The author at Cus and Camille's old property overlooking the Hudson River.

Rory at the location of the old Holloway store in Albany, NY.

The author and Rory outside the Catskill Boxing Gym.

Andre Prieto and author outside Cus D'Amato's gym in Catskill.

Rory at the steps of the infamous Bone Center.

Mike and Rory w/ Glenda and the old Lincoln.

The current Albany Boxing Training Facility.

Gordy in front of the church where he works.

Gordy in his old Brownsville neighborhood.

Mike's childhood apartment on Amboy St.

Muhammad Ali posing w/ "Donkey Don," Mike Tyson, and Rory Holloway.

Mike Tyson and Jerry Buss.

Rory helping Mike during a training session, w/ John Horne in background.

Co-managers Rory Holloway and John Horne w/ Mike in between.

Rory w/ trainer Kevin Rooney.

Mike and Rory goofing off with the press.

Mike wearing the championship belt in the Holloway store w/ Cameron.

Rory and Don King's son, Carl King.

Rory hanging out with Mike in the gym.

Mike Tyson and John Horne behind the newlyweds, Rory and Sheila.

Rory, Sheila, Alba, Mike, and Don King.

Sheila Carrasco and Rory Holloway's wedding, w/ Father Clemmons doing ceremony, and Mike as best man.

John Horne, Rory, Sheila, and Don King.

Rory (2nd from left) showing off his red Corvette to friends.

Mike and Robin Givens w/ Rory on the right.

Rory in Team Tyson gear on the hood of his Rolls-Royce.

Sheila enjoying the convertible Rolls-Royce.

Rory holding his son, Michael Paris.

Rory Jr. w/ Mike Tyson in the background.

Rory lacing Mike's glove while John and Stacy watch, and Mike speaks to Don King.

Mike making his entrance, w/ Rory behind him.

Rory, Mike, and John during a press conference at the MGM Grand.

Rory Jr. holding onto Mike's tiger cub.

Rory sharing a meal w/ Papa J.

Mike Tyson shaking hands w/ Michael Irvin.

Rory raising Oba Carr's hand in victory.

Shorty and Gordy hanging out.

Earl "Shorty Black" Byam.

Bev Holloway dancing with son, Rory.

Stacy and Crocodile getting Mike pumped up.

Rory striking a pose in his Team Tyson cap.

Mike making an entrance.

Mike working the heavy bag while children watch.

Don King, Mike Tyson, and Naomi Campbell at a photo shoot.

Rory and Mike during open gym w/ press.

Mike posing w/ ever-present female fans.

Steve "Crocodile" Fitch in his standard camo.

Rory and old friends, Charlie and Geno.

Rory's oldest son, Rory Jr.

Rory and Mike hanging out with young Rory Jr.

Rory's brother, Capt. Todd Holloway.

Todd w/ his mom, Bev Holloway.

Michael sporting his Yankees cap and tattoo.

Rory's granddaughter, London.   Rory in the gym as his son, Michael Paris, works the speed bag.

Mami and Papi Carrasco in their Manhattan apartment.   Papi Carrasco w/ grandson Michael Paris.

Rory, his mother, and Sheila all dressed up.

Shorty, Rory, Sheila, w/ Gordy in foreground.

Sheila's sister, Alba, dressed to go out.

Bev Holloway (center) and Sheila (far right) hanging out with the girls and Naomi Campbell (right, back row).

Mike and Rory in furs, with Michael & Anna Nateese.

Rory and Sheila ringside on fight night.

Sal DiCarlo, Todd, Rory, and friends out on the town.

Todd Holloway bringing the ball downcourt.

Obar, a good friend, hanging out w/ Todd Holloway.

Shorty Black kicking back at the gym.

Shorty, Gordy, and Rory in their Homburg hats.

John Horne at a press conference, w/ Rory in background.

Sheila and Rory Holloway.

Mike holding Gloria Nia on his lap.

Rory and Sheila's daughter, Gloria Nia.

Sheila w/ her granddaughter, London.

Granddaughter London.

Gloria Nia celebrating birthday w/ London on lap and Lela in background.

The author, producer Kyle Saylor, Andre, Wisdom, Sheila, and Rory.

Andre, producers Kenny and Kyle Saylors, and Rory.

Producer and director Kyle Saylors goofing around.

Andre, Rory, Kharl, Dr. Heuer, and the author.

Andre Prieto and Rory sharing saki.

Rory Holloway and Robert discussing Promax Productions.

The author and Rory Holloway.

The author posing w/ Sheila and Rory in Manhattan hi-rise.

Andre Prieto, financial manager for Promax.

The author with his wife of 24 years, Carolyn Rose.

Mike Tyson Productions Inc.

July 18, 1995

VIA FACSIMILE: 702-731-0187

Don King
Don King Productions, Inc.
871 W. Oakland Park Boulevard
Ft. Lauderdale, Florida 33311

Rory Holloway
1285 15th Street
Apartment 16F
Fort Lee, New Jersey 07024

John Horne
2101 Eagleseh Circle
Henderson, Nevada 89014

Dear Don, Rory and John:

This letter is to express my appreciation for your efforts in obtaining for me a non-refundable but fully re-coupable advance bonus of Seventy-Three Million Dollars ($73,000,000.00) for signing contracts with Set Pay Per view and Showtime Networks, Inc., on one hand, and MGM Grand Hotel, Inc. and MGM Grand Inc., on the other, for their right to broadcast and stage my next ten (10) bouts. In addition, you have negotiated with Showtime for the payment to me of Twenty Five Million Dollars ($25,000,000.00) for my fight which is expected to take place on August 19, 1995 at The MGM Grand Arena in Las Vegas, Nevada.

In consideration of your services, I agree to pay Don King Productions, Inc., thirty percent (30%) of such bonus and to pay my co-managers, John Horne and Rory Holloway, ten (10%) each of such bonus.

It is understood and agreed by me, Don King Productions, Inc., John Horne and Rory Holloway that such advance signing bonus is non-refundable and I will not be required to pay it back. This means that no money will come out of my fight purses to recoup the fully recoverable advance bonus. My only obligation is to participate in the ten

Mike Tyson, President/CEO • John K. Horne, Co-Manager • Rory Holloway, Co-Man

7 Route 534 • Southington, Ohio • 44470   871 West Oakland Park Blvd. • Oakland Park, FL • 3
K (216) 888-9388   Phone (305) 561-

678

Page 1 of letter from Mike Tyson to Don King, Rory Holloway, and John Horne agreeing to pay them the percentages in the Showtime contract, and thanking them for securing the signing bonus of $73,000,000.

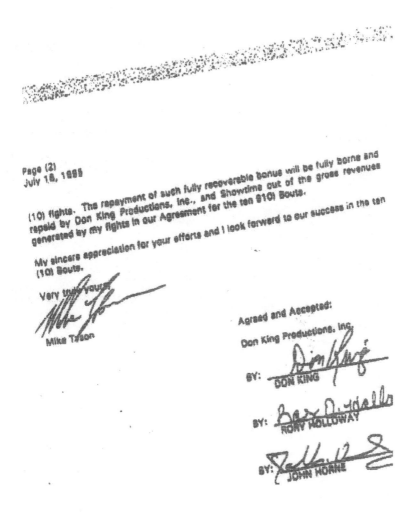

Page 2 of letter from Mike Tyson to Don King, Rory Holloway, and John Horne agreeing to pay them the percentages in the Showtime contract, and thanking them for securing the signing bonus of $73,000,000.

PART THREE

WHEN DID THUGS TAKE OVER MIKE'S CAREER?

*"Those who lead good people along
an evil path will fall into their own trap,
but the honest will inherit good things."*

Proverbs 28:10

CHAPTER NINETEEN

THE CATS

"**W**e weren't the thugs. We was Mike's family." Rory Holloway delivers this statement with complete conviction.

Is it accurate, though?

A comparison of the two eras of Team Tyson seems necessary.

Era #1: From 1982 through 1987, Cus D'Amato was the engineer of Mike's career. The train sped smoothly along, save a few detours, and Mike Tyson was hailed as the "savior of boxing." He was Kid Dynamite. He was Iron Mike. He referred to Cus as his father, and he excelled under the tutelage of Teddy Atlas, and later, Kevin Rooney. He earned two U.S. Junior Olympics gold medals, a Golden Gloves championship, and an unbroken string of professional victories that led to the undisputed heavyweight crown. Few fighters since have generated such global excitement.

In 1988 and 1989, Mike's career hit an uphill grade. He was coping with the deaths of Cus and Jim, and also with Robin and Ruth's attempts at commandeering the train. Lawsuits were filed. Mike fired Cayton. The courts limited the Cayton-Jacobs contract, while still upholding it. For a brief time, Mike kept Rooney as on as his trainer before also giving him the boot.

Sportswriters were incredulous. Had the champ lost his mind? Michael Katz, of the *New York Daily News*, lambasted him for ditching all those responsible for his success.

During this period, Mike's career nearly ground to a halt as his endorsements, public favor, and tumultuous eight-month marriage ended. Rory recognized trouble and moved up from the passenger car to stoke the sputtering engines. Though he faced severe limitations until Mike's existing management contract expired, a new era was soon to begin.

Era #2: It was late 1989, and Rory knew he could not do this alone. In stepped John Horne to claim a co-manager role. Rory functioned as the visionary, charting their journey and enlisting others to come aboard. John was the mouthpiece, addressing the press—a role he relished—and tugging at the ear of Don King. Don hopped onto the train as Mike's full-time promoter, arranging fights with the most advantageous opponents in the most lucrative locations.

Soon, Mike was known as the Baddest Man on the Planet.

But Mike's image became tainted. His loss to Buster Douglas, his first as a professional, was one of boxing's biggest upsets, and though he later regained his title, his grip on invincibility began to slip. He gained a reputation as a trash-talking, womanizing, convicted rapist. Legendary heavyweight George Foreman said that Mike had discredited the sport.

Iron Mike turned into Rusty Mike.

Kid Dynamite turned into Full-Grown Walking Time Bomb.

Boxing historian Bert Randolph Sugar said in a *Philadelphia Inquirer* article, "Some fighters start out as bad guys and end up as good guys. That's the usual pattern. Muhammad Ali, for example, started out as a loudmouthed braggart and ended up as a revered figure. But, with Mike, it's the other way around. He's gone from a good guy to a bad guy."

Did Mike start out as a good guy? Can that case be made?

He was a sensitive kid, no doubt about it. Emotionally damaged and physically bullied, yes. However, none of that changed the fact he was a Brownsville delinquent arrested dozens of times by the age of thirteen. Even under Cus's care, he was expelled from school for his mistreatment of the girls, and when that mistreatment carried over into other areas, he felt Teddy Atlas's gun pressed to his head. These issues were downplayed during his ascent toward boxing greatness. The soft voice and the shy-guy act served as handy disguises for a much darker side.

While it is impossible to compare the two Team Tyson eras on equal terms, there is little doubt Cus's team functioned with less turmoil and distraction. Mike was still teachable, residing in the protective environment of Camille's large Victorian home in small-town Catskill. Cus's eye was on the prize of raising up a second world champion, and he was quick to gloss over Mike's indiscretions. Mike was a troubled black youth in the care of discerning white managers, and few challenged their decisions. In fact, the media was quick to heap praise.

Rory's team inherited an entire different animal. Mike was a grown man when they took over, a reigning world-champion, a millionaire who had never earned a high-school diploma, never worked a 9-to-5 in his life, and was in the throes of a devastating divorce. They found themselves dealing with a beast not only in the ring, where such ferocity was encouraged and lauded, but outside the ring as well. Mike was lewd and crude. He was a troubled black adult in the care of other African-Americans, and the media took them to task.

Who were these lackeys, these clingers-on named Rory Holloway and John Horne?

Where did these guys get off thinking they knew a damn thing about boxing?

Were any other top-paid athletes handled by black managers? Hell, only one *Fortune 500* company was helmed by a black CEO. That told you something right there, didn't it?

In retrospect, the racial bias is hard to deny. Despite making significant leaps in the past two decades, American culture still shows signs of lingering prejudice. Note the recent comments recorded by NBA owner Donald Sterling. Or the hoopla stirred up when African-American Maverick

Carter—aged 23 at the time—signed on as manager for his childhood friend, LeBron James. Carter was simply following a trail blazed by Rory and John Horne.

In the late 1990s, fans shook their fists and blamed Rory and John for Mike's disappointing behavior in the streets and in the ring. They had been teased by glimpses of a boxing god, only to watch his immortality fade away. Surely, somebody was responsible. Who better to blame than Team Tyson?

Rory, what do you say to the journalists who called your team "hoodlums" and "gangsters"?

RORY: Listen, I made a point of making sure our crew had a culture of clean living in camp. They in the gym, they working out, ain't doing no drugs. It was smooth sailing up to fight time. That way when we come to the press conference, when we step into the ring, we were tastefully dressed. My guys, they were always suited and booted, sharp and immaculate. They wearing Versace. They wearing Homburg hats, like the old '60s. Nobody could say a thing, at least that's what I thought.

Soon as the newspapers seen us, they said we was dressed like gangsters. They said we at the press conferences with watches like hockey pucks. What we supposed to do? Put on matching Nike sweatsuits? We do that, they say we thugs.

It was a double standard. We couldn't win. I don't like pulling out the race card, but sometimes it's a real factor. You see some white managers walk their fighter into the arena, they in suits, they in sweats, either way ain't nobody calling them names.

These reporters would come at us. They try to stick that microphone up in my face and get me to say the wrong thing. They wanna get a reaction, then they wanna exploit that. Listen, I didn't go to school for communications and how to talk. I had to learn all this shit on the go. I knew how the game worked, and they never rattled me. Not one time was I caught up with Mike in any public craziness. I ain't never been around one of them incidents. When I was with him, I was in my role as manager. I was babysitter, dishwasher, car-washer, psychiatrist, and best friend. That was it. That was my job.

Were my guys perfect? Hell, no. Boxing is full of kids from the streets, that's where a lotta these cats come from. It's not some issue of color. Whether they from Mexico, Manila, or Brooklyn, that's just the way it is. So when I pulled our team together, yeah, some of them had a past. Nobody denying that.

You look at Cus and his boys, and some of them had pasts too. Teddy Atlas, man, he dropped out of school and took part in an armed robbery. He ended up behind bars on Rikers Island. He still got a scar on his face from a knife fight, took hundreds of stitches to sew it shut. Kevin Rooney, he got charged in Connecticut with driving under the influence and assaulting a police officer. Steve Lott, he had his issues. All these cats was gathered under one roof at Cus and Camille's, and they weren't bad guys, that's not what I'm saying. It's just that when the media got to talking, all you heard was how our team this gang of hoodlums, and somehow that first team, all them white guys, was these upstanding citizens. That just ain't the case.

Most of those in the fight game, they from troubled backgrounds, and boxing is that step up for them. It's their family, their saving grace. Sure, you got some managers who really care, but boxing is the scum of the earth in exploiting these young athletes. It's the nature of the beast. There's no unified board or commission, no fighters' union.

Mike was fortunate, man. Both his teams was full of guys who loved their fighter and wanted him to succeed. Cus and his guys, me and my cats, we had Mike's back.

You say you have no criminal record, and intensive investigation has turned up nothing to contradict that. Are there any incidents from your past that might lead others to label you a thug?

RORY: You want some dirt? Yeah, I did my share of stupid things. I ain't gonna sit here and tell you otherwise.

Listen, my parents mostly kept us busy in sports. That was my way of fitting in. I played quarterback in high school, played basketball, was named all-state. Give my dad credit for teaching me about the sweat of my brow, and my mom for showing me you gotta care about others—high, low, rich or poor, they all deserve a chance. Albany was my people, and I tried to be on good terms with everyone.

I never knew no gang members, but not all these guys I knew was immaculate. Some of them sold drugs. I was friends with them, they cared about me, but they knew I one of these athlete guys who didn't mess with that shit. They knew to keep me outta their business. They didn't grind me like that or try to hurt me or nothing. Sometimes I'd see them walking down the street, and I would pull over. "Hey, you need a ride."

They'd go, "Ro, I'm dirty. Keep going." Silly me, I'm like, "Oh, okay." And I'd roll on by.

That's not to say I didn't try selling some weed once. I was maybe fourteen, fifteen. It started when I seen this relative of mine bring these big Hefty bags into the house, all tied up. He always into something, hustling what he could. And damn, the place smelled like a pot factory. He in there weighing it all, and he seen me. "Get outta here," he yelled. Later, no one's looking, and I grabbed as much as I could outta one of them bags and shoved it into my pocket.

Here was my chance. I seen how guys do it, standing on the corner, hanging out near the telephone booth. Now I'm out there like I'm one of them. "Hey, over here. I got the best deal." My bags was way overfilled. All I know is, I wanna buy me some new sneakers and then I'm done.

Instead, I see the cops coming this way down the street. My eyes get real big, and I'm like, "Oh, shit." They start chasing another guy and they disappear around the corner, but I'm so scared, so paranoid, I take off and leave the bags of weed laying there on the ground. My friend was laughing at me. "Man, they ain't even after you. You gonna give yourself away." That was the end of my big, bad career.

After high school, I got into a situation during my job at Berkshire Farms Division for Youth. One of the kids attacked another kid with a pocketknife. I broke it up, stuck the knife in my pocket, and forgot all about it. I'm driving home that night from Cambridge, Mass, to Albany, New York, I feel that thing in my pocket, and I set it on the seat. Next thing, the lights on my old Lincoln start flashing, blink, blink, blink, and a cop pulls me over, thinking something wrong. He spots that silly knife beside me and writes me up for a concealed weapon. For all I know, that shit went on my record.

Not much later, after Mike won his first heavyweight title, I was coming to the end of my job at Berkshire. I had a real connection with these kids. I cared about them and it was sad to leave, but me and Mike working together now. So the kids made me this special farewell gift, an African stick like a cane, carved and beautiful.

Couple nights later, I'm gonna eat some food with Sal and friends before heading to Vegas on an early-morning flight. I pull up to a restaurant on Central Avenue. Mike'd bought us new cars, and I'm in a convertible Corvette, burgundy, with the top down.

As I get out, these white kids start coming at me. One of them says, "Damn, that's a nice car."

I'm like, "Thanks."

"What's a nigger doing with a car like that?" he asks.

I'm thinking, "Tell me I didn't hear you right."

Then one of his buddies says, "You must've sold a lotta drugs."

I turn around. "Why would you say something like that?"

They start converging on me in the parking lot. I'm backing up. "Why y'all trying to start trouble?" They keep coming. I reach down into the convertible and get my hand on that African stick. This thing looks more lethal than it was, and I'm just trying to scare them off. I don't wanna fight five or six guys. They keep coming, circling the Corvette, getting more aggressive. I'm scared as hell. When one of them rushes me from the side, I swing around and break that stick over his head. Now we're kinda wrestling, this angry mob is on me, and I'm trying to reach the restaurant door. These fuckers gonna kill me.

Outta nowhere, I get help. My brother Todd, he driving by and sees all this, and he and his friends jump out. They throwing punches, beating these guys down, while I get into the restaurant. When the cops arrive, I'm the one gets charged with assault. The judge was known as "Give 'em Time Klein," and I decided to take probation.

About a year later, I'm in a gym at the Jewish community center. I see a few of those same white guys. They come over, tell me they was drunk that night and they sorry for what happened. "Don't worry about it," I told them. "Let's play ball."

Listen, I love my old neighborhood. Even years later, Mike and me still went back to hang out. They treated us like we anybody else. We played ball in the park, and Mike was just as wild on the court as on the dance floor, like he got freakin' convulsions. They cussing us out, calling us all kinda names. It was refreshing, you know. It was cool.

Of course, you always had the crabs who wanna pull you back down.

CHAPTER TWENTY

THE CRABS AND THE SHEEPDOG

If readers were to visit a New England wharf or Seattle's Pike Place Market, they might happen upon a barrelful of live crabs. The crabs clatter over each, clambering up the sides, clawing towards the top. Do they detect blue sky overhead? Do they smell fresh air? Freedom? Whatever the motivation, they seem tireless in their attempts at escape.

And yet few ever make it out.

Why? Because each potential escapee has a dozen of his crusty friends dragging him back down. It is a crab-in-the-barrel mentality that plays out in areas of human interaction.

You mentioned the crabs pulling you down. Can you explain that? As you recruited team members for your training camps, what sort of rivalries and conflicts did you encounter?

RORY: It's sad, man. A few of these guys in Albany, I known them all my life, and they were so jealous of me, of this ride I was on with Mike. They hated to see somebody else elevated. It was that crab-in-the-barrel thing. They thinking, "Shit, if I can't make it, I don't want nobody to make it." It's one thing to envy someone, to be motivated to reach for something more, but it's another thing to be jealous and drag others down. You'd rather hurt yourself and others than let anyone else succeed.

Mike heard the same sorta shit. "Why you employing Rory Holloway from Albany, instead of someone from here in the Brownsville?" Listen, it's just a misplaced thought-process. Some of these guys, they uneducated, and you can't expect any different.

Actually, Mike spent more years around Catskill and Albany than he did growing up in Brownsville. They want to claim him for themselves, that's okay. They have that right. But Mike don't owe them nothing. In Brownsville, you got a lotta empty, rundown buildings, and people always saying how he should've done this or that to help.

Well, he has that right to go back and build something if he want. If not, that's his choice too.

We used to go into the poor neighborhoods with Mike and Don King, bringing in semi-trucks full of Thanksgiving turkeys. Thousands of people showed up, everyone happy. Not everybody bad from Harlem, Brooklyn, the Bronx, that's just not true. There a lotta good people there. You gotta judge each person individually, 'cause everybody got the chance for redemption, right?

You know, even some of my own inner circle I rounded up from Brownsville.

For hundreds, perhaps even thousands of years, sheepdogs have been used to round up sheep and droves of cattle. Humans have modified the dog's natural hunting instinct into a herding behavior, with various breeds employing different methods. Some dogs push the herd forward by nipping at the heels. Others stare down the livestock, guiding their movements by heading them off. Certain dogs use deep barks. Others run alongside the animals to keep them in line.

In many ways, Rory Holloway fit the description of a traditional sheepdog as he herded his team and their fighter. He was trustworthy, alert, and protective, rarely using aggression. He could call upon almost goofy, playful energy to complete a task. According to those who worked with him, his sense of duty carried the day. One former team member said, "Rory is the Phil Jackson, just bringing everyone together and getting the best outta them."

Rory spent much of his time warding off predators such as Craig "Boogie" and Kevin Sawyer. In *Undisputed Truth*, Mike even mentioned that: "My friend Kevin Sawyer who had the beeper shop would beep and tell me he had some girls lined up . . . Don and John and Rory would get so furious when I'd get beeped. They wound up taking my beeper and putting it in the freezer and then they threatened to kill Kevin."

Herding a flock while watching for enemies is one thing. It is an entirely different chore to do so while dealing with a wolf in your own midst.

Mike was ravenous. His appetites were out of control.

When Mike bristled at Rory's disciplinary actions, Mike would bring a girl, or girls, into camp, marching them right past his manager in a show of rebellion. Rory needed more eyes and ears. He needed guys who could divert Mike's attention, focus his energies, and shrug off his attempts at drawing them with him down into the cesspool.

Such guys are not easy to find.

As you gathered your team, did you seek out specific attributes? What was the team's mentality?

RORY: You gotta understand something, everybody says boxing's an individual sport. Well, I disagree. Even though it's man-to-man combat, it's not an individual sport. You develop a camaraderie with your team. These guys got roles to play, they're not just sitting the fuck around. It takes a special kinda person. Their job is to motivate you, to make you the best you can be. It's a process. It's every day, all day. The team live together, eat together, run together. They sacrifice together.

When a fighter really got a good team, a close-knit team, he goes into that ring and he's fighting for his family. Every punch he throws, he throwing it for his team. Right when he wanna give it up, he look back at his team and he decides he ain't gonna let you down, he gonna go that extra mile, he gonna take that extra punch.

He's your warrior, your champion. And you soldiers in his army.

The best fighters, they got that heart of a champion. They don't never wanna quit. They ready to put their life on the line. This shit is for real. Sometimes as a manager, you gotta be that guy who throws in the towel. "You had enough, champ. We'll get him another day, but I'm not gonna let you get your brain beat in. You got too much pride, and it time for me to step in." When he says, "I let you down," that's 'cause he feels like he let his team down. He knows how much it means to us, and we know how much it means to him. We take every punch with him. We in this together.

He lose, we lose. He win, we win.

Period.

Listen, one thing about Mike, he walked the walk and he talked the talk. He took an ass-whooping like a man. He didn't back down. In Toyko he partied, he was outta shape, and he paid the price. He lost to Buster Douglas, but he didn't quit in the ring. He didn't complain. He took his whooping. He came back on the plane wearing his fuckin' black eye like a badge of honor.

Them was hard times. Team Tyson took a lotta heat, but we was dealing with a madman. Each day we figuring out how to contain that. Everything in camp had to be precise. That's where the grunt work happens, the essential stuff. A lot of the stuff you see on TV, a fighter in training 24/7, a lot of it's scripted, edited, just fluff for the viewers. You hear the music, the lights, all the glamour, and it make you wanna jump up off the couch and cheer. The fighter seems like he saying all the right things at the right time.

The reality is there's lotsa challenges in training camp. You wanna create the best environment you can, a culture of winning, a positive synergy. You need guys who committed to that.

That's why I set up our camps strategically, the outer circle and the inner circle. The outer circle, they the guys doing just everyday stuff, you know, carrying bags, getting the newspaper, food and drinks, whatever. I didn't care what they did at night, sneaking out, partying. Camp was a good time for those guys.

Then I had my inner circle. These guys were serious. They didn't go out, 'cause we had to get up the next morning and go running. We purifying our bodies, going through detox. It was a time of reflection, all a part of the process.

I wasn't obligated to go run with Mike, to endure some of that stuff. That's not what a manager gotta do. I could've taken advantage of my friendship and still got my paycheck. But I didn't. I wanted the team to see I'm in there sacrificing too. I want my fighter to be the best he can be. He knows who's in there with them and who's not. We got a fight coming up, and as a manager/trainer/point-man/whatever-my-title, I just tried to make sure camp was running as smooth as possible so my fighter got the best opportunity to win. For me to cheat him of that, I wouldn't have been doing my job.

Today, there's still plenty of talented fighters out there, men and women. Some of that talent gets diverted into mixed martial arts. The UFC's real popular nowadays, and that draws a lotta these kids. I'm telling you, that shit you see is for real. They some incredible athletes. I'd love to see what Mike do in the Octagon. He put his hands on you, you in trouble, especially with them little gloves.

I still got a thing for boxing, though. It'll come back strong, especially if they can unify and cut out the corrupt practices. But is the discipline there in today's fighters? I don't know. We a spoiled culture. We got so much just handed to us. You know, being the champ don't just fall in your lap. You gotta work for it. Gotta pay the price.

Don't get me wrong when I say this 24/7 stuff on TV is fluff. When I say "fluff," I mean they just put the good parts in. For an athlete to get himself up, to take his body to that next level, to take punches every day, it's a mindset. You can't be in front of the cameras driving your kids to school in the van, cuddling with your woman on the couch, you can't do that shit in training. I just believe your mind gotta be someplace else, not on the wife, on the kids. That's the sacrifices a true champion gotta make. He gotta be away from all that. He gotta feel that pain. He gotta know he hurting for a reason, right? He don't need nobody to come in and comfort him. I used to hate that sorta laziness.

Toward the end of Mike's career, you seen him start slipping. Just little things at first, then bigger and bigger. Fighters are creatures of habit, and I knew Mike's thought-process better than anyone, better than any of his trainers. Sometimes we had to do things to counteract that for his own betterment, things to get him doing what he supposed to be doing. Him cussing me out on a daily basis, that was just part of the cost of getting him where he need to be.

My thing was, I gotta keep my boy on course one day at a time, one second at a time. Whatever we gotta do to squeeze that one last little bit outta him, that's what we do. "Yo, Mike, you gotta go a little harder. Mike, you slacking today." Other guys wanna tell him, "Yeah, yeah,

yeah, you looking good." Mike would always ask me what I think 'cause he know I'm gonna tell him the truth.

Like I said, though, this wasn't a project I could do on my own. It was a team effort. Team Tyson was more than the sum of its parts. When Mike was on task, when we in camp, I'm telling you it was a thing of beauty. We a well-oiled machine.

How did you find the various components for this "machine"? Did you have an application process in place or a particular set of criteria you used?

RORY: One thing about me, even as a kid, I had a special ability to be a visionary. I don't look at things from corner to corner, you know. I look from mile to mile. I see things before they happen. I'm a long-distance guy, the way I think.

I believe that's a talent God gave me, to see potential in other people, and the guys I brought in for our team weren't the ones most people gonna choose. They weren't the obvious picks. The media didn't know these guys. They only knew what they saw on the surface, and they made their assumptions. These sports writers got a job to do, a career they building, I understand that, but you gotta take some responsibility for what you put out there. You can't take that shit back.

The guys in my inner circle, they were in this for real. They were solid guys. Take Gordy, for example, here's a man with as much honor as anyone I know.

CHAPTER TWENTY-ONE

THE BOBCAT

Based on Rory's effusive praise of the man, you might expect Gordy Keelen to be a giant male specimen, broad-shouldered and imposing, a warrior with his shield held close and sword held high. He had Mike Tyson as a groomsman at his wedding, and Mike, in his book, called him "my old friend." In person, Gordy turns out to be lean and wiry, the top of his close-shaved head barely reaching my chin. He wears a brushed leather jacket over a buttoned shirt and jeans. He is energetic, talkative, and quick to laugh.

His laughter fades as he drives into Brownsville. These four square blocks were his and Mike's shared stomping grounds years ago.

"This where we grew up," Gordy says from behind the wheel. "We always heard how the white people were the devil, and we gotta get what we can. Well, this was our hell. From back in '79, I was a career criminal, up and down the shops and the streets, picking pockets. I was in and out of jail and group homes. They locked me away in Spofford, same place they put Mike. You think I was upset about that? I was happy, man. That gave me street cred."

He stops at a traffic light. Bathed in morning sunshine, the grim structures and cracked sidewalks look less menacing than in the much-publicized photos.

Gordy nods at a graffiti-tagged building behind a black iron fence. "These projects, man, they hard to get out of. You grow up here, and when your mother dies you take over. What else you gonna do? Things look nicer now, but in some ways it's deadlier than it was when I was growing up. Back in the day, maybe one in twenty of us had a gun. It was knives then. It was all about respect. Even if you lost a fight, at least you went for yours. Now, you got twenty of these kids, they got twenty guns, and the guns're probably coordinated with the color of their shoes. They look at 50 Cent, thinking that if they take a bullet like he did, maybe they'll get rich too."

As if on cue, a pair of youths in hoodies dart around the corner and past our vehicle.

"Them's the motherfuckers that scare me." He shifts in his seat. "You don't look them too hard in the eye, or they might kill you for your cellphone. Not even blink." He puts the vehicle in gear and starts moving again. "These kids and their phones, that's part of the problem, you ask me. At home, no one's talking face to face. Everyone's in his own little world. And at school, how these teachers supposed to get through to the students, to give them an education, when kids are texting on their damn phones right there in class?"

He points. "This is Amboy Street, where Mike used to live. And a couple blocks over, you got the Brownsville Community Center where we hung out. It was day-to-day survival, man. That all changed for me in 1990, when I got sent from Wyoming State Prison into the SHOCK program. SHOCK is Self-discipline, Honor, Obedience, Character, and Knowledge. It was only a six-month program, but it changed my life. It was military-style, four dorms, with these stern drill instructors. They were all white guys, the devil to me, but I learned something from that. These guys rode me hard, had me running, working out, learning discipline. They never let me stop. You let one eye wander, and they were all over you. But they cared, man. They really cared. That changed the way I saw the world, and a lot of the stuff they taught me was biblical principles. When I got out, I still ran every day. I sat tall like I was on parade-rest. I enrolled at Hunter College, and that made my mother proud. She was still alive to see that."

Minutes later, Gordy pulls into a parking lot at Brooklyn's Christian Cultural Center. "This here's the church where I work."

It is a large yet inviting property, freshly painted, with landscaped strips of grass. Inside, ushers give warm greetings and brochures. On any given Sunday, over 10,000 people attend the church here. One of the ushers gestures at Gordy. "This guy here, he's one of the best we got."

Back in the lot, Gordy says, "Before the SHOCK program, man, if somebody asked me to church, I was like, 'Yo, you be buggin'. I wouldn't be caught dead in that sucker.' After I got out, I started coming here, and it's been over twenty years now. I have two grown daughters. Mia, she's a Harvard graduate and works for the Brooklyn Nets. Jhanee went to Virginia State, and she raps and sings. I'm the facilities manager at Bronx Charter School for Excellence, and my God story is bigger than any other story, bigger than Team Tyson and all of that."

From pickpocket to preacher-man. The Lord, as they say, works in mysterious ways.

"I like helping with the kids." He flashes a smile. "Rory gave me a Lexus Jeep back in our team days with Mike, and I wore that thing out driving the kids around, keeping them outta trouble. Those were fun times. I still work with kids at the church, in my neighborhood. They're my life, and they come crowding around, laughing, playing, hugging me. I really love them. One of the toughest things, man, was when I heard one of my boys got murdered. He was a son to me, like my own flesh and blood." Gordy's jaw tightens, and he looks away. "Those were hard times."

As he is about to leave, another church volunteer approaches. His name's Hank, the head of the custodial crew. "Gordy," he says, "we got an elderly woman over here. She locked her keys in her car, and we know you the brother who can get in there for her."

Gordy gives a sheepish shrug. "That's what I'm here for. Gotta help a sister out."

The talents he once used for evil he now uses for good.

Mysterious ways, indeed.

How did you get connected with Gordy? When did you realize he was the type of guy you wanted on Team Tyson?

RORY: Like I said, outta Brooklyn there was a coupla good guys. The Caytons and the Jacobs didn't want Mike to have nothing to do with nobody from there. "Stay the fuck away from those people. Those people are bad." I was the guy who always advocated to Mike, "You gotta have somebody helping you who's from your 'hood. We can give them jobs. You can give back, you know."

Some of these friends of Mike's, I really liked them. One example, Oohie, he genuinely cared about Mike. His real name's William Fagen. He didn't actually work for us, but if we ever needed his help, he was always there. He's still around. He's married now, got grandkids, got gray hair. Mike respected him. He didn't fuck with Oohie.

Gordy and Oohie was tight, but Mike didn't want any of these Brooklyn cats on our team. Mike was a conglomerate. Even though he could give out jobs and change people's lives, he'd tell me, "Yo, stay away from them people. They treacherous." That was stuff Cus put in his head, trying to protect him. I wasn't saying we had to go hang out in the 'hood, but I knew one or two of these guys was serious and had stuff to offer. I wasn't scared if you got dirt on you, if you been to jail, 'cause everybody's good for a second chance, right? And Gordy, he'd just got outta the SHOCK program.

Here's where I'm thankful I had good judgment with people. Me, Mike, Gordy, we're all in my mother-in-law's place one day. Mike was like, "Man, I don't want nothing to do with Gordy. I don't owe him shit. Get that dirt-bag the fuck away from me."

Part of it, Mike was frustrated, and part of it he just showing off. Gordy went out the door wearing this long face, and I followed him into the hall. I didn't have to go out there, I didn't know him from Adam, but I could tell this a good guy. He's at the elevator, got tears in his eyes. These weren't no tears of self-pity. He this hardcore cat who would've fought tooth and nail a year earlier, but now he a changed man. He taking the high road. I said, "Listen, don't worry about it. I got you, man."

Here's Gordy, he had this reputation as a pickpocket. He could walk into an elevator on the ground floor, and by the time you on the fifth floor, he's friends with everyone on-board, and not one of them realizes he been robbed. He could shake your hand and make your damn watch disappear. That was the old Gordy. Real smooth. Sounds crazy, right? But I seen there was something else in him, and it was one of the best decisions I ever made. Turns out he one of the most trustworthy guys you ever wanna meet. He's not out to hurt you, but you mess with his people and he gonna fight back. He's like a bobcat, small and fast and fierce. You throw him into any type of environment, whatever situation, he gonna figure it out. He's highly adaptable.

The next time Mike seen him, he said, "What the fuck's he still doing around?" I said, "He's with me. He works for me now." And Mike was cool with that. He figured if I'm okay with it, then he's okay with it.

Listen, I'm a real rational guy. I'm not a genius, not complicated. I'm like a third-grader, man. One and one is two, two and two is four. It just makes sense. That's how I live my life, how I make my decisions. Straight-up rational. When I chose these guys for our team, I wasn't walking around thinking, "What is he gonna bring to the table?" It was about trust, about relationship. If we decide we in this together, we in this together.

From the root to the fruit. Any other way just gonna hold us back.

Ain't no better example of that than Shorty Black. Like Gordy, he had some stuff in his past, stuff that people whispered, but I just knew Shorty was my guy.

CHAPTER TWENTY-TWO

THE BULLDOG

Earl "Shorty" or "Shorty Black" Byam, a black man built like a fire hydrant, grew up in a street culture where survival was paramount and respect was everything. He had his first son at the age of 15, and he learned early on to step up and be a man. In his own words, "If I earned a dime, my son would get a nickel of it, that's the way it had to be. Nobody told me how to earn that dime, though. I had to figure that out on my own. I thought I was in control, but I wasn't."

He understood better than most that life is precious, that he should make each day count. As a husband now of over twenty years and as the father of three children, he cherishes the moments with those he loves.

What does he do for work with the Team Tyson's days behind him? In a twist of irony, the same city that would put a guy like Earl Byam in prison has employed him for nearly a decade. Shorty helps with power-distribution maintenance in the New York subway system, working as a third-rail specialist. The pay is good, and for good reason. That third rail carries the system's "juice." Even a simple brush against it could electrocute him with nearly a thousand volts of direct current.

For Shorty, a man born on New Year's Day, it is yet another reminder to make each day count.

It seems, Rory, that you had a knack for picking out troubled guys as members of your team. Why did you let a man like Shorty get involved with Team Tyson?

RORY: First time I met Shorty was in the early 1980s. His older brother, Caesar, he was attending Albany State University, and I was dating a girl who went there. We all met through mutual friends, then Shorty comes rolling up from Queens one weekend in a Jaguar. That meant a lot to him, coming up to see his brother. Well, I saw him get outta the car, short and dark, chest like a barrel. Next thing, me and Mike're riding around with him, and we all just clicked. I could tell this guy was solid. And sharp too, always coming up with this philosophical shit, dropping jewels on us. You know, he's even published books of poetry.

Shorty loves basketball almost as much as he and Caesar love boxing, and he'd be the first to admit he didn't expect much from no ballplayers from upstate New York. He from the city. What some country kids gonna show him on the court?

Summertime, he packed a buncha guys from Queens into his car and drove up for a game. I dropped forty points on them. He couldn't believe it. His guys, they all haggling him, giving him a hard time. Next time they come up, they make him promise that he not gonna let me drop forty on them again. I scored only thirty this time, and later Shorty told me he felt good about that. He could live with thirty.

Shorty's from a close-knit family, very attentive to his mother. Queens had a lotta celebrities back then—LL Cool J, Run DMC—and they all knew Shorty Black. Across the board, unilaterally, everyone said he was as solid as they come. One day, I found myself in a bad area of Queens, these rough cats gathered on the corner. I'm just that kid from upstate, right? I'm scared to even get outta the car. Then I hear somebody say, "Yo, that's Shorty's guy. Back off." He was respected, man.

One time, somebody stole Shorty's new car, a Mercedes-Benz. Well, the next morning, it's right back where they found it, washed and waxed, an apology note inside. I'm telling you, nobody fucked with him.

By the late '80s, me, Gordy, and Shorty, we were like the Three Stooges, right? Shorty got this fly Corvette by then, and we cruising around. Sometimes we just playing pool, maybe we going to the movies. Shorty'd get mad in the theater, "Man, that's not believable. C'mon, you can't fuckin' go through a door like that, you can't put your fist through a window like that." Me and Gordy, we're laughing, telling him he gotta quiet down 'cause he's scaring folks. "You sound like the angry black man."

Shorty was a serious cat. I'd go and bounce ideas off him, and he always good for some wise advice. He says, "God gave me two ears and one mouth, so I should listen twice as much as I talk." That's how he is, man. He takes his time, thinks stuff over. I could always count on him.

Did I purposefully pick these cats with checkered pasts? Hell, no. I ain't crazy. Like I said, I seen something in them. And Shorty, for example, he was all lined up to go into the Air Force before he became part of Team Tyson. He's a smart, committed guy. Listen, whether you squeaky clean or got some dirt, whether you a big-shot lawyer or a street sweeper, that don't make no difference to me. I'm looking beyond that. Oh, so you're the Wolf of fuckin' Wall Street? No, thank you. That's not the sorta guy I want on my team.

When Mike was in jail those three years, things got real tight. We didn't have no upcoming fights, no money coming in. I was hurting bad, running low on cash. Me and John had access to all Mike's stuff, his cars, his accounts, but we weren't touching none of that, and I was too embarrassed to ask Mike for help. How that gonna look, my man sitting in prison and me begging for a handout? That's not the way I roll.

So Shorty, one day he comes over to my house, and we in the hallway talking. He's like, "You alright, Ro?"

I tell him, "I'm alright."

"You sure you're alright?"

"Yeah, I'm alright."

He holds out this bag of money. "Put your hand in there, man. You take what you want, however much you can hold." Then he just walks away.

Listen, I could call Shorty right now. "Yo, man, I'm having a problem with these guys. They threatening me and shit." He'd be on the next plane out. If he had to hitchhike, he'd be here. You can depend on him.

I took pride in having the best camps for my fighter, and these were the kinda guys you want there with you. We'd hear guys from our opponent's camp, they out partying. I didn't catch my boys in no damn club. Not my inner circle. We in the gym working out at midnight. Gordy and Shorty, they dialed in. They up every morning at four o'clock, running with Mike. Mike out there and look behind him, we running. Gordy, he right there like Forrest Gump. "Run, Forrest, run." Shorty, he ran slow as a damn turtle at first, but by the end of training he was the best runner out there. If you couldn't do that shit, you didn't belong.

We looking at twelve to fifteen weeks of camp, with maybe fifteen guys on payroll—trainers, sparring partners, security, cooks, whatever—and they all had a part to play. We had $1,000,000 for camp expense. I'm signing those checks, and I ain't letting you just take Mike's money. You had to earn it. My own brother, I kicked him out 'cause he just sitting around. You don't do right by Mike, you fired. Period. I don't care who you are, I gotta protect my fighter from distractions. Way I saw it, we was preparing for war.

Mike was always unpredictable. One time we was setting up camp in Flagstaff, Arizona. We rolled into town like rock-stars, got this eighteen-wheeler parked outside the hotel. Rooms arranged, kitchens and everything, technicians wiring in big-screen TVs. Mike shows up for two days and says, "Fuck this place." He takes off. I don't have time to argue with him, not now. We got a fight coming up, so we gotta pack up and move to the next location. That was probably $100,000 down the drain. He'd just move on impulse, so we gotta be prepared. Like we the Boy Scouts of America, except this kid ain't no Eagle Scout. He's a big freakin' baby, and we chasing him around.

Once we were settled, I tailored stuff to Mike's personality, strategically setting things up like a chess game. I gave a gym bag to Gordy. "Here you go, with Mike's gear, boxing shoes, everything he need to work out." Then one to Shorty. "You got a bag too. If he goes off-location, if he in the mood to work out, he don't got no excuse. You ready."

The longer camp went, the more tense things got. We gotta sit up under this ferocious beast. He's irritable. He anxious. He cussing. He ready to fight, to get his hands on someone. He going through sexual withdrawals.

This whole time, I don't see my own wife. I put Mike before Sheila. She knew coming in that my boy was priority. If she couldn't deal with that, we probably wouldn't be married today. My Ferrari, my Lamborghini, they just sitting back at my mansion. I ain't enjoying any of that, right? If my fighter gotta go through this shit, I do too.

Gordy and Shorty, they made sacrifices of their own. They got family and friends they setting aside. They weren't going on no vacations or none of that. They got that paycheck in their hands, and it was going straight home to take care of their families. They in this with both feet—chasing after Mike, keeping the champ on task.

You gotta always be on your toes, man. Always anticipating what's next.

I needed these guys. I needed that adaptable and fierce bobcat, and Gordy was the man. And how'm I gonna get this done without a bulldog like Shorty to push us through?

The day of the fight, when we walked with Mike into that arena, that was a true honor, an absolute privilege. Mike still talks in interviews about how he wasn't going into that ring alone. He knew we there with him. It wasn't no show. Then you got John Horne who didn't go through camp, didn't put in the sweat and blood. Usually John off doing meetings, working on financial stuff, but he sure loved that spotlight when we walk into the ring. Man, that made Gordy and Shorty mad. They busted their asses for that honor. You look at their faces, you see them wearing it on their sleeves, and you know they belonged there. Only certain kinda guys made that cut. Them two, when they stepped into that arena, they was walking on holy ground.

If I was in a war and sitting in a foxhole, there ain't nobody I want in there with me more than Shorty. That's the guy you want beside you. Shorty, he the summer dog—summa this and summa that. If Gordy was the bobcat, Shorty was the bulldog. A true junkyard dog, just as loyal as can be.

The bulldog is a distinctive breed, recognized by his wide head, muscular shoulders, rolled neck, and formidable jaws. During World War II, English Prime Minister Winston Churchill was caricatured along those same lines for his stubborn resolve against the Nazis and unwavering support of his own people. Yes, the bulldog comparison seemed apt on a number of levels.

Before legislation banned the mistreatment of animals, this particular breed was used for centuries in the sport of bull-baiting. Wagers were placed on which creature could grab a tethered bull by the nose and bring it down. It was a dangerous business, and the dogs were often gored, trampled, and killed in the process—not to mention the damage to the bulls. In the 1800s, these events were popular across England, thus the emergence of the Old English Bulldog.

Thankfully, those cruel days are over. While the dog still has a reputation for being fierce and aggressive, the American Kennel Club says its disposition should be "resolute and courageous (not vicious or aggressive)," and its demeanor should be "pacific and dignified."

Once again, the image of Sir Winston Churchill arises.

Or, at Rory's prompting, the image of Shorty Black.

How did Mike get along with Shorty? Was it primarily a working relationship? Did he recognize Shorty and Gordy's contributions to the team?

RORY: In his book, Mike talks about his "friend Shorty Black" and mentions that he had "a little rinky-dink bar in Queens." Listen, Mike wasn't gonna let nobody hang around if he didn't want them. You gotta remember, he the boss. We all working for him. A guy like John Horne could get under Mike's skin, and when we out and about, Mike always saving his ass. But John wasn't there in camp each day. Camp was different.

Years later, when Mike ended Team Tyson and got new managers, it just shows how they didn't understand the value Gordy and Shorty brought to the mix. These two guys had Mike's back unconditionally, and even after I was out, they would've stayed if Mike had asked them. They would've been right there with him to this day, for better or for worse. Forget the job working the third-rail, or the job as a facilities manager and church worker. Shorty and Gordy were true friends. Friends to the end.

Shorty is tenacious. If he was still with Mike, there wouldn't have been no Jackie Rowes, no Craig "Boogies," no Shawnee Simms. He would've run those motherfuckers off. I'm just telling you, man, he would've run them off the right way. Maybe that's why Mike got rid of all of us, clearing room for the cesspool crew.

You know, with this book, Gordy and Shorty finally got a voice. They were unjustly put in a tough situation, being on the team and being friends with me. They took a lotta heat. Everybody in the world, all these cats in Queens and Brooklyn, they wanna know what really happened with Mike, where'd his money go. To this day, Shorty and Gordy gotta listen to all that, respond to all that. It's the shit they have to go through.

What people don't know, what nobody talks about, is the hard work these two put in. Team Tyson was about humility before honor, and these guys lived that. You think they did it for the recognition? For the limelight? For the money?

Hell, no.

They did it outta their love for Mike. Outta duty to the team.

Shorty and Gordy, they pushed the champ, but they could laugh with him too. We had some fun times together, the kinda memories you don't never forget. You know, some of the craziest stuff happened with us and Mike's tigers.

CHAPTER TWENTY-THREE

THE STALLIONS

The tiger's feline beauty and grace cannot mask its predatory nature. Reaching upwards of 600 lbs., it is a deadly-efficient hunter, stalking prey through any type of terrain. It is capable of blinding bursts of speed and breathtaking leaps. It aims for the back, sinking in curved claws, dragging down its quarry, clamping fangs into the neck.

Keeping a tiger in captivity is akin to leaving a loaded gun on the coffee table. Put such a weapon within reach of enough humans, and eventually someone is going to get hurt.

In 2003, Roy Horn, a partner in the illusionist act of Siegfried and Roy, was mauled and paralyzed during one of their Vegas shows. In 2008, a man was cleaning a cage at an animal farm in Missouri, when a tiger vaulted a ten-foot gate and mauled him. He tried to convince hospital staff he was attacked by a pit-bull. Soon after, a sixteen-year-old zoo employee was set upon by three tigers after he tripped in their enclosure. That slight movement, that moment of weakness, triggered something in the creatures.

Tigers seem to be everything Mike aspires to be— beautiful, deadly, and unbeatable. When it comes to their predatory nature, Mike could get that same chilling stare, that same focused stillness. As for feline grace, he had to rely upon some of his performances in the ring.

Not so much on the dance floor.

Either way, the man was a danger to himself and others, a fact his handlers were wise never to forget.

Is it true that Shorty had some dealings with the tigers, both humorous and dangerous?

RORY: He had both, definitely both. Like I said, Shorty is dependable. You call him at one, two, three in the morning, he gonna answer and be right there. Whatever you need done, he gonna see it through, and he loved Mike to death. But Mike, sometimes he just didn't respect these guys. Mike is a narcissist, the world revolves around him, and in any situation he thinking what's in it for him. Thing is, with Shorty, you can't piss in his face and tell him it's raining. You can't do that.

You gotta understand, Shorty has a short fuse. I seen it playing ball with some guys in Vegas. We in this gym, we running up and down the court, and I take this hard foul. This big guy, he standing over me. Suddenly Shorty's right there, staring up at this dude. "You don't wanna do that," he says.

The guy's smirks. "And who is you?"

Shorty doesn't bat an eye, doesn't move a muscle, just says in this low voice, "I'm the Grim Reaper."

Gordy hears that and he's like, "I'm done. Shorty, he's going there. I don't wanna play no more, Ro." He walks away and sits down.

The next night we in there again, and there's these young kids playing us. They good, but they arrogant. They talking trash to Gordy, trying to get in his head. Shorty, he's had it up to here, and he stares them down. "Oh yeah, you think you're tough? Well, they make little body bags too." He's that bulldog, man, and these kids back away like they afraid he gonna bite.

Shorty's mumbling to himself, "I'm just tired of playing with these cats. What's wrong with people, huh?"

So here's Shorty in Vegas, on his toes, ready to do whatever Mike needs. Well, Mike was very—how shall I say?—unorthodox. He wasn't into normal stuff. He hands Shorty this bag and says, "I got $250,000 in my safe. Go get it." Shorty comes back with the bag filled, and Mike says, "Fly that to Cleveland. I got some breeders waiting there at my place. Give them that money so they can mate their tiger with mine."

The entire flight Shorty's fuming in his seat, thinking, "What the hell? I didn't join the team so I can help some tiger-bitch get fucked." His people back in Queens were just trying to live another day, and here he's carrying around a quarter million bucks so that a pair of tigers can get hot and heavy. What kinda twisted shit was that?

That wasn't the only time Team Tyson traveled with cash on hand. That's the way we rolled back then, and it wasn't just chump change. I'm going through the airport on a trip, got a camera bag over my shoulder. Security tells me to open it up. "Yes, sir." I unzip the thing. The officer, he stares down at these stacks of money on top. He feels inside, slides his hands along the edges. What's he think he gonna find—drugs, a bomb, a lap dog? I tell him, "It's all hundreds in there, all the way down to the bottom." His eyes get big, and he just zips it back up and hands it to me. "You have a good day, sir."

If we traveling on the road, we usually had Mike's tigers to worry about. They in the car. In a cage. In a hotel room. You think that scene from *The Hangover*, the tiger in the bathroom, you think they just made that stuff up? They should've had a note, "Inspired by actual events."

Listen, these tigers was serious business, especially when it come to feeding them. You can't domesticate them. They're predatory. You better feed them on time, every day, on the dot. If not, they get kinda mean. Say they eat at 3:00 p.m., you better keep that routine. They got a ticker in their head. You don't keep them waiting till 3:05 or 3:06. You do that, you risk losing your hand.

We had Kenya in Mike's garage one time. You don't want her in the house when you can't be watching over her, right? You know how a cat can stink up a place, well, imagine a tiger. You ain't scrubbing that urine stain outta your carpet, no way. So I'm a little late for feeding time, and that was bad news. I open the door, and Kenya had literally torn open the roof of Mike's Maserati. Peeled it back like a damn sardine can.

We fed the tigers mostly chicken and horse meat. How we did it, we would grind it up and put the nutrients inside. They loved that ground-up horse meat, had a real taste for it. And that led to a problem in Vegas.

Mike had a neighbor who owned these beautiful horses. Man, that scent just drifted over the walls, right? One of the tigers slipped out of the enclosure. Mike wasn't always real careful about that, 'cause in Cleveland he let them wander around the property. On the other side of that wall, this white stallion's running around, mane flowing. He can smell too, and he probably spooked by the crouching tiger. That tiger's instincts kicked in and it leaped down, going after the horse. It probably wouldn't know what to do with it, being domesticated and all, but we never found out. That poor stallion, it just dropped over dead of a damn heart attack. You think you got problems with your neighbors? Man, you have no idea.

Mike just don't know the right thing to say sometimes. I remember a time just after he finished a fight, we standing in the Hilton lobby, everybody excited 'cause he won. Here comes Sylvester Stallone with his entourage. He walks past and says, "Yo, Mike, I'll put you in my next *Rocky* movie? You like that?"

Mike frowns. "I don't even lose for play. Nobody gonna beat me, not even in imitation." Sly looked at him like he crazy and just moved on.

I'm thinking, "Whoa, Mike just turned down the Italian Stallion."

Another time, late at night, we're in a restaurant with Sean Penn and Anthony Michael Hall, that kid from *The Breakfast Club* and *Weird Science*. Sean was known as a bad boy, and Mike was trying to get them two riled up, get them into a fight. Always stirring things up. He just liked hanging around these cats, especially older actors, mobsters, anyone who could tell him stories about the '50s. That was Mike's thing, man.

We driving along in L.A. once, and no joke, we turn and see Tito Jackson sitting there. Mike doesn't start in with small-talk or nothing. He says, "Tito, it true that your dad beat you kids? That's some messed-up shit."

This world we were living in was unreal. Surreal. Always a different challenge. On top of that, you got the people who wanna play divide-and-conquer. That's why I chose guys like Gordy and Shorty, guys who weren't in it for the money. Hell, they'd do this for free. It was a ballsy move going with them two. I mean, I lost friends and family 'cause of that decision, but nothing was more important than protecting Mike and his interests.

Yeah, people accused us of being this buncha thugs—and you definitely don't wanna disrespect Shorty, that ain't cool—but we were all married men, family men. One of Gordy's daughters, she works for the Nets. The other, she's into music. Shorty, he and his wife, they putting their kids through school. Earl Jr. is a grown man, and Marcellus, he was named after Cassius Marcellus Clay. Troy, he was a preemie baby, so small he could fit in your hand. He's excelling in college now, running track, awards and scholarships like you wouldn't believe.

These guys in my inner circle, they were stand-up guys, as solid as could be, and they still that way today.

These tigers, though, it wasn't just me and Shorty who had our dealings with them. Gordy faced his situations too, and usually they were embarrassing.

CHAPTER TWENTY-FOUR

THE TIGER CUB

Despite sitting atop the food chain, tigers are dwindling in numbers. Worldwide, only an estimated 3,000 remain in the wild.

Which makes it all the more surprising that 7,000 exist in the United States.

Tigers are displayed in zoos, circuses, casino lobbies, and Vegas acts. As pets, they prowl the homes and apartments of animal lovers, breeders, rappers, and celebrities. Michael Jackson reclined with one on the cover of *Thriller*, the bestselling album of all time. Tigers were presented to two U.S. presidents, Van Buren in the 1800s and Eisenhower in 1960, and became an extreme status symbol after the popularity of movies such as *Scarface* and *The Hangover*.

Their dangerous nature only adds to their appeal, making them an unbeatable item to show off to one's friends. "Oh, you got a Rottweiler?" Stifled yawn. "Well, come out back and see what I just bought."

Caring for these creatures is a financial nightmare. If the average citizen cannot afford steak as a nightly meal, imagine providing for the daily needs of a four-legged meat eater. A tiger can consume more than three dozen pounds of beef a day, with a bill well over $100. Tally up the costs of supplements, enclosures, and other expenses, and an owner is looking at $50,000 a year for one big cat. That is if he keeps his pet lean and mean. Let it gorge, and he may as well kiss his retirement fund farewell.

Mike was one of the rare people who could afford his tigers. He loved them. He slept with them. *Ring* magazine, among others, photographed the beast with his beasties.

Appearing one night on *Conan*, Mike was asked by host Conan O'Brien, "Did the tiger ever hurt you in any way?"

He answered, "On one occasion, I went 'Give me a kiss,' and she put her head in and—boom. I had gold teeth back then, and she knocked my teeth out because her head is like concrete."

Mike has said in recent interviews that he would like to own tigers as pets again, except that he cannot afford them, and his wife Kiki will not allow them in the same living space with their kids.

Give the lady props for that.

"I'll have to have my own little private compound," he told the *Daily Express*. "When tigers fart, it smells like hell. You don't want that around the house."

With Mike's tigers acting as your team mascots, the possibilities for embarrassment seem limitless. What were some of Gordy's encounters with them?

RORY: Gordy was a different guy after SHOCK, a full three-sixty. That's when I met him, and he was heavy into religion. He stopped smoking, stopped drinking. No more drugs. To Mike, this guy was a little irritating sometimes. You think I cared? That the kinda guy we need around. Real disciplined. On top of his game.

Gordy lived for a while with Mike on First Avenue, and they'd go running around the Reservoir in Central Park. Gordy be bouncing ahead like a rabbit, yelling these army chants, "One left, two left, three left, four." It was just what Mike needed, and at first that shit was fun. But Mike, sometimes he resisted the daily grind. Sometimes he'd get to cursing. "Shut the fuck up. You getting on my fuckin' nerves!" Gordy would keep his chin up and continue running.

When camp come around, Gordy was always ready. Shoes laced, bags packed. Whether we training out in Amish land in Ohio, or we in Vegas, or Flagstaff, wherever, I knew I could count on that man.

He was funny in camp, though. He had narcolepsy, where he just nod off sometimes. For a while, he had a digestion problem too, Crohn's Disease, where he in the bathroom a lot. He even wore them adult diapers. We out running and training, so he gotta be prepared, right? It was funny, but it wasn't funny. I felt bad for him, you know. He ain't the type to back outta doing the work 'cause he got some bowel issues.

One time, we had Mike's tiger wandering around the house. Kenya, she this beautiful cub, about forty pounds at the time. She's curious, poking her nose into everything, hiding, swiping at your legs. Like a big kitten, you know. Gordy runs off to the bathroom, stomach gurgling, and he doesn't get the door all the way shut. Next thing, Kenya drags something out across the carpet into full view. It's this saggy Depends. Shorty's like, "Phew." Someone else who don't know about Gordy's issues, they like, "Look at the size of that diaper. You must got a big baby around here."

Gordy took a lot of flak, always good-natured about it. He was a straight arrow. He up reading his Bible each day. He not pushy about it, but he knew what he believed and he ain't gonna hide it, right? Mike would try to sneak these girls in, and Gordy knew what Mike was like. Next thing you know, Gordy has these girls telling Mike how they not gonna give it up so easy, how they respect their bodies and he should too. Mike, he's yelling, "Gordy, you motherfucker, you messing with my girls' heads. Enough with all that religion and shit. You a downer, man."

Playing pool, that was a favorite team activity. One night, we was in the billiard room, holding our cue sticks, racking up the balls, and there's Gordy leaning over the table about to break. Mike starts flapping his gums at him. "Yo, Bible-man, you gonna preach to them balls? 'Praise the Lord, brother. Amen.'" You see Gordy's mouth tighten, but he ain't saying nothing. He puts the cue ball in position. "Give it to 'em, Gordy." Mike still taunting. "Hallelujah. Give 'em that old-time religion." Gordy throws his full weight behind his stick and breaks the balls. The eight-ball, it rolls right to the edge of a pocket and drops in. One shot, and he's won the damn game. Shorty's like, "Don't mess with the preacher-man, Mike." Mike just turned and walked upstairs.

Let me say this, I didn't care what my guys believed, 'cause the name of your religion don't always tell me what's in your heart. I wanted guys I could trust. Mike, his mother was Catholic, he got baptized in a Baptist church, and he converted to Islam. None of that really stuck. He like a lot of us, just trying to find something stable and real.

Gordy and Shorty, they the kinda guys who gonna be in the daily struggle with you. On the table, on the bed, Mike'd leave diamond rings worth over $1,000,000, wads of cash, watches worth $100,000. He had so-called friends he bring over, they leave, and that shit is gone. We tried to minimize the losses best we could. Gordy was my eyes and ears. He'd gather up Mike's stuff when we left a hotel. Gordy and Shorty, they the conscience of the team. They never stole a damn dime, and Mike knows that.

Gordy went above and beyond, man. He cleaned up mud, piss, blood. No shame. Mike liked rough sex, and when he get busy in his hi-tech love nest in Vegas, Gordy was the clean-up guy. Gordy had nothing to do with what went on in that room, he a straight cat, but he'd go in afterward like a forensic technician, gloves on, picking up after the champ, doing the laundry, washing them sheets. The most beautiful girls could be sitting there, and he over there sweeping the floor, picking up trash. They laughing. They calling him a square.

You think that didn't hurt? You think it didn't get under his skin? Let me tell you, Gordy was a man's man. He doing that for the team.

The crabs in the barrel, the friends of mine who wonder why I gave Gordy and Shorty a job and not them, they just wasn't built for that. They'd ask Gordy why he clean up after these cats like a damn slave. And Gordy, he said, "Let me explain something to you. When you get up and go work for that white guy, polishing his shoes, cleaning his car, you do it with pride. Why shouldn't I have that same sorta pride doing it for my friends? I'm proud. I wouldn't wanna be doing nothing else."

I heard that, and man, that was deep. He was absolutely right.

You look at the NBA champs, the NFL, that's how they win. The Seattle Seahawks are Super Bowl champs 'cause they walked around with that attitude of "it's us against the world." That's what it takes—that tight-knit group, that humble pride, that commitment and loyalty.

Can you share other examples of Gordy's commitment and of his involvement with the tigers?

RORY: Man, anytime Gordy got near the tigers, something funny seemed to happen.

Mike's tigers were usually kept in Cleveland. He had three of them there, later four. His house didn't really have a proper built-in sanctuary, but the laws in Ohio were more flexible. Each state is different. In Nevada, you had to have a proper enclosure, so we had to get one custom-built at Mike's place in Vegas. If we on the road, though, lotsa times we took the tigers with us. Most places back then weren't real strict about crossing state lines with these exotic beasts, but we still worried about getting pulled over, right? We were the traveling rockstar-circus-carnival act.

One time Gordy, he's driving from Ohio to New York. He got a damn tiger in the back, blankets and stuff over the cage so you can't see what's inside. We're a few minutes behind in another vehicle, and the traffic comes to a grinding halt. We inching along, inching along. We finally get up there, and it's Gordy, man. He nodded off, his narcolepsy, and veered into a ditch. He's shaken up, his ego bruised, but he's okay. A cop is talking to him, making sure he not under the influence or nothing.

We pull over, and we tell the officer how we part of Team Tyson, how we headed to the next fight. He's all smiles. "You drive carefully, boys. You take it easy. Best of luck to the champ." The whole time, we just hoping he don't ask Gordy to open the door and pull that blanket aside. For all we know, one look at that tiger and the cop might've fainted on the spot. We'd have to get on his radio. "Officer down. Officer down."

It was always something crazy. I mean, we dealing with the Baddest Man on the Planet. Whether it was his tigers, or his women, or his negative influences, it was always work to keep this train on track and steaming ahead.

A whole Roman legion couldn't do that job to satisfaction, but we brought in some security guys to help us out. And Anthony Pitts, that man was a godsend.

CHAPTER TWENTY-FIVE

THE GORILLAS

Mike Tyson has no patience for bullies. He suffered childhood taunts for his bulk and thick glasses, and he discovered the power of his own fists when a neighborhood tough killed one of his pet pigeons. Under Cus D'Amato, he learned how to defend himself and to anticipate the moves of his opponents, while striking back with deadly force. He still gets emotional when speaking of the confidence that gave him. "I knew I'd never be fucked with again."

Even in the animal kingdom, Mike does not tolerate such behavior.

On a private tour of a New York zoo, he saw something that disturbed him in the gorilla enclosure. A big silverback was bullying the other gorillas. The victims were large and powerful, yet their eyes betrayed a childlike fear, and this sparked something in Mike. He offered $10,000 to the attendant for a chance to get in the cage and "smash that silverback's snotbox."

The attendant declined, saving the man or the beast—maybe both—some medical issues. Undoubtedly, the man deserved a raise, to offset the ten Gs he passed up.

Mike has not always unleashed his protective instincts in the smartest ways or places. In August 1988, he risked his own boxing career outside Dapper Dan's Boutique. Located in Harlem, Dapper Dan's catered to celebrities, and Mike arrived at four in the morning to pick up a tailor-made suit. As he stepped back out to his parked Rolls-Royce, he came face-to-face with an old nemesis, Mitch Green.

Two years earlier, Mike had been guaranteed over $200,000 for his bout with Green. Managed by Carl King, Don King's adopted son, Green was guaranteed only $30,000. That rankled Green. Although he lost the fight, he believed he deserved equal pay and respect, and he spent months pestering Mike for a rematch.

Green stepped toward Mike on the sidewalk. He ranted about previous injustices and how promoter Don King had robbed him. A *Sports Illustrated* article in September 1988, reported that Mike fired back: "Don King robs me, too. That doesn't make you special," a curious admission from a man who waited eleven more years to take Mr. King to court.

According to witnesses in the early morning light, Green made the first move, and Mike countered with a hard right that snapped back Green's Jheri-curled hair and sent him to the hospital for stitches in his nose. Mike broke his hand in the process, thus delaying his upcoming fight with Frank Bruno.

Green later won $45,000 in a civil suit against Mike, his closest thing to a rematch.

This and other incidents made it clear that Iron Mike needed bodyguards—to shield him from others, to shield him from himself, and to shield others from him.

Mike's troublesome behavior is well-documented. What did you do to avoid such pitfalls?

RORY: People always ask me, why didn't you do this? Why you didn't do that? Mike took over the controls, and we was a train-wreck waiting to happen. We didn't have time to leverage things in his favor. We was barely keeping this thing on the rails.

You think we needed to protect Mike's ass? Maybe that was part of it, but I instructed our guys to protect him from himself. Our boy wander off, you let me know. He call up Craig "Boogie" or Kevin Sawyer, you distract him. He try to hook up with some girl and start grabbing and groping, you step in and get him back to camp.

Before Anthony Pitts came on-board, this shit was wearing me out. The closer it got to training time, the worse it was. Mike wanted his freedom. He would be up all night, everyone else snoring, and he was like a ghost. You wake up and he's gone.

He vanished one time right as we getting ready to go to Vegas. I called John. "Listen, I know you don't like getting your hands dirty, but you are getting paid, right? I need your help to get our fighter on the plane." John hated that, but he came to New York, and we tracked Mike down through all these traps—various girls in the 'hood.

We finally caught up with him, and I said, "C'mon, Mike, we gotta hit training."

He shook his head. "I'm not going. I don't wanna train."

John said, "You got a fight coming up."

"Motherfucker, don't tell me what to do. Matter of fact, I quit."

I said, "Man, you just don't wanna leave these streets. Well, this shit still gonna be here when you get back."

Mike climbs into his white Porsche 911. "I'm not going with you," and he takes off.

He's the worst driver ever, and it's like a cat-and-mouse game with us and our chauffeur chasing him in the limo through alleys, down one-way streets the wrong direction. He stops in the middle of the projects and jumps out. "I hate you bastards." He picks up a brick and throws it through our windshield. "Stop following me!" He looks at the local cats gathering around, then points at us. "Kill these two motherfuckers!"

We're scared now. Our driver whips the limo around and we bolt. Screw Mike. Screw camp. Few minutes later, something bumps us hard from behind. It's Mike, and now he's the one chasing us. He's ramming us with his Porsche, smashing up his damn car. The dude's gone crazy. We get stopped in traffic, and he runs up and yanks open our door. We scared he's about to clobber someone. He takes one look at our faces and then he just starts laughing. "Okay," he says. "Let's go to the airport. I'm ready to go."

We knew we needed a real security guy at that point, and Anthony Pitts was a lifesaver. He was someone John Horne knew from L.A., a long-time employee of Magic Johnson, and John brung him in to head up our team security. He was a big guy, very cool, very professional, and he gave me some much-needed rest. I mean, I had to close my eyes every once in a while, right?

Anthony took Team Tyson to the next level. He got us radios, and we all had our own handles. He was "Team 1." I was "L1" for Leader One. John was "L2." Shorty was "Team 2." Gordy was "Groove 2." Mike, he used a couple different handles. For a while he was just "Arnold," and later he was "Deebo," like that guy in the movie *Friday*.

Now when we were in camp or in town, wherever, the guys could hit me up like, "Mike is over here," or "Mike is over there."

Mike'd grab the radio. "Motherfuckers, you calling Rory and telling him what I'm doing?" He'd play tricks on these guys and try to sneak off. He had girls secretly stashed away in nearby hotels. If he got free, he'd start messing with us on the radio. "Where security at, huh?"

I would call Anthony. "Team 1, where's Arnold? He with you?"

Anthony would pause. "He is, sir, but he ain't."

Mike's a big kid at heart, and that rebellious side is definitely there. How you gonna discipline him, though? I tried to withhold things, give him clear goals and rewards, but he was the boss. I was limited. When he was younger, he didn't have the distractions. He had his own self-discipline. The longer this went, the more that slipped.

Mike used to hold off on sex before fights. That was a tradition among fighters, like you gotta recharge your testosterone. Well, he got fed up with that and told me he can have sex whenever he want. We jogging early one morning on the trails around a golf course, and it's still dark, sprinklers going off. Mike sprints ahead. Suddenly, he's just gone in the darkness. I'm like, "Where the fuck is he? Where'd he go?"

He had a girl hiding in the bushes, that's where. Back at the gym, he's real defiant about it. He tells us to put the best sparring partners in, and one after another he knocks these cats out. "See." He glares over at me. "What I tell you?" Anthony catches my eye and just shrugs.

Mike was difficult. You and me, the average Joe, we all get the Monday-morning blues, right? When Mike got like that, he tried to manipulate those around him. "Man, I'm wore out. Cut me outta these gloves. I ain't sparring today." Real calm, I'd say to the team, "You take those gloves off him, and you fired." One time he was so pissed at me, he stomps outta Johnny Tocco's gym and wandered along the Vegas Strip with his damn gloves still on. He's sulking like a kid, asking tourists to help him get loose.

All this was part of our job, being a pincushion as he's building up aggression for the next fight of his life. We had our fun times, but our team had to stay strong.

Someone like Eddie Murphy, his team would set things up ahead of time, his security paving the way at the club, the restaurants, the airports. Mike didn't want none of that. He wanted to be a regular guy. Well, we had a rule. No layovers. 'Cause if Mike on layover, he gonna wander into whatever city he in, find the lowlifes, and be gone for days. That's where Anthony played a role in holding Mike back. And if he couldn't do that, he stuck to him like glue so he couldn't disappear for good.

Team Tyson, one day we in the airport waiting on a flight, everybody spread out with luggage, grabbing food, using the bathroom. We got our radios with us. This overzealous cop, he stops Gordy for "being a black man with a radio in the airport," and that really upset Gordy. The cop hears us doing roll call. "Team 1, in." "Team 2, in." "L2, in." He figures Gordy some kinda drug dealer, so he cuffs him and holds him overnight. That was a mess— literally, with him and his Crohn's Disease.

Poor Gordy, man.

Mike bailed him out, and even though they didn't charge him with nothing, that really hurt Gordy. Here he'd cleaned up his life, and they treating him like a criminal.

Anytime we in the airport, it was like running the gauntlet. Soon as we got Mike on the ground, for a camp or a fight, I was ready to kiss the ground beneath my feet.

At times, the stories of the team have a criminal edge. Is it true that Anthony Pitts got into a fight with security personnel from another team? If so, how did that start?

RORY: It's true, alright. And it all goes back to Mike 'cause he the biggest instigator in the fuckin' world. He's just a hardcore guy from Brownsville, from a group home, from the streets. He functioned best in chaos. If camp too smooth, his mind started going, you know what I mean? He gotta stir up some shit. He just had to do it, and I could see this coming. I didn't know what it gonna be, when it gonna be, but something about to happen and you better be prepared.

The first Razor Ruddock fight, the Cayton-Jacobs contract was finally done. Me and John, we had been managing already, but this was our first official fight. Well, Mike stirred it up at the press conference. He says to Ruddock, "You're so sweet. I'm gonna make sure you kiss me good with those big lips." The media loved that, of course. They all scribbling away on their notepads. "If I don't kill you," he adds, "then it don't count."

In my mind, that fight was a defining moment in how tough Mike was. Before that, he usually had these quick knockouts, but Ruddock was the real deal, one of the hardest-hitting guys, catapulting people into the air. Well, Mike took his best punch, took it like a champ, and was like, "Hit me some more. C'mon." By the seventh round, Mike had Ruddock hurt and the ref jumped in.

Even I thought it was a premature stoppage, and Ruddock's corner, they was understandably furious.

A melee ensued. Both corners rushed into the ring, guys throwing hay-makers, poking at each other's eyes. It was a mess. Officials called us in later, showing us slow-motion videotape, trying to identify who did what. I'm shaking my head, real serious. "No, sir, the one in the black shirt, I can't tell who it is throwing that overhand right."

Of course, the whole situation put some bad blood between the two camps, and created a big thing for the second fight. We scheduled the rematch for nine months later. In the meantime, this Muslim cat who was part of Ruddock's promotion team, he just had it in for Anthony Pitts. His name was Kevin Ali. They'd squared off in the melee, and Ali took it so personal that he became like a stalker.

One day we at Don King's office, a posh, uptown place in Manhattan. No black people around. We took over the block, hanging out in the nearby stores, Versace and stuff. Me and Mike, we go up into Don's office to work on details of the rematch, and the secretary steps in. "There's a Mr. Ali here, and he wants permission to fight Anthony Pitts."

Don's like, "Get him outta here with that shit. We ain't gonna have no fight."

When we go back downstairs, Ali is outside. Mike sees this, and he's just itching to make it happen, ready to take a punch himself. He looks from Anthony to Ali. "C'mon, you wanna fair one?"

Ali says, "Yes, I wanna fair one."

"Okay, then." These two gorillas, they face off, and all of a sudden, two punches—bam, bam. Anthony hit this dude, and Ali crumbled. He didn't even get no shots in. They started at the same time, no sucker-punches, and Anthony just dropped him with these old-man punches—goosh, goosh—like George Foreman. Ali is spread out and bleeding on the pavement, and Anthony, with his adrenaline flowing, goes over and starts stomping on him. I dove in, caught him in midair. Don King's yelling. There's this whole commotion. These poor white folks, they thinking we come in and just took over their neighborhood.

As it turned out for the rematch, Team Tyson and Team Ruddock both ended up on the same flight out to Vegas. Bad news. Our team's in the back, plane take's off, and Mike starts throwing spit wads at these guys' heads. He throws one, then makes this innocent pose. I'm like, "Mike, you so obvious, man." He throws another one. About the fourth time, these guys get up and come to the back. We scrapping on the plane, water flying everywhere. I'm like, "Lord, please don't let nobody grab and open this door."

The FAA called the cops in Vegas, and when we hit the ground, it like something out of a movie. Cop cars everywhere, lined up along the tarmac. We got off the plane, everybody acting real calm. Mike's like, "Hello, officers. Is there a problem?"

The second fight went the full twelve rounds, and Mike won again.

Chalk up another victory for Team Tyson.

Getting to the fight and winning as a team, that was always our ultimate goal. Not the purse. Not the cheers. Not the glory. We doing this for Mike, for each other, for our kids. Each and every fight was our destination and reward.

CHAPTER TWENTY-SIX

THE APE

Boxing is a grueling sport. Only those with a certain mentality and determination can endure its physical and mental grind. While speed, power, and endurance are all vital components, the fighters who shine the brightest and last the longest have a quality that cannot be taught. It goes beyond talent and raw skill.

They have heart. A big fucking engine in their chest.

It keeps them punching when others would quit, standing when others would collapse, coming forward when others would run.

The Gospel of Luke, Chapter 10, Verse 27, says: "You must love the Lord your God with all your heart, all your soul, all your strength, and all your mind." It is a life prescription given two thousand years ago that still has potency today.

Heart. Soul. Strength. Mind.

Arm a fighter with these weapons, and he will be damned near unstoppable.

Despite Mike's early obstacles, or perhaps because of them, he developed into a man with the heart and soul to fight to the bitter end, the strength to overcome, and a mind to process and learn from his victories and defeats. He is in the public eye again, and it remains to be seen whether he will prove himself a champion over his own weaknesses and addictions.

To bet against him would seem unwise.

You were present at Mike's first professional loss. Do you take the blame for that?

RORY: As his manager, I always shared the blame. That was my guy. He win, I win. He loss, I loss. We one and the same.

But would he let us do what we gotta do to help him win?

That's where our problems started.

Before the Douglas fight, Mike was a monster in the gym and in the ring. He was scary good. He just went into this beast mode where nobody gonna deny him what's his. He won his first thirty-six pro fights, most of them by knockout. Even after he became champ, he had that "me against the world" mentality. We be walking along the hallways in the Hilton, and he would eat leftover food off the damn room-service trays that guests set out. We called him a Viking.

He was a beast in all the best ways, a freakin' animal when he laced up those gloves. No robe. No socks. No frills. Just down-and-dirty business.

He in the gym this one time. This huge white guy, a Canadian fighter, he thought he could deal with Mike. He looked like he know what he doing, so we let him in to spar with the champ. The bell rings, Mike takes two steps toward this guy, throws a hard right. The guy's head turns halfway around and he drops like a harpooned whale.

Days before a fight, Mike would go to a different place in his head.

This was his beast mode.

I'm telling you, it was a frightening and beautiful thing to watch. Like a switch went off somewhere inside him. He'd walk into the room, and you'd feel it. The tiger was on the loose. He chewing on towels, chewing on paper. No more joking, none of the goofing around. This was this calm before the storm, his eyes turning dark and distant, things building and swirling and beneath this eerie stillness. The warrior was ready for battle. The beast was in that zone. Mike'd be in the car talking to himself. "Kill him, kill him, kill him. I'm gonna kill that motherfucker." Before he faced off against Larry Holmes, I caught him shadowboxing in the dressing room. "I'm gonna crush him," he says. "I'm gonna fuckin' crush him." You seen that in the ring, the way he was throwing his arms halfway through Holmes' body.

Things was coming easy for Mike, maybe too easy.

I'm telling you, he just wasn't the same after everything went down with Robin. That took something outta him. The beast found other ways of feeding his hunger, and that's when he started calling up Kevin Sawyer, hooking up with these girls in L.A. Now we gotta chase him around, trying to get him on the plane to Toyko. Even in-flight, I'm worried. You better lock up the damn stewardesses, Mike Tyson on-board.

Then he gets to Japan, and he's not taking this seriously, not putting in his time at the gym. He says it in his book how he didn't want me or Don King or Anthony Pitts around, 'cause we getting in the way of him doing it with the Japanese maids.

Man, it ain't no surprise to me he lost that fight. Jay Bright, Aaron Snowell, they did their jobs in training, but Mike just wasn't the same guy.

Brick by brick, piece by piece, he was coming apart.

First Robin, then Buster Douglas, and next it was all that stuff with Desiree Washington and the rape trial. When Mike come out of prison three years later, he wasn't himself. Here, we signing these big Showtime contracts for him, we got the whole world waiting to see this beast we about to unleash—like we got Godzilla locked away or something—and the whole time, I know Mike ain't half of what he used to be.

While Mike was in prison, you tried to diversify and manage other young fighters. What happened in those situations?

RORY: I managed two or three other guys.

One of them was Oba Carr, from Detroit—"Motor City," he was called. He was a welterweight, and he got that engine, right? He worked his way up, got a title fight, and lost to Felix Trinidad in the eighth round after knocking him down in the second. That was tough. So we worked him back up and arranged a second title shot.

The fight was in Madison Square Garden, against Ike Quartey. The Garden was packed. That was a real action-packed fight, and at the end I thought we won. Instead, they raised Quartey's hand. Afterward, Oba Carr and me, we sitting in the locker room. He was so beat up, eyes swollen shut. He'd put on such a brave, gallant performance. His head was down. The lights were low. He said, "Hey, man, I'm sorry I let you down." Those words cut through me, 'cause I know this man fighting for me.

I gave him his check, and he could barely see it through his puffy eyes. Before the fight, I'd floated him a $300,000 advance. He said, "I probably owe you almost half this check now." I said, "Don't worry about it. You keep it, okay. Maybe next time."

I know business is business, but sometimes there's something bigger than business. How'm I gonna look this warrior in the eye and take his money? He just put his damn heart on the line. I couldn't do that, man.

When fighters lose, though, they gotta blame someone. That's just how it is. Lotsa guys fire their managers, their trainers, figuring they need to change things up. Who am I to say? After Oba Carr lost, he let me go. In an ESPN interview, he told the commentator, "I had bad management." The commentator asked him,

"How could it be bad management when they got you two title shots in eighteen months?"

Hey, it's the nature of business. You take the good with the bad.

Another guy I managed was Ike Ibeabuchi. Now this guy had issues. He was a big Nigerian, built like the Incredible Hulk. Size 17 shoe. He come looking for me, wanted me to manage him. "I with you," he said in his accent. "I want fight Mike Tyson." He was raw, he smelled, and his damn feet dug into the canvas like claws. The man did have talent, so I signed him after checking with the Nevada Commission that he ain't already with somebody else. I gave him a $50,000 signing bonus, and then brought Don King on as promoter. Don walking around his house, rubbing his fingers together. "Rory, you found us another champ, bling, bling, bling."

Next thing I hear, Ibeabuchi's in trouble at the Treasure Island in Vegas, refusing to pay this call girl he slept with. "I pay no one nothing," he said. "She should pay me." He brooding like a damn ape. This man's even crazier than Mike. I was gonna hand her $10,000 just to put this thing put behind us, but that wasn't what this girl was after. It was a matter of principle to her, and she wanted an apology from Ike. But Ike wasn't budging. "You're not in the bush," I told him. "You're in Vegas. What's wrong with you?"

Yeah, you see where this is headed, right?

The next day, I get another call, and he's gone and done the same thing in another Steve Wynn hotel. Shit, I had another train-wreck on my hands. The incidents with these call girls was just the start of the problems. This guy was more trouble in ten months than Mike was in ten years.

Without even telling me, Ibeabuchi went off on his own and arranged a fight. I turn on the TV, and he's in the ring beating Chris Byrd, a future title contender, a good fighter. Ike looked good, but he was signed with me. I could've sued him for doing this behind my back. So I went to see him in Arizona, figuring we can still work together if we talk this out. I walk into his living room, and he sitting there in the darkness with a damn shotgun on his lap. He got this look in his eye, like he gonna shoot me on the spot, and his mother had to get called in just to save my skin.

That was the end of managing Ibeabuchi. With the right training, he could've been a long-time champion. But I was done, man. I didn't need that shit.

Ibeabuchi found new managers, won some fights, and got the WBC heavyweight belt. They nicknamed him "The President." In the title match, he and David Tua threw over fifteen hundred punches combined. That's some serious firepower.

Eventually, "The President" ended up in prison for rape. He was like Mike Tyson on steroids, just this big, angry dude. He in his cell knocking guards out left and right. They even used video of it as instructional material for other prisons. That was in '99, I think. He's been denied parole a buncha times, and he was about to be released this year before it got hung up again. When he gets out, he says he still wants to box.

I ain't waiting for "The President" to call, I'll tell you that.

No, thank you.

You remember those Toughman Contests they used to have on TV? That's how I found my next fighter, a skinny white kid named Danny Batchelder. He looked kinda like you. He's knocking these grown men out— boom, boom. Just a country kid, hardcore guy, with rocks for fists. He used to train in a barn. I'm thinking, "I like this kid."

He came to Vegas with me, under my wing. We called him "Danny Boy." He could've been champion, and he went on a good run. Then he got caught up in all the stuff with Mike, that whole mess after biting Holyfield, and Danny cut his ties.

He called me recently. He been fighting his whole life, and now he back from retirement and fighting again. I hope it works out for him.

You know, some of these guys got that heart. They just can't quit.

Fight fans, they like to argue about the champions of the past. Who was the greatest? The hardest hitting? The best chin? I'll tell you who I think, but in the end, it's the biggest heart that counts. That's where you gonna find your real champions.

CHAPTER TWENTY-SEVEN

THE WHALE AND THE BUTTERFLY

The boxing community enjoys knocking names around, keeping alive the perennial debate about who is the greatest heavyweight of all time. Polls are released. Lists are compiled. If a favorite fighter of one's own generation is left off, heated reactions are quick to follow.

Despite being in nearly every discussion, Mike Tyson is frequently left off the list, but when it comes to the list of those who never reached their potential, he is a surefire bet.

From a boxing standpoint, when did you see Mike's skills and determination slip?

RORY: Before prison, Mike would've fought an alligator to be champion. He wasn't doing it for the money. He was doing it for a different cause. Afterward, the paycheck was his main motivation. That old discipline and drive just wasn't there.

Why you think I found a blowhard like Peter McNeeley? I knew we needed to build up Mike's confidence, and here's McNeeley, this big, boastful Irishman. I found him in a bar in Boston, talking like he can take on the world. I almost believed the man myself, the way he was selling it. I didn't know he gonna go down in the first round the way he did—not even like a harpooned whale, just a big beached whale.

You think fight fans wanted to see that? Hell, no. Neither did I.

It was a constant job working on Mike's psyche, rebuilding him. You know, at his first fight back in his early teens, he almost snuck out and rode away on the New York subway. Underneath his tough front, he fragile, and that always worried me. Closer we got to a fight, the more I'm holding my breath. I'm crossing my fingers, my toes, everything I can cross, hoping he don't leave us high and dry.

Before a fight, we had these closed gyms. No press. I wasn't protecting Mike so much as protecting his mystique, his marketability. I wanted people thinking we got the damn bone collector in there. Sometimes he would get that old focus. Sometimes he knocking out five sparring partners in one training session. When that happened, man, we used that. We milked every bit. We'd leak it to the news, then we wrapped these guys in tape and gauze and had them carried out on stretchers.

Sometimes that closed gym was just so the media didn't know our boy had up and disappeared again. "Where the hell is he?" I wish I knew. Probably out in L.A. again, on a damn mission to get the women. No price is too high, no pussy too low. We'd put a robe on one of Mike's sparring guys, throw a towel over his head, tell him to run from the gym past the reporters and hop into the limo with its tinted windows. We buying time till we can tag Mike's ass and get him back where he belong.

Before the second Frank Bruno fight, I seen Bruno in the jewelry store. I'm standing behind this sucker, and he has muscles coming outta his shoulders, his neck, his ears, his hair. He's standing six-foot-seven. He's even bigger than I remember. I'm like, "Holy shit, this guy is huge."

My nerves is bad. I know Mike isn't training as hard as he should, but his problem is, sometimes he just crazy enough not to worry about nobody in the ring. I go back to camp, splash some water on my forehead. Mike in there watching TV, and I come in like I been jogging. "Whew," I said. "I just seen Frank Bruno. I hate that fucker."

"Where you seen him?" Mike asks.

I drop beside him on the couch and take this big breath. "He out running. Man, I hate him."

Next thing I know, Mike calls out, "Anthony, go get my sneakers. I'm going for a run." And later he knocked Bruno out.

See, that was the psychological game I had to play with him. That was Dr. Rory at work. If I just told him to get out there and run, he ain't gonna do it. He ain't gonna put his heart into it. These were the types of things we had to do to keep him on task.

When he wasn't prepared, you can't blame all that on me or on John. We couldn't get no cooperation. Mike has zero patience. He's spontaneous. Hell, for a two-minute press conference, I'd have to start working on his mindset five days in advance. I'd explain everything to him. "Friday night you gotta be here . . . boom, boom, boom." Thursday night, where's Mike? I hear he's flown outta town again. "Man, Ro," he says to me over the phone. "I just forgot."

My blood pressure was through the roof. I couldn't take one relaxed breath till my fighter in the ring and touching gloves with his opponent. That's when I know we done our job. That's when I finally heave a sigh of relief.

Who would you list as history's greatest heavyweight boxers? Where does Mike fit on that list?

RORY: Man, what the public seen of Mike at his best was only a glimpse of how good he could've been. I seen spurts and spots of genius, like when he come into the gym and bite down for two or three days straight. I witnessed things that it's hard to fathom somebody else could do better. Mike believed the more relaxed a fighter was in the ring, the more deadly and proficient he gonna be. He'd push his knuckles up into his gloves, aiming to blast his fist through the back of his opponent's head. Nobody had the kinda power he had. He was so fast, man. So accurate. He shifty and unpredictable, throwing combos from different angles. He was a true student of the sport. Thank Cus and Jim Jacobs for that, showing him the old films, pointing out stuff about boxers of the past.

When you look at the best fighters, they all unique but got that same never-say-die component. Mike admired the gutsy fighters like Duran and Chavez. He loved the way Marciano broke people's wills. He emulated that. He would stare guys down, and when they glanced away for even a split second, he knew he broke them.

Go way back, and man, I gotta show respect to bare-knuckled fighters like John L. Sullivan, "The Boston Strong Boy." The man was a straight-up racist, right? He said, "Any fighter who'd get into the same ring with a nigger loses my respect." But he was tough, man. Then along comes Jack Johnson. He's black, knocking out cats left and right, dominating the world for almost ten years. He didn't care what nobody thought. He dated white girls, and that got under a lotta people's skin. Oh, they hated him. Doing what he did, when he did, how he did, he was one of the greatest of all time.

After that, Jack Dempsey, Gene Tunney, Rocky Marciano, Sonny Liston, they just some old-school bad-asses. Joe Louis, "The Brown Bomber," he was quiet and polite, but that boy could hit you like a ton of bricks. Joe Frazier, George Foreman, they were some true champions. Larry Holmes, he had forty-eight straight victories, but he just never excited the crowds. He deserves credit, though, for what he did.

At the front of boxing's Mt. Rushmore, you gotta put Muhammad Ali. Ain't no question. He was fast, strong, intelligent, quick on his feet, and the man had one helluva chin. He changed the sport. He used fame and money as a platform like no one before him. And man, he knew how to put on a show. "Float like a butterfly, sting like a bee . . ."

You know, there's been this running debate. If Ali and Tyson met in their primes, who would win? Floyd Patterson thought Mike would get beat. Bill Cayton said Ali would win by decision. Teddy Atlas, he believed Ali would win 'cause he a stronger, more stable person at his core. Even Kevin Rooney gave the edge to Ali.

Listen, I can't argue that. In no way am I gonna diminish Ali and the things he accomplished. He deserves every honor and accolade. He was a true example to the young fighters who came up after him, and Shorty'll tell you that "Ali had a love for Mike that was beautiful and beyond."

Let me say this. I think Mike was absolutely amazing. For a man of his stature, his size, he was so explosive, so talented. I was privileged to see some of this stuff. I don't blame fans for being frustrated that he never reached his full potential, and they aren't half as frustrated as me. I wanted to be a part of that. Instead, we was chasing him around these bars and hotels. We couldn't keep the man tied down.

You grow up watching athletes like Michael Jordan or LeBron James, you know they something special. Jordan had that work ethic and incredible will to win. You couldn't question that. LeBron, he's professional, loyal, and disciplined. And with Mike, I knew ever since he beat Ferguson back in the '80s, I knew he had the ability to be extra special. He showed it a few times, but we won't ever know for sure 'cause he couldn't sustain that focus. We just won't ever know.

You ask me, though, Mike Tyson would've been the greatest of all time.

I'm not just saying that as his friend, but as a boxing fan. His potential was astronomical. Like Tupac with music, he had all the talent in the world, and then—boom!—it was just gone.

CHAPTER TWENTY-EIGHT

THE MOSQUITO

Tupac Shakur was named among the 100 Greatest Artists of All Time by *Rolling Stone*, and the young rapper has sold upwards of 80,000,000 records worldwide. He had multiple number-one albums, including the first to ever hit that mark while its artist was in prison, and 50 Cent said, "Every rapper who grew up in the '90s owes something to Tupac."

Performing as 2Pac and Makaveli, Tupac influenced not only other young black men, but males and females across racial lines. His music was raw, honest, catchy, and conflicted. His tunes are still used by advertisers, movie producers, and fighters walking into the ring. Every day, his name and image are duplicated by graffiti artists around the globe.

On September 7, 1996, Mike Tyson walked into the MGM Grand arena with a 2Pac track penned just for him. Tupac cheered Mike on as he knocked out Bruce Seldon in the first round.

In the hotel lobby after the fight, security cameras caught Tupac getting into a confrontation and beating an alleged member of the Crips. The rapper hopped into a vehicle with Suge Knight, CEO of Death Row Records, and moved off into snarled post-fight traffic. The desert night was warm. Not a care in the world. They flirted with girls in nearby cars, inviting them to a party.

At approximately 11:15 p.m., a Cadillac sedan pulled alongside, its windows came down, and weapons opened fire. Though the crime has never been solved, most believe it was a retaliatory attack by the Southside Crips.

Tupac was struck multiple times, and died six days later at twenty-five-years of age.

Tupac and Mike were two game-changers of their generation. They had met years earlier at the Palladium in Hollywood and formed a quick bond. "He was only 125 lbs., but he was just fearless," Mike said. "I've never met no one like that before." Both men came from broken homes. Both had parents with criminal backgrounds. Both had a leaning toward literature and violence. And both spent time in state prisons on sexually-related charges.

In fact, Mike was still behind bars when he warned Tupac in 1994 that he needed to calm down. "I look up to him something horrible," Tupac revealed on *The Arsenio Hall Show*. "I was like, whoa, it's time to calm down."

Tupac and Mike were complex individuals. They desired kindness and love, while struggling with a brooding unrest. In their efforts to succeed against all odds, each of them relied on a sense of humor, an ability to mix with any crowd, and a bad-boy magnetism that attracted the ladies. They bridged the black-and-white divide without ever denying their roots. They made tens of millions of dollars while disrupting the calm yet murky waters of white America.

Tupac was the mosquito, buzzing around your ear and refusing to leave.

Tyson was the tiger, pacing and licking his chops.

Both wanted to bleed society of its sins, to peel back the layers and reveal its awful and beautiful truths. An ESPN documentary, *One Night in Vegas: Mike Tyson and Tupac Shakur,* said: "Tupac is Tyson with a microphone. Tyson is Tupac in a boxing ring."

When Tupac died, it shocked the nation. Mike grieved the loss of a personal friend.

A year later, Mike ended his own career in nearly as dramatic a fashion, and the void of these two game-changers festered like double gunshot wounds to society's midsection.

Robin Givens wrote in her book that "Michael was part of the advent of hip-hop culture . . . He helped usher it in . . . It was a culture that considered him king." Do you agree with that?

RORY: You know, the night Tupac died, Mike was supposed to meet him afterward at the club. They were tight, and he was shook up about what happened.

There was no talk back then about Jay-Z, about Nas. Tupac and Biggie was the only things that counted, West Coast and East Coast, the two biggest icons and getting bigger by the minute. It's unfortunate that propaganda made them go at each other like that. Together, they could have made magic. Mike could've been the mediator, 'cause he had that thing, he had that respect. He wasn't scared of nobody.

Tupac was climbing fast at that time, making an enormous impact on the way kids dressed, the way they talked, the way rappers thought. His lyrics were so powerful, always about life, the current situation, police brutality and all this stuff.

Mike was doing the same through boxing, this young guy, free-spirited, speaking his mind. He quoted Machiavelli, Che Guevara, Arthur Ashe. He was a different kinda warrior that kids related to. He made hisself a part of the people. He just walked the streets with the common man.

Mike wasn't living like a common man, though. He had this house out in Farmington, Connecticut, a place 50 Cent later bought. I found it for him through one of my mom's real-estate friends, for sale by this Ukrainian guy who was trying to get back to his own country. The place was ridiculous, over 50,000 square feet, sitting on seventeen acres. Nineteen rooms, thirty-seven bathrooms, a gun-range, racquetball court, elevators, nightclub, heated driveway. I talked him down to $2,800,000.

I put up $800,000 to hold this for Mike. That was my gift to him, and I thought it was a place where he could get away, have fun, stay outta trouble.

Mike's birthday was coming up, and we put on a party that no one who was there will ever forget. My friend, Wisdom, helped arrange transportation for everyone using seven Ferrari flatbeds. There was over two thousand people, with *E!* helicopters circling and taking pictures. We had every detail covered. No drama, no confusion, no troubles. The rock-star traveling circus was in town, and nobody wanted to miss it.

We had Oprah there, Tom Cruise there, Ray Allen there. We had every A-list celebrity, B-list celebrity, C-list celebrity, every rapper and singer. A band was playing outside and a disco going inside. Models were there. Naomi Campbell was trying her best all night to get to Mike. Mike's probation officer was there, and drunk as a damn skunk. I heard a black guy in the food-line with Donald Trump, and he's like, "Damn, I'm in front of Mr. Trump in this line."

After we bought the house, Mike didn't really stay there much—and later, Monica got it in the divorce settlement, before selling it to 50 Cent. Man, nothing I did could settle Mike down. He was more comfortable in the 'hood than in that palace. He just trying so hard to be a regular guy that he couldn't just be a regular guy.

That was the kinda attitude that made Tupac and Mike bigger than life. It was a special era. The two of them, yeah, they were the kings.

Controversy? They thrived on that shit. Listen, these cats were on the cutting-edge of black economic empowerment. It was like people been waiting for them.

During those years that Mike was in prison, I'm telling you, boxing was dead. There was no excitement, nothing really going on. None of the barbershops were buzzing, no conversations around the water cooler. Then he got out, and it like everything come back to life, the water flowing through the desert again.

When Tupac died, it was a sad time, incredibly sad, but he was the martyr for the cause. These young rappers today still carry on his name. Their consciousness about society, the way words flow off their tongues, they were all affected by Tupac. They respected how even during his time in prison, he up on the tables preaching.

If Mike hadn't got caught up in the women and all this extracurricular stuff, I think, just like Tupac, he would've had a lot to offer, to young people especially.

Mike loved hip-hop music, and when he listened to Tupac's stuff in the gym and in that car, that got him fired up. He was a fan. In return, the hip-hop community loved Mike. They liked his rawness, his realness. They liked that he come from poverty. He felt comfortable with these people. He be laying up in the projects, middle of a drug war, and he's snoring away. Someone fires off an AK-47, and he just thinks that shit funny.

He was a street ambassador. His talent was something different, 'cause he had that thing where these guys respected him. The Crips and the Bloods could be about to shoot each other, and he'd walk up in the middle of that, no fear of dying whatsoever. "Hello, my brothers." Bullets are flying past. "Let's not fight, let's just chill out." He wasn't scared. I'd sit back thinking this shit gonna get him killed.

Instead, these hardcore gang members, they're like, "Yeah, man, let's chill out."

One day he saved John Horne's ass, right? We was in L.A., going to the club—me, Mike, John, Anthony Pitts, and another security guy named James Anderson. We stopped on our way, and Mike got up on top of this row of mailboxes, sitting there swinging his legs, chillin', talking to these girls going by. Then some guys walked past, they well-dressed, and they recognized Mike. "Yo, Mike, wassup?" They all clasped hands.

"Yo," said Mike, "wassup, my brothers?" They said something about being Crips. Mike's like, "That's cool, man, that's cool."

John jumps in with his squeaky-ass, annoying voice. "Man, all that stuff is bullshit. I wear red, and don't nobody mess with me."

It went from smiles to stone-cold killers.

These motherfuckers pulled their shit out and they ready to blow John away. John lived in L.A., so he should know better, but now's he put us in a serious situation. These guns are real, these guys about to bury a body, and my heart is racing. It all happens so fast that Anthony didn't even have time to reach for his weapon.

Mike throws himself down from the mailboxes. He's like, "Yo, man, fuck that shit. Kill me!" He thumps his chest. "Kill me now, right here. Kill me!"

These Crips just started laughing, they're cracking up, and that diffused the whole thing. One of them points at Mike as they're leaving. "Yo, Mike, you better tell your man right there, 'Don't play like that.'"

Mike just had that way, you know. Listen, it may be misplaced, but the black community has this code of honor, this sense we gotta help each other out. It's not just about being "a self-made man." We a team. It's that same sense of community that drew all these unsavory characters to Mike's fights. I'd look around the arena, the ringside seats, and there's all these pimps, whores, and drug lords. It like a convention, a damn family reunion—East Coast, West Coast, everyone in the same spot. And nobody could get the buzz started like Don King, crowding people into town a week before a fight. Hotel owners loved him. He filling their houses, right?

Hell, the most-wanted criminals were arrested at some of these events. The FBI just waiting for some scumbag's head to pop up, like a kid hunting gophers.

And where's Don King in all this? He up in the ring before the fight, big smile, waving his little flags. "Only in America, only in America."

There was a big-time gangster from Miami, he flew out for one of the fights. We making our way through the crowded hotel, hardly room to move, and this guy comes outta nowhere. He got a top hat on, glasses with diamonds along the edges, a gold neck chain that's like fifty pounds, and a ring that had these two boxers on it and covered all four fingers of his hand. He looked like something out of a freakin' movie.

Mike says, "What's your name?" One of the guy's rings could whirl, and he spins it. "World-famous Convertible Burt, that's me." He spins that ring again—whirrrr. And of course, Mike is hooked. We get out to our car, and Mike invites this guy to get in with us. We riding. The guy's spinning his ring. He saying, "I'm famous as you, Mike. I don't need your money." He pulls a roll from his pocket to prove it, and he has like $70,000.

Next thing you know, Convertible Burt was a fixture. He put together a party at this hotel in Florida, and we went down. I'm watching after Mike, playing babysitter. Anthony's there too. Then we headed back to New York, and by the time we get home, it was all in the news that some people came and shot things up in the hotel, in the very room we was in. They were coming after Convertible, but that could've been us.

I'm telling you, God takes care of fools and babies.

As for Convertible Burt, he ended up in prison, thirty years or something like that.

In some ways, you seem to glorify the shadier aspects of Mike's relationships. Do you think that enabled his self-destructive behavior?

RORY: Some of this stuff that happened, it's just plain entertaining. You know, who doesn't like a good story, all the juicy details? You drive past a car-wreck and you wanna turn and look, right? We're drawn to it somehow.

Like I said, though, we were handling a rich, grown man, stubborn and spontaneous. After Mike got outta prison, his first fight was against McNeeley, and I rushed him away from all the liquor at the after-party, back over to his place where we could control what went down. We set it all up, a good time had by all. Well, that barely made a splash in the news, right? 'Cause Mike wasn't screwing up.

Our team did what we could—security guys, best friends, trainers, every which way to stay in his ear. He talks in his book about how me and John were "always trying to get me to stay away from the gangster rap crowd, but I loved those rappers." It wasn't the individual rappers as much as the crowd. We could just see it, the cesspool sucking Mike back in. Thing is, once my boy made up his mind what he wanna do, if you lay yourself down, he gonna run you right over.

I believe if Tupac was still alive, the two of them would still be good friends. They was just two misunderstood guys, right? They might've helped each other.

Mike took his death hard, and he scared me when he started playing with guns.

CHAPTER TWENTY-NINE

THE POLAR BEAR

When asked why they did not corral their fighter, Rory Holloway explains that Mike was an adult, a man who did as he pleased. True, but he was also a world-class athlete. Wouldn't it be wise to call upon that discipline?

A fighter goes through various stages during his apprenticeship in the "sweet science." He acquires specific tools for his trade. He puts on a groin protector, gets his hands wrapped before slipping on padded gloves, and bites down on his individualized mouth-guard. He learns how to move in the ring and shift his weight, how to dodge and dance away from danger, how to cut off angles and corral his foe. If he wants to succeed, he avoids common sparring problems and masters defensive skills.

He does not lunge his punches. He finishes them.

He keeps his guard up, his chin down, and his eyes on his opponent.

He settles himself down when he gets angry, staying mobile and unpredictable.

He conserves energy, delivering crisp, clean punches.

Seems reasonable that these same attributes should apply to a fighter's management team as they face the public and the media. Shouldn't they be anticipating blows to their fighter and dodging them? Keeping their guard up and conserving energy?

As time dragged on, Mike's team seemed to slow down and lose some of their step. The fatigue was catching up, and it was easy to blame them any time Mike performed sluggishly. In turn, Mike's lackadaisical training might have been dulling his team's performance. So who was responsible?

As Rory and his team struggled for answers, their fighter showed signs of mental instability. The years in the ring and the spotlight were taking their toll.

Do you believe certain athletes, boxers in particular, deal with mental issues because of the physical trauma they put their bodies through?

RORY: That's been documented more and more, right? I think a lotta NBA players got issues, bipolar, whatever. Beasley from Miami, he's one example, but they dealing with it. The NBA, MLB, NHL, NFL, they don't always know what product they getting, and sometimes they end up with damaged goods. At least they got good support systems in place to help these athletes find the best help they can get, to protect both the players and the public. These teams have PR people who deal with things internally and try to spin it for the media.

Boxing don't have a good support system. Each boxer is like his own private company, dealing with this stuff on his own. He can hire and fire who he wants, but he don't always understand having someone around him for his best interest. Especially, you know, if he's a bit mentally off.

It's rough for these young guys. They don't wanna look weak. Meanwhile, they dealing with mental pressures, physical aches and pains, and emotional stuff fans might not ever know about. They cry. Underneath, they just regular people.

Mike, he lost so many people close to him. He was always grieving someone, always looking for a fix to get him through, whether it was women, or drinking, or guns.

At Mike's house outside Cleveland, the local sheriff's department helped guard his compound. They on patrol twenty-four hours, monitoring who goes in and out, and there was a nice security lady named Maria in the booth at the front gate. Mike sweet-talks Maria into letting him shoot her gun, and all of a sudden he got a new fetish.

My boy always goes to extremes. Now he starts buying all these weapons, stacking up like he preparing for a war. He out there all through the night—pow, pow, pow!

We tense, man. We tense. This motherfucker got a new toy.

He's out on his estate one day, in the woods with my brother Todd, and all I hear is pow, pow, pow. "Let's try this one, Todd." My brother grabs the gun—bap, bap, bap, bap, bap! "Here, try this one, Todd." They laughing, right? And I'm just shaking my head.

I go outside, start cussing my brother out. "You can't have this guy shooting guns. This shit ain't funny. Mike shouldn't even have his hands on this stuff."

That makes Mike mad. He's like, "Man, Ro, you such a fuckin' killjoy. You get on my nerves. These my guns, this my property, and I can do what I want." I'm trying to explain to him that if one of these bullets misses a tree and goes onto the next property, someone's gonna get hurt.

"Fuck you," he says, "I know what I'm doing. Look, watch this shit.'

Powww! Powww!

He's just crazy. I go back in the house and call Don King.

While I wait, I'm watching through the window with John. I'm paranoid, but John's so paranoid he needs psychiatric help. Mike's still out there rushing around, firing off rounds. Anybody comes around, he's gonna kill them. Todd's just as bad, they encouraging each other, two shadows bouncing around. "Here, Todd, tie this to a tree." Mike hands my brother this big white teddy bear, like one of them Coca-Cola polar bears or something.

They got this thing strapped up, practically glowing in the sunlight. "Do it, Mike. See if you can hit it now." They so amped up, they can barely hit the thing.

I'm like, "Get the morgue ready. Somebody gonna die." John's shaking his head. "I can't live like this, man. I can't keep living like this."

Brother Early was a cook for the Kings, a tall, distinguished man. He'd help out at camp, feeding our team. He was the James Brown of soul food—grits, fried chicken, ribs. He pulls up the driveway in a brand-new cargo van that Mrs. King just bought. He delivering food to the house, probably a distraction sent by Don. Things is quiet for a few minutes. Me and John can breathe again. Supplies are coming in from the garage.

Then Mike and Todd reappear. Mike's got a .357 Magnum, and he wants to see if a bullet will go through the van. He starts blowing the van away. Boom! Boom! He runs around to the other side. "Yo, look at this shit, Todd. It went right through."

Don King arrives, and he's scared 'cause the champ got guns. Don's shaking his head. "Who shot up the van? This my wife's new vehicle."

Mike says, "It was Isadore, he shot the fuckin' van."

Isadore was a driver for both the Kings and us, a cool, reliable cat. He says, "Mr. King, I didn't shoot the van."

Mike steps closer. "Isadore, you shot the van, right? It was you."

Isadore nods real slow. "Yes. Yes, I shot the van."

Another time, we outside, and Mike was showing me his German Luger. The thing wouldn't fire, and he turns it around, looking to see if there's an obstruction. I grabbed the gun away. "Man, what's wrong with you? You don't look down the barrel of a gun."

He's like, "I ain't stupid, Ro. I know what I'm doing."

I flipped off the safety and emptied the clip into the ground. He could've killed himself, but you think he cared?

Considering the obvious danger and liability, did Team Tyson take any preventative measures?

RORY: Absolutely. We reached the point where it was time for an intervention. We had to do something to shake Mike outta this 'cause he in love with these guns.

So me, John, and Don King come up with this plan. We talked to the Sheriff's Department, figuring they got a role in this, too. Don was a donor of theirs, tied in with them, and he pulled some strings in this little town. We know we can't do this alone. He says, "Listen, here's what we gonna do. I'm gonna roll up on Mike's place along with all the cop cars, and we'll scare the shit outta him. They'll take the guns and act like they raiding the house."

The day comes. I'm in the house with Mike, checking my watch. Mike has this elaborate system, all these cameras, where he can sit and see what's happening at the front gate. He's looking at these cop cars coming up the driveway, and he gets himself a gun in each hand. He leans back in his chair like something outta *Scarface*.

I'm in back of him, thinking, "Yeah, they coming." Mike's not budging, though. I said, "Mike, I think they coming for you. We gotta put the guns up."

He says, "I'm not going nowhere. I'm ready for 'em."

"What you mean, you ready for them?"

His fingers are flexing around the gun butts. "I'm not stupid. I'm not scared. Let 'em come, Ro. This is my house."

"C'mon, man, just put the fuckin' guns up."

He says to me in this real eerie voice, "Let 'em come. We'll let it happen. We just gonna go."

What the fuck? All of sudden, what we thought was gonna be an intervention just turned into a possible hostage negotiation.

I wanted to call Don on the radio. "Abort. Abort."

By now they at the front door. Mike jumps up and goes to meet them. He sees the cop, looks at me and Don, then points his finger. "What's all this? You guys fuckin' snitched on me?"

Don's like, "No, champ. No."

Mike says, "You motherfuckers ain't gonna arrest me."

He storms down the steps to his white Lamborghini truck, first one ever made. He revs the engine and skids off down the driveway. He clips a cop car, and just keeps going. The cops are scratching their heads, thinking, "This is some crazy shit."

When Mike was fun, he was fun, the biggest prankster of us all. We would laugh, we'd joke. Wisdom, he talks about how Mike was a gracious host, very generous, courteous, and accommodating. He wanted you to be fed and comfortable. He never acted like he better than you or above you.

But he had this split personality, and that was the side that scared me.

Guns've never been my thing. They just trigger stuff in me, stuff from my past. Don't get me wrong, 'cause I had it better than lotsa kids growing up. I ain't saying I come from some rough neighborhood—that's not how it was for me up in Albany—but I seen things no kid should have to see.

I'm talking about things that happened under our own damn roof.

CHAPTER THIRTY

THE ROOSTER AND THE HEN

The Holloway family lived under two different roofs during their tenure in Albany, New York. Rory spent his earlier years on Tunis Street, known as "Tuna Plaza" to him and his buddies. Later, he and his family resided over their convenience store at the corner of Clinton Avenue and Swan Street. Though the building now houses a quiet attorney's office, the store was once a hub of neighborhood activity.

To this day, locals speak nostalgically of the store's fish fries, and of the successful Pop Warner teams coached by Willy Holloway. Bev Holloway is just as revered, not only for her daily dedication to the store's operation but for her selfless assistance to many troubled kids.

If Bev came upon a sexually-abused young girl, she was there with listening ears and open arms. If she learned of child beaten and neglected by a drug-addict parent, she was ready and waiting with a plate of food and a heartwarming smile.

Remarkably, Mrs. Holloway raised not only her four biological boys—Cameron, Rory, Todd, and Chris—but six other children whom she legally adopted. One of her adoptees, Tyra, was born in prison before coming to the Holloway home. Another, Darlene Chapman, was a nine-year-old victim of molestation when Bev took her in. Darlene went on to become a Philadelphia top cop and an educator in the D.A.R.E (Drug Abuse Resistance Education) program.

While Bev played the part of mother hen and gathered her chicks under her wings, she was also dealing with a husband who could be overbearing, if not downright volatile. His most abrasive behavior was aimed at her and her two oldest boys, the reasons for which she kept to herself—and which Rory discovered years later on his own.

Bev Holloway was living day-to-day.

Work. Cook. Smile. Try not to set Willy off. She had an entire brood to watch over, and her own well-being was the least of her concerns.

In the midst of a crowded household, were you aware of any confrontations between your mother and father? What were the family dynamics?

RORY: We had a lotta good times in our home. It was always active, man. Grand Central Station.

I don't know how my mother did it. She couldn't even afford to take care of the kids she had, but she found a way to take care of somebody else's kids too. She went through the process. She went through the courts. She treated us all the same, loved us all the same, and you'd never know from the outside looking in who was adopted. You get brought up in that situation, and it teaches you humility, right?

Me and Cameron was pretty close. He was a typical big brother. After high school, he got himself a brand-new car, did his thing, and left to live with my mom's sister in Connecticut. I didn't blame him. He probably faced the worst of it from my father, and he had to get out. The way Cameron puts it, "We was living in a house of horrors." He still deals with that, you know. He can still tell you how he got whipped with that extension cord. Still tell you about the night we saw my dad push a gun in Mom's face. These days, Cam keeps mostly to himself, works out a lot, and eats healthy. I love my brother. He's a good guy.

Chris, he's like four or five years younger than me. He was pretty athletic, a good ballplayer, but he had it rough always trying to compete with me and Todd's legend, so to speak. All us brothers were very competitive. Chris played quarterback, but everybody talking about Rory. Chris played basketball, but he always hearing about me and Todd. He created this thing in his mind where he'd jump up off the couch, try to tell you he the best. I'll say this, he is a very detailed guy, and he made a helluva coach. He's so good, so sharp, the way he teaching the fundamentals. He has that patience. Basketball, baseball, whatever, he just helps kids excel. And he's an excellent father.

Our adopted brothers and sisters, some of them were too young for me to know, but Darlene was a little older. She was tough. She stuck up for her brothers. What she's doing today, after what she been through, I have so much respect for her, man.

Outta everyone in our family, Todd was the real bright spot, the one you couldn't ignore. Ask around Albany, and people still know the name Todd Holloway.

He was this fixture, this local hero.

Todd was a year younger than me, but he was like the sun our family circled around. He was just full of energy, full of life. What you see is what you get. And that really bonded him to Mike. He was Mike's chaos pill. They were two peas in a pod, whether out in the clubs or shooting guns.

Todd was the only one of us boys who could really fight. As a kid, I never got in fights, but he was in one every other day. If my mom was a hen, man, Todd was like a rooster. He didn't never back down. It's funny. I was always losing another best friend 'cause Todd would fight them. I'd say something to my mother, and she'd yell at him that he shouldn't be doing that shit. That's the crazy thing, right? She wouldn't stand up for herself to my father, but when it came to her kids, she didn't let us put up with crap from nobody. This guy named Baron was trying to bully me, and when Mom heard about it, she lead the pack straight to his door. She knocked. Baron answered. And she's like, "You been talking about my boys? Rory, you tell him. You gonna deal with this now."

Todd never needed backup. Man, he was a force all on his own.

My father put him and Chris through Christian Brothers Academy, a prestigious private high school in town. It was all-boys, real expensive. When he first started there, he just about the only black kid. He wearing a military uniform, very disciplined. Out on the basketball court, he put that school on his shoulders. He gave it swagger and heart. It was a buncha white guys, and he got them talking trash and playing with confidence. They got flair, they got flava. They went from nobody on the sports scene to somebody. He was my father's pride and joy. "Todd, the best. Todd, Todd, Todd . . ."

You gotta remember, Albany the state capital, right? You got doctors, lawyers, judges, senators, a lot of them who come from CBA and even played with Todd.

Man, they all remember Todd Holloway.

He was more popular than I ever was, I'll tell you that. He graduated and went to Texas A&M. He set school records that still stand to this day—most minutes played, most conference steals, high up the list with points and assists. "Todd was one of the greatest competitors I ever coached," Coach Metcalf told ESPN. "Everybody on the team liked him . . . He probably won more games for us in the last ten seconds than anyone else on the team."

There were hints of trouble, though. One day I'm with Todd, and he goes into a public restroom. He's like, "I gotta pick my stash up." I said, "What're you talking about?" He goes over to take a leak, and this freakin' guy taking a leak next to him drops an envelope and walks out. My brother comes out with the envelope, and it's stuffed with a stack of hundreds. "What's this shit?" I said. "You gotta give that back." He laughed. "You crazy, man, this my payoff."

I'm not condoning that. But listen, if you aren't gonna pay these college athletes, at least set up some sorta lifetime insurance for them. A lotta them don't make it to the pros. If these kids end their career with knee problems, back problems, concussions, they in trouble. They don't got no recourse, and here these schools been making tens of millions of dollars off them. Coaches at the top schools, they making like $8,000,000 a year, and the NCAA's making a fortune off your jersey. But you sell your own jersey, you in trouble. It ain't right.

Todd was so talented. He even worked out for some NBA teams, but his heart just wasn't in it. He wasn't caught up in the glitz. Hell, he only wore two different shirts. He just a free-spirited guy.

I loved my brother more than life itself. When he started messing around with drugs, I was getting these phone calls. I'd be gone with the team, but I'd try to talk with him. I kept promising myself, "After the next camp, after the next fight, I'm gonna go up there and spend time with my brother and take him outta that. After the next one."

The next one never came, and then I get the call he's dead. Todd is dead. They said it was a heart attack, brought on by complications with his asthma.

Man, I carry all kindsa regret for that, for not being there.

You never realized how many people adored Todd till he left this earth and went to a better place. His funeral in Albany, you had the governor there, the mayor, a military formation, white horses, hundreds of people following the carriage through the streets. Like the vice-president just died or something.

That was October 2004, and not a day goes by I don't think about Todd.

What was the secret you learned about your father that gave you an entirely different perspective? How did you respond to that discovery?

RORY: You know, as a kid, I seen my father jump on my mother. I seen the bodies fly. I seen the violence. I know what she went through, how it tore her down. She never really talked about it, even to this day, but I could see how that damaged her, and I wanted so badly to rescue her outta that.

Whatcha gonna do? You're just a kid, and these your parents.

My father was always on me and Cameron. He didn't never encourage me. I'd go to Coach Pierce or Jerry Spicer, and these men would listen, they'd tell me they believed in me and to keep my head up. Those two guys meant so much to me, man. I just couldn't see why my father do us like that. He wanted to toughen us up, I guess. He taught us to be strong, to work hard. He put that roof over our heads. I give him credit for that. But why you gotta tear me down?

Then, when I was maybe eighteen, nineteen, I found out something that put it all into a new light. This one weekend, I gone to visit relatives in Hartford, Connecticut. Uncle Fool, he was there, and he drunk all the time, always spouting some craziness. People just laughed at him, nobody taking this shit seriously. Well, I found him in this half-empty bar, he up on a stool. He looked over at me. "Hey, Tommy."

"I'm Rory," I told him. "Bev's son."

"Oh." He's rubbing his eyes. "You look just like your daddy Tommy."

Tommy? What the hell?

Back in Albany, I sat down on the bed with my mother and asked her about it. She admitted that my biological father was a guy named Tommy Johnson. She spoke highly of him, said he was never abusive to her, but he got himself in trouble with drugs and got locked away. She needed something better for me and Cameron. We was just little kids at the time. She doing it for our good.

Now I wanted to meet this cat, see him with my own eyes, and decide if this for real. Mom said he was remarried, a family in Hartford, but she got his number for me. We set up a meeting on Blue Hills Avenue, and soon as I seen him, I knew Tommy was my father. Like looking in a mirror, right? No special bond or nothing, but I knew. We didn't talk longer than ten minutes. We met up a coupla more times, and I met some of my half-brothers and sisters. Tommy didn't make no effort, though. It was on me.

All this helped me understand things at home, why Willy treated Cameron and me the way he did. Todd and Chris was his real sons, and he could've just put us outta his house. Least he still watched over us, right? He never threw that in my face.

I saw Tommy every once in a while, but we never got close. One time, me and Mike pull up in this cheap white limo, and Tommy gets in. "I hear you doing good," he says. "You think you could give me a hand, you know, like maybe $15,000?" I was so offended, I started cussing. He snaps at me, "Hold on now, I'm still your father." Mike says, "Motherfucker, you aren't his father. Get the fuck outta here. I'll kick your ass." Tommy knew better than to mess with the world champ.

A few years back, Tommy got ill and he passed. Me and my half-brother, Polka, we got to be friends, and he wanted me at the funeral. I couldn't do it, though. I saw no purpose. Was I supposed to cry some crocodile tears? I barely even knew the man.

You know, when I started making good money, I finally had my chance to do something I been wanting to do a long time. Me and Sheila, we packed up my mom's stuff in Albany, and we moved her in with us. We lived in Guilderland then, just on the outskirts. When we went to Vegas, she came too. Just getting her outta that situation, giving her back her life, that was one of my proudest moments. That felt so good.

Of course, my father was bitter at me for rescuing her the way I did. I don't regret that, but I regret that he don't know my kids. He's never met my daughter. They could sell him cookies outside the supermarket, and he wouldn't even realize it.

He's the one gotta live with that. It ain't a burden I want on me, and I just gotta move on. You can't always control what other people gonna think and feel.

My mom lived with us until she was well. All the people she grew up with, her childhood friends, they in Hartford, and that's where she is now. That's really home. She's still so loving, so wise. Just a beautiful, beautiful woman.

Listen, all the money, the stuff, it can up and disappear, but helping the ones you love, that's a good feeling. You think you can steal to get that feeling?

No, you gotta earn it.

PART FOUR

How Did Mike's Millions Disappear?

"Don't wear yourself out trying to get rich . . .
In the blink of an eye wealth disappears,
for it will sprout wings and
fly away like an eagle."

Proverbs 23:4-5

CHAPTER THIRTY-ONE

THE JAILBIRD

Earning money was never a concern of Mike's. As a kid, he took what he could find, legally or illegally.

As a teenager, while he lived under the care of Cus and Camille, all of his needs were provided for. As a young man, he earned tens of millions fighting under his original contract. Now, in his late twenties, he marked his time as a prisoner of the state, receiving physical nourishment (cafeteria food), mental stimulation (classic literature), and sexual release (female prison employees and outside visitors).

"Only in America," as Don King would say, "only in America."

However, in August 1994, Mike faced a dilemma. He had seven months until his release back into society, and he had only $20,000,000 left to his name. What about taxes? What about the millions in loans to repay to Don King? How would he maintain the lavish lifestyle to which he was accustomed? One can imagine him staring into a bowl of his favorite cereal, Cap'n Crunch, and realizing what he had to do.

Return to boxing.

What a drag, man. What a downer.

That meant working the heavy bag, hitting the pavement, jumping rope, doing sit-ups, and giving up on the snack cakes and treats. It meant answering to his team, dealing with security guys, and preparing for press conferences. He was getting too old for all of that shit.

If this sounds a bit out of touch, remember that Mike was a self-proclaimed extremist. For him, it was "the top of the world or the bottom of the ocean," and he was feeling cynical after his perceived mistreatment by the U.S. legal system. In his own words regarding that time period: "My insanity was my only sanity."

So, back to the fight game. Back to what he knew best.

When it came to management, he had plenty of options. There was a steady stream of visitors ready to hand over bags of money for his signature on a contract. Boxing promoters and managers, everyone from Donald Trump to Butch Lewis, made gestures. Instead, settling on those he trusted and knew best, he gave Rory Holloway and John Horne authority to pursue contractual agreements for him.

Team Tyson was about to make history again.

Rory helped set the blueprint for the way contracts were formed in the years to come, not only in boxing but in sports at large. Shorty and Gordy point out that he did it without all the research tools and algorithms available to coaches and managers in today's world of athletics. Mike could not see it. Even John could not see it, because he had only dollar signs in his eyes. Quietly, relying on his instincts and people skills, Rory breathed that same air of the Pat Rileys and Phil Jacksons, and proved himself a "Zen master" in his own right by blending different walks of life into a cohesive team, by creating a brand before "branding" was commonplace.

It is public knowledge that you helped engineer the largest contract in sports history at that time. Did Don King have a hand in it? Did you worry that his involvement might open the door for future theft or embezzlement?

RORY: Let me tell you how we put this together. Mike's getting outta prison, right? He's not getting outta college. If we'd come to him with even a $3,000,000 signing bonus, he would've been happier than a sissy in Boys Town.

But, hey, I figured we had nothing to lose. Aim higher, a lot higher.

So we over at Seth Abrahams' place in Greenwich Village. He was this boxing impresario, the head of HBO. He lays this deal on the table, says, "Wouldn't you like to have a friend who makes this kind of money? That's more than Shaquille O'Neal makes."

I glance at it, and it's an offer of around $80,000,000. I'm practically broke at the time, I got Gordy sleeping at my place, and it takes all my willpower not to show my surprise. "Nah," I say. "That's not gonna work. We talking to someone else already, and you gotta remember, Mike's eating nails. He's bending bars." My voice is steady, but I'm talking pure crap. "If they don't let him out soon, he gonna break out. These other guys're, they offering us $150,000,000."

Abrahams frowns. "You do know he's in prison for rape, don't you?"

"Yeah, but this is the market. Listen, I'll get back to you."

Next, Butch Lewis calls me. He's like, "Are you sitting down?"

"No, whatcha got, Butch?"

"I got an offer for you. How does $10,000,000 sound?"

I'm real calm. I'm like, "Only $10,000,000? Are you saying that's just for me?"

He gets upset. "No, that's for Mike. What's wrong with you? Don't you realize Mike's in prison for rape?"

"Butch, I'm tired of everybody telling me where Mike is. I know where he at, and I know what he in for. I just talked to HBO, and they offered $150,000,000."

What I got to lose, right? I'm playing these guys against each other.

That's where Don King came in. He calls up. "Hey, brother." His voice all sappy and smooth, and I know what's coming. "Brother," he says, "we together, and I hear you been having some meetings."

I say, "Listen, I wanna be with you, Don, but I just talked to some guys—can't give you no names, 'cause I signed a non-disclosure—and we talking about a $150,000,000 for Mike. I can't turn that down."

He got excited. "Ro, listen, you gotta give me seven to ten days to see if I can beat that number."

He called on the eighth day. During that time, me and John had leveraged the best we could. John likes to say he handled all our business and I handled training camps, but that ain't true. He couldn't do nothing without my signature and involvement. We was a team, and that's how it went. Don't get me wrong. He did a good job negotiating contracts for Mike. He definitely played a part.

So now, Don's taken our groundwork and got a $373,000,000 deal on the table over at MGM. This took a Herculean effort by all, and I make sure there's no moral or performance clauses in this thing 'cause that sure as hell won't work, not with my boy.

Then, right as Mike's being released, it all comes to screeching halt. MGM's president, vice-president, and CEO all decide they don't want no part in this. They're like, "We ain't giving a fuckin' jailbird this kinda money. Never been done before."

We at a stalemate now.

So what we do? We went around them and set up a meeting directly with Kirk Kerkorian, the owner. We over at Kirk's house, one of the richest guys in America, and we brought Mike in. Mike was smooth, man. He's that boxing historian, and he sees Kirk has a personal scrapbook in his office. Guess Kirk used to be an amateur fighter long ago, and Mike starts spouting details of Kirk's record. You talk about changing things in a hurry? Kirk went from being hunched over to straightened up. Before we left there, Kirk was on the phone telling his guys to give us that deal.

I hand-delivered a check to Mike, his cut of the $73,000,000 signing bonus.

A deal this big was unheard of back then. And on top of that, there was a "Keep Mike Tyson Happy" fund of $25,000,000. Talk about spoiling our boy.

As Don King put it, "The price of pussy just went sky-high."

Man, there were top guys at MGM who resigned over this. The Showtime janitors and secretaries, they were all mad 'cause they ain't getting their bonuses. They thinking Team Tyson took everything. Hey, I just kept asking, and they kept giving.

Was all this worth it to MGM and Showtime?

They came to us later and offered an extension, if that tells you anything.

At that point, Mike was on pace to be the world's first billion-dollar athlete. Don King was lining up fighters so Mike could rise from the ashes and work his way back to the top. Did I worry about Don? Damn right I did. Everybody knows what he capable of. But why you think these tycoons, the Steve Wynns and Kirk Kerkorians and Donald Trumps, so willing to work with him if it's such a bad idea? 'Cause he's an incredible guy at building that hype. Keep your eye on him, sure, but he's the best at what he do.

All we had to do now was help Mike stay on task. We had a script. He train, he fight, and by the time he thirty-five years old, he can retire a very wealthy man.

Thing is, he wasn't that carnivore he once was. Sure, he would fight to entertain, fight to earn a prize, but the beast had tasted other things. His appetites had spread since those early years back in Cus's gym.

On the day of Mike's release, you were there. Many fight fans thought he would be even more vicious in the ring after prison. Was he just chomping at the bit, ready to fight again?

RORY: Not exactly. On March 25, 1995, we rolled up in this sleek black limo at the Indiana Youth Center. It's early in the morning, all these reporters and photographers crowding in, and we hurried Mike into the car.

Listen, I'd been visiting him the past three years, and I knew he ain't the Mike of old. He's just old Mike. He never thought he'd live past thirty, so to him twenty-eight's like retirement age. He's washed-up goods. We had to sell it like he something more. And he's a felon who's done time on sexually-related charges. Our society's not real forgiving about that. Take Tiger Woods. Soon as word got out about his affairs, he lost millions and millions in endorsements, and he ain't been the same since.

Mike was real prickly after he got out. He was back to the real world. He respected Shorty's opinion, him being a straight-shooter, and pulled him aside. They shared their faith in Islam, and Mike wanted to know if he should go right away to the mosque to pray since that might look good for all these reporters around. Shorty told him, "You can go pray now, if that's what you wanna do. Or we can go back to Cleveland and pray in private. Don't you worry about no one else."

Even weeks after that, though, Mike was still on edge, still feeling the pressure from all sides. Shorty was with me, and he's like, "What's wrong with this guy? He outta prison, he got millions of dollars. Fuck this. I don't need to put up with his shit." I did my managerial duties and talked Shorty into sticking with us.

To Mike, the money is just paper blood, that's all it is. He never got around to paying Don King back for the millions Don floated him the past three or four years. He just goes right back to his old spending ways.

Before prison, Mike got a lot of his clothes in Vegas. There was this furrier, Anna Nateese, she and her husband did all Liberace's stuff, these elegant coats and tails, all different colors. The Nateeses were older, real nice, and Mike was always a gentleman around them, asking to hear stories about Liberace and Elvis. He loved that stuff, loved wrapping himself in them big robes. "Man," he'd say, "this shit heavy."

Now that Mike was outta prison, we took him to New York, to a guy named Dennis. Dennis was best friends with Wisdom—in fact, that's how I first met Wiz—and Dennis had a clothing store. He carried all the hottest lines, tied in with all the best designers. I told him, "Mike Tyson's my man, and I wanna bring him in here."

"Bring him in," he said. "We'll put together two or three outfits for him."

That became our new place. Mike spent millions there on suits and shoes, filling up closets with this stuff. Pretty soon, all the rappers, players, pimps, they all shopping there 'cause they know it's Mike's go-to spot.

The money he was getting paid, Mike figured he gonna face King Kong in his first fight. He was nervous. When I showed him tape of McNeeley, he couldn't believe it. "This the bum I gotta fight?"

"That's him," I said.

He smiled. "Well, let's start training."

CHAPTER THIRTY-TWO

THE NIGHT OWL

In the mid-1990s, Mike Tyson signed the largest sports contract in history and packed arenas for his fights. By 2003, he was a footnote in boxing history, a man selling off assets, going through a second divorce, and declaring bankruptcy.

Where did all that money go?

Eric Brown, a longtime friend of Mike's and the best man at his wedding to Robin Givens, once said that Mike got treated as a "human ATM."

Mike himself claimed, "Everyone in boxing makes out but the fighter."

Really? Consider the signing bonus from the Showtime contract alone. If half of it was split between his managers and promoter—per the contract they all signed, don't forget—Mike still put $36,500,000 in his own pocket. He made forty percent more than both Rory and John, and twenty percent more than Don King.

Of course, not all fighters do so well, but certainly Mike was not hurting for cash. It is akin to John Grisham griping that everyone in publishing makes out but the author. Consider this: if, from sheer boredom, Mike broke down his career earnings into $10 bills and lit one bill every second of every day with a flamethrower, he would still be setting fires decades later. Work it out on a calculator. Or call *MythBusters* to test the theory. He would torch more $10 bills in a year than many Americans make in a lifetime.

Regardless, the pressing question is whether his managers were stealing from him. He claims they were, and even throws a few low blows at them in his book.

Rory, Mike alleges that before one fight, he put you and John Horne up in the Hilton, where you bought

gold watches from the hotel shop and charged them to his bill. He goes on to suggest you also stole hotel towels. Are these accusations true?

RORY: Mike is one of the most giving men I ever met in my life. He was my best friend. If I wanted a fuckin' gold watch, I could've asked him for it and he gonna get it for me. That's the type of guy he is. But I wouldn't ask him, and I definitely ain't gonna steal it from him. He says I was charging watches to a hotel bill? If I was, why'm I gonna steal a damn towel instead of charging that, too? It don't even make sense.

And listen, Mike didn't put us up in hotels before a fight. We was his managers, and the hotel rooms were part of the contract, but while John was lounging in the hotel, doing what John do, I was with Mike those weeks before a fight. If you called the hotel, I wasn't there. My room was empty. Why? Because I'm in camp with my boy.

Here's an example of how Mike was. He bought us all these brand-new cars, these $450,000 Bentley Azures, right off the line. First ones ever made. Me, John, Don, Mike, we all had one. He did this on an impulse, thinking it be cool, Team Tyson in matching Azures. If you working for a guy like that, why you gonna steal from him?

I never stole a thing from the Hilton.

And I sure as hell didn't steal from Mike.

Let's be clear, the fringe benefits of being Mike Tyson's best friend, of being his manager, those things were overwhelming. I'm not gonna say they wasn't. It was incredible. I had phenomenal opportunities and things I got to experience. Then again, we was abiding by our contract and earning our keep.

In the early years, Mike couldn't pay us what a normal manager earned. Cayton was still getting his cut, and we had to wait. About the time we became official, Mike landed hisself in prison, and we waited another three or four years. There were no guarantees, 'cause Mike could've chosen anyone he wanted as his managers. I wasn't in it for the payday, that's the truth.

We did finally make some money, though. When we helped Mike earn more money, we made even more money. Not one of us was complaining, and there was no reason to be greedy. This train was rolling.

Over the years, we used team resources to bring in financial gurus, Price-Waterhouse, whatever, just to provide advice for Mike. You think he paid any attention? He wanted none of that. He was like, "What the fuck do I care?"

Was it my job to tell him no? Listen, if I said no to Mike's spending, people would've accused me of trying to hoard and steal from him. Instead, he spent it like it going outta style, then he accused everyone else of making it disappear. Talk about one fine magic trick. He made David Blaine look like an amateur, the way he fooled the world into falling for all this.

Money never meant a thing to him. He spent it faster than you could burn it.

In his three years after prison, Mike Tyson netted over $120,000,000, thanks to the "bad deal" he signed. With his earnings, he maintained a home in Southington, Ohio, that was an ode to decadence. Over 25,000 square feet, it sat on sixty-six acres. It boasted 100-inch TV screens, a chandelier that weighed half a ton, a bedspread made of fox-tails, over seventy pairs of size 13 shoes in a walk-in closet the size of many people's master bedrooms. His garages housed Porsches, Mercedes-Benzes, Range Rovers, Bentleys, Rolls-Royces, a red Lamborghini Countach, and a black Ferrari Testarossa.

During one shopping spree, he bought ten BMWs, four Rolls-Royces, and several more Bentleys. He also bought a home in Vegas for $3,000,000, which he poured millions more into during renovations. In one month alone, he was known to drop $5,000,000. In his marriage to Robin Givens, he once purchased her a $2,000,000 bathtub as a Christmas gift.

He annually paid a tiger trainer $125,000 to watch after his tigers. He paid even more than that to cover their food costs. When an animal lover climbed into his tiger enclosure and was bitten, he felt sorry for the lady and gave her $250,000.

He paid over $100,000 each year for gardening alone.

Jake Tapper of the *Washington City Paper* pointed out that "These tales of poor Tyson and the mean streets were legendary, but it is often overlooked that Tyson lived like a prince from age thirteen on."

Of course, not all of his money went to cars and women, fun and games. The IRS wanted their portion as well, and he mailed them over $10,000,000 each time April 15 came around.

One can only imagine the amounts on his future Social Security checks?

Mike also dealt with various lawsuits. Robin Givens, for example, filed a $125,000,000 libel suit against her estranged husband. Desiree Washington threatened to sue Mike over a venereal disease she thought he must have passed to her. Monica Turner eventually divorced him and won a settlement of $9,000,000.

Mike admits in *Undisputed Truth*: "I couldn't even count the massive amount of money that my management team paid out to keep the gold-diggers and ambulance-chasers away. Rory and John Horne used to actually leave Johnny Tocco's gym before I would and approach the girls who were waiting for me . . . 'What do you want from Mike?' Rory would ask the girls. 'If you cared about him, you wouldn't be here.'"

Here's the real shocker: Team Tyson's largest single payout for their fighter's sexual indiscretion has never before been made public.

It is no secret that your team forked over large sums of money, usually to women, in an effort to make certain troubles go away. What was the largest amount ever paid?

RORY: December of '95, we was in Philadelphia getting ready for the Buster Mathis, Jr. fight. It was set up with Fox, and we getting good money for it. The night before the fight, I get a call from John Horne. He needs me to meet him over at this hotel. Says it's urgent. Don't wait.

I walk in, and there's Special Prosecutor J. Gregory Garrison. Mike's still on probation, but he's been out of prison eight, nine months.

So what the hell's this guy doing here?

Garrison was a shit-talking guy, medium-build, pasty white. He'd stick out his chest, try to be intimidating. He was all "Lights, Camera, Action." He didn't care about justice, about right or wrong. He was a shyster, plain and simple. He did a TV interview with Barbara Walters alongside Desiree Washington, and later wrote a book about Mike's trial, called *Heavy Justice*. He just loved seeing his name in lights.

Well, here you go, Jack. I'll give you some of that attention you love.

I took a seat in the hotel room. Garrison's over there, looking smug. He pulls out a tape-recorder and plays us this tape. Mike's on there profusely apologizing to a girl over the phone, saying, "You know how I am, baby, I get a little rough sometimes. I'm sorry if I hurt you. I'm sorry, baby."

Clearly this girl was a set-up, and if Mike was an average guy off the street, it might sound less incriminating, but he was a man with previous allegations.

It's the dead of night, face-to-face in this room, and the prosecutor says, "Listen, we can settle this now, or we can let this go to court. It's up to y'all."

Garrison wasn't there for no heavy justice. He was a night owl, looking for prey.

What we gonna do? If we don't agree to a deal, this prosecutor gonna make sure Mike faces Judge Gifford again, and she gonna be like, "Go Directly to Jail. Do Not Pass Go." Far as we was concerned, there's only one option what we could do.

We ask Garrison what he wants. He knows the kinda money Mike's making, it's public knowledge, and he says real cool and cocky that he'll accept $20,000,000.

He is out of his fuckin' mind.

We talk him down to $3,000,000. Agree to give him half up front, the other half after Mike gets off probation. So that's what we do. We draw up the paperwork to make it legit, and we hand this shyster a check. We don't even tell the champ.

"And justice for all . . ."?

Don't take off that damn blindfold, Lady Liberty. There's no justice here.

Team Tyson was in the cross-hairs. We was always on-guard, always on-duty, always ducking and dodging trouble. People had no idea what we was doing on a daily basis to keep this train chugging down the line. It was a united, concentrated, complete team effort. After the Holyfield fight, that's when people finally saw it for themselves, saw the beast we been dealing with.

CHAPTER THIRTY-THREE

THE CROCODILE

Mike Tyson vs. Evander Holyfield II . . . The Sound and the Fury.

This was the rematch everyone wanted, and when it occurred at the MGM on June 28, 1997, it was history's best-selling Pay-Per-View fight to date. Nearly two million viewers plunked down money to hear the sound and feel that fury.

They had no idea what they were in for.

The previous year's match between Tyson and Holyfield had ended in an eleventh-round TKO victory for Holyfield. Mike had slacked off during camp, whereas Holyfield had trained at altitude for four months. Mike later confessed he had lost his love of boxing in prison and become a three-round fighter, preparing only for the quick finish.

With the rematch in mind, Team Tyson tried to shake things up. They had trainer Jay Bright step aside so that highly-experienced Richie Giachetti could come onboard. They also gave Steve "Crocodile" Fitch a more active role, though he had already been with the team for over two years. He was an ex-con who walked around in army boots and fatigues. He had worked with other fighters, such as Oba Carr, and his boisterous personality reminded older fans of Muhammad Ali's Bundini Brown.

Put bluntly, Crocodile liked to yell.

"C'mon, you dirty flea. You maggot! Bite. Bite down!"

He considered himself a master motivator, and prided himself on not using profanity in front of boxing fans, since many of them were youngsters. Mike said the guy was inspiring. When Crocodile showed up at press conferences, he always gave reporters something to work with. "Is it supposed to be a funeral in here?" he would bark. "You don't fall asleep with the Crocodile around, baby, because I'm going to bite all day."

That June evening in Vegas, Crocodile led the way into the ring for the rematch, boasting a black vest with large white letters: "Loved by Few, Hated by Many, Respected by All." Fans were on their feet as the fighters entered the ring. The electricity in the arena was palpable.

Showtime, folks.

George Foreman had warned years earlier that Mike "needs to be sheltered like you would shelter a lion or a tiger. You lock him up, except when you want him to come out and jump through a few hoops." This particular night the warning was heeded too late.

Holyfield was taller than Mike, yet during the course of the fight he ducked down and came back up at awkward angles. His hard head kept catching Mike in the chin, in the forehead. Mike felt groggy. He clenched with his opponent. In the first fight, head-butts were an issue Team Tyson complained about, and yet Referee Mills Lane seemed oblivious to the same problem now. The crowd cheered as Mike turned more ferocious.

When the next head-butt occurred, Mike went ballistic. "I lost my cool . . . the worst thing a soldier can do," he later admitted. "At that moment, I went insane . . . didn't care about the Queensberry Rules . . . I wanted to inflict as much pain as I could on that man."

It was the beginning of the end for Team Tyson.

Sitting ringside, what did you see? Was the head-butting a true concern or a convenient excuse for two losses in a row?

RORY: Mike didn't need excuses. He knew how to take a beating like a man.

You have to understand, leading up to the second fight we tried to get a ref who would protect Mike from the head-butts. We seen the way Holyfield done that in the first fight. He beat Mike fair and square, definitely had Mike's number, but he gave my boy a concussion in the process. We didn't want that to happen to him again.

Well, when their heads started colliding, when it started again, Mike got disoriented and he just panicked. You put him on the streets, you corner him, he gonna fight. Well, he must've thought he was out on the streets in that moment.

I'm sitting there, and I watch him come up like Jaws.

The first bite, I'm in shock, like I just seen the bite but can't believe it. The second bite, I seen it clear as day. I'm like, "He just bit him for real this time!" He spits a piece of ear on the floor, and my minds racing, wondering how we gonna get outta this one. I'm scared to go in the ring and be anywhere near that flap of skin. I'm like, "Mike, you nasty. You just took this guy's ear off."

Crocodile was the hype man, and people heard him yelling, "Bite, Mike. Bite down!" Later, Holyfield's wife even tried to sue Crocodile for it, not realizing that he just encouraging Mike to try harder and not give up.

It was complete chaos. The fans, they were shocked and furious. Holyfield was cool, but the boxing officials, the judges, announcers, it was all kindsa crazy.

John was amped up. He told the Showtime guys, "All I know is Mike got a cut over his eye three inches long, and Evander got a little rip on his ear that don't mean nothing. He jumped around like a little bitch." John's emotions took over, and the things he said really hurt our cause. He was protecting his fighter, but you gotta be wise, no matter what you're feeling in that moment.

When they asked me what I thought, I said, "We just hope Holyfield is okay, and I wanna see if Mike's okay."

Mills Lane, he tried to say the head-butts was accidental, but he must've been wearing blinders or something. It was plain as day. Those blows were as bad as any uppercut. We had to get Mike outta there, 'cause he had a gash in his forehead that was gonna take dozens of stitches to close.

We got our fighter into a car outside the arena. The crowd at the MGM seemed to know where we was at, and they yelling at us, calling us names. They angry, right?

This little white kid comes to the window, and he says, "You're a punk, Mike." Mike jumps outta this moving car and next thing, Mike's chasing this kid and I'm chasing Mike. The kid jumps over a bush, Mike jumps over a bush, and I jump over a bush. Up and over, up and over, up and over. Soon as the kid fell, Mike catches up. The kid's screaming, Mike's hovering over him ready to throw a punch, and I dove in. "You can't do this, you can't hit this kid." I corralled Mike back to the car, and we took off. Whole time he's growling, "I'm gonna kill somebody. I'm gonna kill somebody."

I'm like, "Omigod, this is not my night."

As all this was happening, my career was coming to an end. I just didn't know it yet.

People wanna blame Crocodile, wanna blame us. Listen, Mike's his own man, and this stuff goes as far back as Cus. Mike'll tell you that Cus taught him to be ferocious. He says, "If Cus told me to bite, I'd bite."

Mike just had that animal instinct. He loved them tigers for a reason. I used to think it was fun at first having them around as pets, and then I realized these things was hunters. They killers. Their psyche, Mike was really into that. The tigers are like four or five hundred pounds, and he out swimming naked with them in his pool. Sheila can tell you how our kids was over at Mike's house in Vegas, they go to the window, and they see him coming outta the pool, his pimply, black ass dripping wet. "Mom," they said, "Mike was in the water with the tigers."

A tiger tamer, he can't overpower the beast, right? Instead, he's trained to understand the body language, to predict the tiger's movements. Well, I'd watch Mike in the ring, the way he pacing back and forth. It was eerie when he in that beast mode. You see all these muscles moving, almost like he's gliding. Whether he moving to the left or to the right, his eyes were on his opponent, not even blinking. It almost hypnotized you. Your feet, they just stuck in the ground.

As his handler, I had to be watching all the time. If my boy about to do something crazy, I'm trying to divert his attention. If he got that look, I'm trying to take the tension off. Man, that ain't something you do through a phone or beeper. This was a 24/7 job. If he wanna sit and watch karate movies, then that's what I do. I'm not into those movies, but if that's what he like, that's what I like. Whatever it takes to keep the beast occupied.

Well, the beast got loose that night in the ring.

The tiger showed his stripes.

I thought maybe we could pull the team together after that, pick up the pieces, do damage control, but there wasn't no way that was gonna happen. All that tiger shit was about to hit the fan.

CHAPTER THIRTY-FOUR

THE SNAKES

After the night of the Sound and the Fury, the Nevada State Athletic Commission fined Mike $3,000,000 and revoked his license for a year. While the money was nothing to Team Tyson, the twelve months of down-time were cause for serious concern. He had not gone that long without a fight in over fifteen years. Training routines and fights kept him on task—and only barely—so a layoff this long spelled trouble with a capital S-E-X.

And Mike was soon to add another flavor to his alphabet soup: D-R-U-G-S.

The two-time heavyweight champion, the highest paid athlete in the world, the iconic international superstar was about to change tracks and head this runaway train over the edge into a bottomless chasm.

Team Tyson was doomed.

"It was a Greek tragedy," Mike once said, in his self-aggrandizing manner, "only I was the subject."

Some fans voiced their rage at the former champ, saying they would never pay to see him fight again. Others swore they would offer up their firstborn to see what he did next in the ring. Mike still had three fights on his existing contract, and Showtime recognized the earning power of such a polarizing figure. They offered an extension of $150,000,000. If his team took the deal, he would be one step closer to that billion-dollars-earned mark.

Except Mike was driving the crazy train again. He had been on this thing over half of his life, with no signs of it slowing or stopping, and he just wanted to bring this journey to an end.

Stoke the engines. Aim for the cliff. Take another bite of alphabet soup.

Did you see the contract extension that was offered by Showtime? Why didn't you capitalize on that and try harder to keep Mike on task?

RORY: I held the offer in my hands. It came to us right after the bite. Even after my man's been fined and suspended, he's being told there's more money around the corner. Man, that just boggled my mind. It was this pattern, though. Each time Mike do something stupid he got more attention. He punches a guy in the face. He pinches a girl's butt. He gets sent off to jail. No matter what it was, his fame and his paychecks just got bigger and bigger.

You have kids of your own. What you think gonna happen if you keep rewarding their bad behavior? What you think gonna come of that?

This ain't rocket science, man.

And shit, I was just as guilty, 'cause all we did was spoil this fuckin' guy.

Here, he just bit Holyfield's ear, and he gets offered an extension. Showtime's, like, "It's unfortunate what happened. We're still with you. Nothing's changed. You'll still get your money. Oh, and how about another $150,000,000?" Math wasn't my favorite subject in school, but I was smart enough to know this was one helluva deal.

Right away we were doing damage control with the press, getting Mike some medical attention, setting up for our next run, but I knew all the down-time was against us. Now Mike's running loose, like a nightmare come to life. Don't you dare go to sleep, boys and girls, 'cause Freddie Krueger in town.

It was a perfect storm. Mike was tired. His wife, Monica, was tired. Our team was tired. And all the usual suspects out there just waiting to get their hands on our boy.

That contract never happened, and I'll tell you why.

Now Mike's depressed, and he's mad at the world. Nobody protected him from the head-butts, so it's everybody else's fault he done what he done. He holes up in a usual spot, Trump Tower in New York, and he got all this free time for Craig "Boogie," Jackie Rowe, and Shawnee Simms to get up in his ear. They putting things in his head.

And not just in his head.

Man, before this I never known Mike to be on drugs a day in his life. Maybe before we met, but not on my watch. He done a thousand piss tests, clean as a board of health. Years later he got caught, during the Savarese fight, I think, but I didn't know that Mike. Who that guy with the tattoo on his face? I don't know him. And I wasn't gonna be the guy who give you a needle. I'm not gonna sit there and watch you do it.

So he's holed up, and I go to visit him. The hotel door opens, and he in there with magician David Blaine. They both look stoned. They glazey-eyed. Craig "Boogie" was there. I ain't no square from Delaware, and now I'm even more worried about my boy. I'm like, "C'mon, Mike, let's get you outta here."

That's not what he wanted. After the Holyfield fight, he just wasn't the same guy. He lost his respect for himself. You know, lost his giving nature. He just lost it.

This my friend, though. I'm still believing we gonna pull through.

Then I start hearing the whispers.

Jay Larkin, executive producer of Showtime's boxing, once said, "This is a fluid business. It's like a bag of snakes. You throw it in the corner, and it changes its position." When did you realize that people around you were changing position?

RORY: Mike's weakness let these snakes in. He got everybody scrambling. He already talking with Shawnee, and she working him. On the other side, he got pressure from Monica. She wondering where all his money going. What they gonna do now that he's suspended? She's just trying to protect her family and their future. Well, Mike ain't about to tell her he's blowing a fortune on girls and drugs. How that gonna sit with his wife?

So Mike gets Jackie and Shawnee to start working Monica. The three women, they in it together now, conspiring to cut Mike loose from his team.

One day back in Vegas, I'm in the fitness center. I didn't hire Crocodile because of his brain, so I wasn't surprised when he come through smiling, telling me how Mike's talking to Shelly Finkel about managing him. Why'd he divulge that to me when I'm Mike's manager? I said, "Let me explain something to y'all. If Mike do choose that road, his career gonna go down the drain so fast it ain't even funny. So for you to sit here like a cheerleader on the sideline, you don't know what you're doing."

Finkel was this older white guy, clean-cut, mild-mannered, a Wall Street office, all the things America can accept. Fighters went to him thinking he gonna be their savior.

In contrast, this guy was the devil in disguise.

I know Monica brought him in, part of the plan to switch Mike's management, but he didn't have Mike's best interests in mind. He lined his fighters up like an assembly line. And I seen for myself how Finkel was years ago in Atlantic City. We there for the fight with Larry Holmes, I was in this restaurant, and Finkel's at a nearby table, holding court with these business guys. It's all about how Mike was an animal, and Finkel would never work with a guy like that, never let him in the house or around his daughters.

Now he wants in on the action. He thinks he'll just change the names on Mike's contracts and rake in the same money. You could see it, all these people with horns on their heads. If you could hover above, you'd see them circling the train. Finkel figured he gonna take over Team Tyson, switch out the engine, and keep on rolling.

Problem was, Mike's heart was the real engine, and he was losing steam fast. He loves hard and trusts easy, and this wasn't really about the mismanagement of his money or career. It was about those people who came in and mismanaged his heart.

I lived in Vegas then, right around the corner from Mike. He gets back to town, comes over a coupla times, two, three in the morning. We talking about his troubles, all this stuff after the Holyfield fight, and I'm thinking maybe we back on track. Then, a few days later, he's back in this shell where he won't talk with me.

That came from Monica, and he let it happen. Protecting his marriage, I guess. She started choosing sides, firing all the people I had, hiring a new security detail. What she did was, she weeded everybody out. The people she kept had to convince her they was against me. "I'm firing anyone who's close to Rory and. . . boom, boom, boom." These people started staying away from me like I had a disease. Snap. Just like that.

It wasn't just Finkel trying to slither in here. The door was still open, and this guy named Jeff Wald tried to get in too. He this entertainment manager, a California guy, used to work with Roseanne Barr and James Brolin. Jeff first got to Mike through Don King, and now he starts trying to take him away. Jeff's team, they wanna manage Mike, and they're telling him he'll be in movies, be on a music label, make millions of dollars. Mike was looking for a way outta boxing, and this sounded good.

It was just how these guys sucked you in. They gonna make you a star. They never did nothing for Mike, though. This was eleven years before *The Hangover*.

Don King, he's a street guy at heart, and he wasn't gonna sit by during this.

He flies out to see Jeff. He meets with those guys, and Mike's there too. Don says, "Listen, motherfucker, if Mike wanna be with you, that's fine, but at least pay Rory Holloway and John Horne. They still under contract." Mike jumped up. "Fuck that. I'm not giving them shit. Rory and John already made enough money off me."

Is this the guy who once told me, "We ate bologna together, now we eat steak together"? Is this that same guy? So, now I'm not allowed to share a bite?

See, that's how Mike thinks. He don't realize that a manager deserves to be paid. It's all "me, me, me." He doesn't wanna deal with his business, with his contracts. "Just give me $30,000,000, that's all I wanna hear." He don't understand what we did to get him that shit, the hours we put in, the sweat and the stress.

Even then, Mike and me tried to talk.

He come over to my house one morning, and we sitting in these chairs calm as can be, just like me and you here. I said, "Mike, listen, Monica and them are trying to get you to breach your contract. If you do, you're gonna end up owing Showtime $25,000,000. You don't wanna mess with that." He said, "I know, I know. Don't be concerned. I don't wanna talk about that shit, man. So how you doing? I love you, Rory. Forget about all that. C'mon, let's go for a ride."

We had these choppers, these custom-made Harley three-wheelers. It was hot that day, and we drove it up in the desert, Red Rock Canyon. We just talking and riding around. Then we went to a gun shop with all these weapons and knives. There was this long knife, like a hatchet. Mike's holding it, talking crazy. "I like this shit."

He swings it back and forth, and the store owner, he jumps back. "Whoa, Mike."

Hanging up on the wall was this bazooka. Mike's like, "Does that work?"

"Yeah, if I load it up."

"Can I buy that?"

"No, Mike, it's just an ornament."

Mike shakes his head. "You know how many fuckin' people I could kill with that?" He was scaring me with that talk.

So he takes this big knife and we get back on the choppers. It's hot as hell, like a hundred and ten degrees, and I'm wearing flip-flops, never thinking we be gone that long. We get back to the house. We're in his bedroom, where it's cool. I figure here's my moment to bond and talk some with my boy. He starts in about how everyone's trying to get him to do this and do that, how it's stressing him out, how he's going fuckin' crazy. I tell him, "Mike, man, you just gotta take a step back and look at the big picture."

The phone rings as he's in his closet getting dressed. He's on there getting into an argument. I can tell it's Monica. Well, she must've scolded him and said to get me the hell outta there, 'cause he comes out of the closet, and I swear to God, he was like a different human being. Whatever Monica said to him, she hit the right button and he made his choice. He has a serious face, has that fuckin' knife in his hand, and he says, "Get out."

I'm like, "What?"

He says, "Yo, man, go. You gotta leave. Just leave!"

In the boxing ring, the knockout always comes from the punch you don't see. Well, I never seen that coming. This my man, right? What's he doing?

You know, Mike could've just come to me and said, "This not working out, Ro. I appreciate what you done, but me and my wife wanna go another direction."

I would've said, "Okay, well, here's the pros and cons, and if you need me to, I'll take a lesser position. I'll take less pay. That ain't no problem with me." Then, if he still wanna end it, if he wanna take his head and ram it into a wall, that's ultimately his decision. At least we're still friends, right?

I wrote a letter to him, figuring Crocodile could get it to him. Well, Crocodile never delivered it. Later, Crocodile became the biggest conspirator in Mike's drug use, and them two dragged each other down for years. Nowadays, Crocodile's got his shit back together, up every morning like clockwork, working out, reading his Bible, living clean. He's got a motivational gym or something out in Vegas. Like I said earlier, everybody deserves a second chance.

And I tried giving Mike that second chance.

I went over to his house the very next day, thinking I'm gonna talk to this fool. They had security at the gate, but I seen Mike standing up on his porch. He turned his back and just walked inside. Then the guard flashed a gun on me, like he gonna shoot me. This was some retarded shit, and I wasn't gonna get myself killed over it.

I wrote one last letter, like four pages, and gave it to a security guy to deliver to Mike personally. The guy threw it in the garbage, since they all working for Monica now.

Monica was still real cordial with me, like we good. She called up this one day, won't never forget. She said, "Rory, what's happening with my husband's money?"

Well, at that point there's a lot he doing that he don't want her knowing about, and it was part of our bro code that I don't tell nobody else about his financial affairs. That's not good business. As partners, you gotta have that trust. So I told her, nice and calm, that if Mike wanna know something about his finances, he can dial me up and I be glad to talk to him personally and confidentially.

A few minutes later, the phone rings again. It's Mike. "Rory, you slimy, no-good, motherfuckin', punk-faggot, piece of shit . . ." He's yelling, it's this stream of profanity like he ain't never said to me in our entire lives together.

In that moment, he broke the bro code. He let these women get in his head and turn him against me, and all I'm trying to do is protect my boy. This was all happening so fast that my head was spinning, my knees was wobbling. I'm getting hit from every angle—Monica, Shawnee, Jackie, Craig "Boogie," Jeff Wald, Shelly Finkel.

I'm in the trenches trying to fight for my guy, for his future. He's bleeding out. And all I can do is put fuckin' Band-Aids on a gunshot wound.

He slammed the phone down, and it was the last time we ever talked.

I'm still shaking when the phone rings a third time. It's Shelly Finkel. About now I realize he's sitting there with Mike and Monica, and they all making their move. I'm still on the contract as Mike's manager, but here's Finkel telling me how he's arranging stuff for Mike. "If you act right," Finkel says to me, "I think I can find a place for you."

I was so insulted by him saying this to me, the guy who helped build Mike's team. And I know Mike's standing right there, not saying a damn word.

Mike wrote to me in February of '98, a termination letter that came through his attorney. I actually got the thing after it was all over the news that he fired me and John. "I loved Rory," he says in his book, "but I had no choice . . . I hope Rory doesn't take the firing personally."

Mike should've come to me like a man. How can I not take that personally? We friends, we business partners, let's discuss this like civilized adults. He trivialized my friendship, and that hurt me more than anything.

Me and John released a joint statement, saying, "I think there is sometimes a frustration and misunderstanding that can occur in the best of friendships and business relationships, and that's how we categorize this." In other words, we weren't going to point fingers or fire back publicly. We were leaving room to work this out and keep his contract in place. We protecting my boy's chances for the future.

Instead, Mike says, "There was my answer. Rory had cast his lot with two scumbags. I had been let down and betrayed by someone I would have died for."

You say you'd die for me, then fuckin' talk to me instead of running off with these people who don't know you like I do, who don't care about you like I do. Once again, you letting other people pull your strings.

When Mike fired me, it was like he put a curse on me. "I no longer with Rory."

And everyone else said, "Me neither."

I kept waiting for him to call and reveal his end game. He was just posturing, that's what I thought at first. Then people told me he on TV denouncing his team, and that's when I realized this shit was for real.

It turned all cloak-and-dagger, like nobody wanted to be seen close to me. Mike didn't assassinate me with a gun, he did it with his words. He shot my confidence, my reputation, and my relationships to pieces. Right now, if my cellphone rings, I know it's one of five or six people.

That's it. I keep my friends close. Back then, at the height of all this, I was so popular I needed five phones to keep up with all the people calling me.

Money doesn't just change you, it changes the people around you.

That's a sad fact I learned.

Friends, even some family members, they were changing because of what I got. They didn't come and ask me for things, they just expected I'm gonna come to them and say, "Hey, here." They wanted a handout here, a leg-up there. When that stopped happening, they started looking for reasons you don't deserve the things you got.

The one who hurt me the most was LaTondia. We was close, like brother and sister. I met LaTondia at a health club in Vegas, we started talking, and she was a go-getter, very smart in business. She became my personal secretary, and even now people know her as Rory Holloway's former assistant. She was paid outta my salary. She worked for me, not Mike. When everything went down, she left and went to work for Mike and Monica. She played both sides, like good-cop/bad-cop. Right to this day, she don't know what that did to me. That cut me deep.

That's fine, Mike, you wanna make me the fall guy. You wanna fire me and John, blame us for making you sign a bad contract. But what did Shorty do to you? What did Gordy do? What was the methodology behind that? They didn't handle your business. This shit was systematic, getting rid of the guys you knew could think for themselves.

Shorty is one of the most practical, reasonable, unfiltered guys I ever met in my life. He is wise beyond his years. He a man's man. He didn't take my side, didn't take Mike's side. He didn't make no assumptions. He didn't do none of that.

Gordy, all he ever done is clean up after Mike and keep things running smooth. He busted his ass in camp. He was a go-to guy.

I would've been happy if Mike kept them two around, 'cause then I know at least somebody got his back. What they do to him? They had kids, houses, mortgages. Their reputations got dragged through the mud. And to this day, man, neither one of them gonna say nothing bad about him. Especially Shorty. He'd put his head on the chopping block before he badmouth Mike Tyson.

The guy who deserved what he got outta all this, the one rat in the bunch, that was Don King. Ain't no way around it.

CHAPTER THIRTY-FIVE

THE RAT

In the 1980s, Bill Cayton and Jim Jacobs put together an HBO contract for upwards of $3,000,000 per fight—with Bill, Jim, and Mike splitting the money in thirds.

In 1995, Rory Holloway, John Horne, and Don King put together Showtime contracts for upwards of $30,000,000 per fight—with Rory and John each getting ten percent, Don getting thirty, and Mike getting fifty. That was nearly ten times more money than Mike earned under his previous management.

Why, then, was the latter Team Tyson vilified?

If Rory, John, and Don had been a trio of middle-aged, conservatively-dressed, white guys, would they have been praised for pulling off such a lucrative deal under such adverse circumstances? A man outta prison just got how much money?

These days, if an athlete signs a fat contract, no one cries foul that the agent got millions as part of the cut. In fact, other athletes go banging on that agent's door, hoping this savvy fellow might work similar deals for them. Or when a promoter such as Bob Arum gets his massive paycheck from a Manny Pacquiao fight, the sportswriters do not take him to task for it—though Dana White, head of the UFC, once accused Arum of sucking the life out of boxing.

When it comes to race, Don King used that issue as a tool. He sold himself as the Great Black Hope for many of the young fighters he worked with, the only one they could trust.

You say that Mike broke the bro code by letting women create a rift in your relationship. What was

the code Don broke by robbing Team Tyson of millions of dollars?

RORY: First, let me say this, I don't know that the media was racist toward us. Ignorant, yes. You know, there's a difference between racism and ignorance. Racism gets into hate, but a black friend of mine, he spent the night at his white friend's house and overheard the mom asking, "What do they eat?" She was just being ignorant, like we African-Americans eat Martian food or something. You know, I think it's just best that we all give each other a chance. Be in each other's worlds. Show some respect.

Mike once told *USA Today*, "I go to England and Scotland and white people love me. I come back home, and black people hate me." It's complicated, right? The way I see it, we was the first black guys managing an athlete of that caliber, making that kinda money, and the media was just ignorant about us. They heard our grammar, looked at the clothes we wore, and they made assumptions.

Was some of it racist? I don't care about a black box or white box or Hispanic box. I'm not into that. All that "we brothas" talk, that was Don King's thing.

The code he broke had nothing to do with color. It was about business, and he stole from his partners. That ain't cool, under no circumstances.

Mike says in *Undisputed Truth*, 'By introducing me to sign this deal with Don . . . they made $22,000,000 each on my fights after I got out. If they had been real managers, they would never have allowed me to sign off on any deals that Don brought me.' How do you respond to that?

RORY: If I go into the woods, kill something, and drag it back to the campfire, I don't deserve a piece of that? Is that what Mike's saying?

I believe John and me, we put together the best deal we could for our fighter. We did a damn fine job and deserved a percentage. Was Don making a helluva lot of money from this? Were we? Yes, we were. Even so, Mike would've netted less under any other deal he was offered. Plain and simple.

Listen, Don was greedy, but he wasn't stingy. While Mike was in prison, Don floated him almost $9,000,000 over those three years. If Mike thinks me and John got some of that, he's wrong. Me and John didn't see a dime. Don was just hedging his bets with Mike, keeping him on the line for the day he was free and able to fight again. Did that pay off for Don? You bet it did. Did Mike ever give him that money back? I don't know. Guess that's between him and Don.

Either way, Don got his money back in the long run. You know, he's just one greedy guy, always looking for more crumbs. Ask anyone who knows him.

Me and John, we started poking around and found out that Don was holding onto earnings from Mike's international sales. Millions of dollars worth. And the more we investigated, the more shit we found. He wasn't just taking crumbs, he was building a damn bread factory—paying his daughter nearly $50,000 a year to run Mike's fan club, paying his son a six-figure "consultant's fee." And he doing this with Mike's own money. I mean, the guy's just being brazen about it.

Give John credit, 'cause he always saw Don like a father. He thought they was close. But that didn't stop him from agreeing we gotta confront Don about this. We could've gone to Don and said, "Hey, we know you got your hand in the cookie jar. Let's make a deal. Give us a couple million, and we keep our mouths shut." We could've done that.

Instead, we went to Don's house unannounced, waking him up at 5:00 a.m. There he is, standing in his bathrobe, surprised to see us. Probably figured we was bringing him some bad news about Mike. Not this time. We figured we'll nip this in the bud and get him to make things right, but we'll do it privately so we don't threaten Mike's Showtime contract in any way. Just keep the train rolling.

We laid it all out there, all the details of what we found, and started grilling Don about Mike's business affairs, specifically the monies from foreign sales. Don stayed calm and poured himself a cup of coffee, as if he knew this gonna be a long morning. He was in complete denial mode. He said he needed a little time to look into this. John got louder, his voice echoing through the house, veins popping out on his neck. Don refused to give in.

We set up a meeting with Mike to discuss what's going on. Well, the word gets out, and that gave Monica and the people she'd been plotting with their "ah-ha!" moment. It was just the ammunition they needed. Now they could go after Don, throw in Rory and John as guilty parties, and cut all ties so they can start fresh.

Of course, Showtime gonna be happy too, 'cause now they have an out. They can ditch this "Keep Mike Tyson Happy" fund and renegotiate a deal more in their favor.

Don King is a shrewd guy. He'd predicted all this stuff years ago, telling me that Mike was an Uncle Tom, a Jefferson Davis, that he was weak underneath and when the shit hit the fan he was going to throw us under the bus. I didn't believe that, man. I thought Don's brain must be frying under all that hair. But Don was right. He was absolutely right.

Now Don was the master chess-player trying to think ten moves ahead. He saw the tensions, all these fractures, and he knew his best bet was the old divide-and-conquer game. United, we might take him down, but ain't nobody gonna take him down alone. So he's telling John stuff about me, telling Mike stuff about Don. He tells me, "It hurts me to see the champ do this to you, Ro. He's the godfather of your kids, ain't he? How he just leave you behind? How he do that to you and Sheila, to Paris and Nia?"

I told you about Mike's sex tapes earlier, right? Well, as all this is going on, I told Gordy to gather up the tapes, maybe sixteen or seventeen of them, and seal them in a bag. He took them back to New York, and we locked those suckers away at my mother-in-law's place. Turned out to be the right move.

See, Don knew about Mike's love nest, too.

One day I'm in Vegas, and Don calls me up to this boardroom, all these lawyers around the table, and he plays a news-clip of Mike talking crap about me and John. He says, "See how he treat you, Rory? What I tell you?" I wasn't saying a word. I smelled a rat. "We need your help, Ro. Get Mike's tapes for us, man. Bring us those tapes."

I knew he wanted them to leverage his position as promoter, right?

I'm not a confrontational guy. I nodded. "Alright, I'll get the tapes." The minute I walked out that building, I called Sheila in Manhattan. "You know the bag I got locked up?"

"Yeah."

"Take it downstairs and burn it up, burn everything in it."

You think I couldn't have used that footage for my own gain? You think I couldn't have blackmailed half the women on those tapes—*Sports Illustrated* swimsuit models, celebrities' wives, Miss Universes, whoever? Hell, I could've sold that stuff to *Vivid* or *TMZ* or the *National Enquirer*. Instead of selling off my cars and property later, I could've divvied that shit out and make a fuckin' fortune. I just wasn't gonna do that, outta respect for my friend and all those women.

Sheila called back a little later. "Honey, it's done," she said. "Papi and me threw it all in a barrel and burned it. It's all gone."

Over the years, I had plenty of opportunities to rob my friend, to take advantage of situations. Right after Mike divorced Robin, he pulled out all his money from the bank on a cashier's check. You remember how I told you about that? That was back in '89. Well, I carried that check around for months. I'm talking about $9,000,000, in my name.

You think I ever touched that?

Hell, no. That wasn't mine to spend.

Another time, Mike left a bag of cash on the couch in my basement. It was a cool hangout spot, fixed up with a pool table and an aquarium. My cleaning lady, a real loyal woman, she seen it there for weeks and just worked around it. She knew not to poke around. Thing is, Mike didn't know it was missing. I didn't know it was there.

We in camp when Sheila calls and tells me she found this bag with $100,000. "That must be Mike's," I said. I looked over at him. "You lose $100,000?"

He gives me a blank look. "I haven't lost nothing."

"Well, this is Sheila, and she says you left some money in our basement. What, you think we need a loan?" It was this funny moment, 'cause we all doing good at that time. We laughed about it, and he bragged to the guys in camp about how he could trust me with his shit.

As soon as we flew home, Sheila had his money waiting.

Don King has never confessed publicly to any thievery. What steps were taken to get back the money he stole from Mike?

RORY: Eventually, Mike and his lawyer sued for the $100,000,000 that Don stole. Mike was right to do it. We seen that for ourselves. Don ended up settling for $14,000,000. Well, Don ain't giving you nothing of his, not one dime, so if he gave Mike money, he was laughing the whole time 'cause he knew he owed him a whole lot more.

Legally, as a manager, I could've sued Mike for breaching our contract when he went to Finkel. Years earlier, Mike broke his contracts with Cayton and Jacobs but had to keep paying anyway, after a court decision. This was the same situation. I had three more fights under our contract together, almost $10,000,000 still owed me. Even the chairman of the Nevada State Athletic Commission said Mike couldn't just drop us. "It would be very hard for someone to sign with someone else, knowing he already has a valid contract."

But I ain't that guy who's gonna sue his friend.

When it comes down to it, I don't care if you got tattoos, look tough, talk tough, spout off about how you gonna take a bullet for me. That don't make you a true friend. It's about your character. The loyalest guy might be the scrawniest cat in the world. Sometimes you don't know till you put it to the test, and when all the money was gone, I found out who was with me. I got guys like Gordy and Shorty. And Papa J, there's a true friend. He gonna be there when I'm sick. He coming through for me, no matter what.

I used to say to Mike, "How you know these girls really love you when you start out by giving them hundreds of thousands of dollars? Don't just give it to them. Let them earn it. See who is really in it with you, the trials and tribulations."

It's a great feeling when you do find those one or two real friends. It's even greater when you find a woman who loves you unconditionally. She still smiles when shit ain't funny, still scratches when you ain't itching. You can't buy that. There's no substitute sugar. That's the real deal right there.

Well, I never thought Don was a friend. Not one day in all those years.

Me and John filed our own suit against him for the $100,000,000 he owed. Don right away, he started sending Range Rovers over to Dennis' clothing store, trying to buy me off. "Just take the car, Rory."

I'd say, "Give me at least a million, million and a half in an escrow account, then we talk."

"You ain't getting nothing. Mike's the one who done all this to you. I can't believe he do you like that. I'm trying to help a brother, giving you some cash to keep you rolling. Now sign this deal, and we put this all behind us."

"We're going to court, Don. You know that's where we headed."

He turned serious then. "Listen, man, you can't win this."

"We'll let the judge decide that."

"I'm telling you, Ro. You can't win. You know who I got on my side, dontcha? You know who my friends are?"

When he said that, my skin turned cold.

"Bush," Don told me. "That's my guy. He's been at functions at my house. I helped get him elected. I could call him on the phone right now. We connected. I'm telling you now, you gonna feel bad if you keep on the path you've chosen. Best if you just take what I'm giving you and shut up."

Was this just more of his bullshit?

Who knows? All I can say is, the judge threw the whole thing out before we even got started. We had enough evidence for a fair trial, but now I had nothing left to work with. Maybe it was my pro bono lawyer's fault, 'cause he was terrible. Hell, he barely knew the names in the case. Or maybe Don really did have connections.

Either way, Don was free and clear, the guy who was all about "the brothas" and "we in this together" was now nowhere to be found.

Don King still dabbles in boxing, but I really think all those years in the cesspool caught up with him. He's like eighty-five now, and his wife passed a few years back. What's his fortune doing for him these days? Did it bring him happiness?

From Day One, I knew the kinda guy Don was, but like the Wynns and Kerkorians and plenty of others, it was a gamble I decided to take. Well, it came back to bite me.

What hurts the most, though, is the way it hurt my friend.

CHAPTER THIRTY-SIX

THE CHEETAH

Joyce Carol Oates met with Mike while he was in prison, hoping to penetrate the psyche of this complex individual. A prolific author and winner of numerous awards, she wanted not only to understand Mike, but to understand the psyche of boxers as a whole. In her own words, boxing was "the quintessential image of human struggle, masculine or otherwise, against not only other people but one's own divided self."

Considering Mike's dual personality, his struggles are not unexpected. He carries within him a desire to dominate and control, as well as a desire to give generously and bring happiness to others. These traits of his are well-documented.

He admits, "When I had money, I was an animal. I was so belligerent." Yet he still cares for pigeons as pets, cupping the fragile creatures in hands that could tear out a man's throat.

To this day, he is as intriguing as he is mystifying. He once said, "If you think God will help you, quit your job and see how much He cares." It is the type of pop-spirituality that earns him fans, yet fails to take hold of personal responsibility as a gift instead of a curse. His life and career have been caught constantly between those two extremes.

What happened for Mike career-wise before his reemergence in The Hangover and his Broadway show, Undisputed Truth? Did you watch any of his fights after your Team Tyson days?

RORY: First, Jeff Wald and his Hollywood promises never panned out.

These women, the ones he let tear everything down—Shawnee Simms, Monica, Jackie Rowe—do you think any of them are still around? Mike ended his professional relationship with Shawnee after he was in her wedding. He and Monica got divorced, and she walked away with a lot from that deal. As for Jackie, I don't know, but I doubt Kiki's calling her on the phone much.

Mike's fights, man, it was just too painful for me to watch. Within two years, he couldn't even fill an arena, and in his bout with Norris, he got a third of what he was making with us. Mike bragged how he was keeping all his money, how he the man now. Really? He still paying a manager's fee, a promoter's fee, and he netted $5,000,000 instead of $15,000,000 with Team Tyson.

You a dummy, Mike. How else I gonna say it?

He says that even after he made $20,000,000 from his rematch with Lennox Lewis, he was "fucked financially." Does that sound like a man in touch with reality?

So you wanna be Rory Holloway? You wanna be John Horne? You really want that job? When other managers came in and took over, Mike wasn't on no drugs. He didn't have no tax problem. He owned all his cars and his houses. He was making $30,000,000 a fight. Now look at him.

People underestimated what we did for Mike. This shit wasn't easy.

These guys from Magic Johnson to Spike Lee, everyone who gets involved in business with Mike, they think he gonna listen to them. Magic thought he'd help Mike, and there's no doubt he would've been a great mentor under normal circumstances.

Thing is, he wasn't the kinda guy Mike needs. The kinda client Mike is, it just wasn't gonna work. He isn't a protocol guy. You need to be able to get gritty, get down in the streets, chase him around. Magic probably thought he had the golden child, and he gonna get him on the straight and narrow. Then he realized he just took the Chucky doll into his house. "Man, I gotta get Chucky outta this place." No more than a week or two after he got involved with Mike, Magic walked away. "Take him, take him!"

You know what I mean? Like when you drop off a kid somewhere, and they call fifteen minutes later. "Come get this kid, he's bad as hell."

Mike's a guy from Brooklyn with that same gritty, gutsy mentality. He never changed who he was. He stayed in character. I couldn't stop him, I could only deter him. No one could stop him. At the end of the day, Mike Tyson gonna do what Mike Tyson do, and he will tell you to kiss his ass in a heartbeat. That's Mike.

Finkel limped him along through a miserable last few fights. You see Mike in there, pudgy, slow, outta shape, stomach as big as his ass, over two-hundred and fifty pounds. What the hell? Is there something wrong with my TV? Adjust the ratio, this ain't right. His fight against Danny Williams, it broke my heart to see him like that.

Somebody should've been arrested letting my boy fight in that condition. These sportswriters who say they all about journalistic integrity, they weren't saying nothing about it. You didn't hear them on ESPN the next morning calling Mike's people and trainers "these dumb-ass managers," which is what they called us.

And Mike's in there looking like the marshmallow man.

Shit, after what these various managers put Mike through, I don't blame him for being on drugs and drinking. I'd be drinking too.

This might not make sense to some people, but Mike is a follower, not a leader. He's that kid who just wants to be part of the gang, you know.

Years after all the troubles that sonofabitch Special Prosecutor Garrison caused us, I seen Mike run over and shake Garrison's hand on TV. Mike did the same thing with Teddy Atlas, smiling, apologizing, talking redemption. For some reason Mike just love shaking everybody's hand when the camera's rolling, but to me, it's phony as shit.

What kinda man is you, Mike? You gonna kiss the asses of these guys, but you don't say nothing to the guys who stood by you, who cared for you, who shared your pain? You let others denigrate Team Tyson like we nobody.

I just don't understand that.

When Mike got outta prison, he was still in a cage. And it wasn't long before I looked around and I'm like, "Damn, I'm trapped in here with him." That wore me down, man. I never knew what gonna happen, or when he gonna turn and snap. We did our best to tame the beast, and most of the time it worked. It was a beautiful thing. Then there's that one moment when the beast turns on you, and suddenly you are in deep shit. That's just the way it was.

One time I'm in the car, this beautiful young lady, she's hanging out with us, and Mike starts groping her. He pounces on her like a cheetah on a rabbit, his tongue down her throat. She's wincing. He didn't care. Years ago we was having fun voluntarily with the girls, and now he was a monster. He had guys bringing him women like they bringing him McDonald's. It was sad, man. You know, Kevin Sawyer, his West Coast pimp, he ended up committing suicide.

There's always a price. That way of living, it don't come free.

And it was costing me. I felt like shit. I started looking at myself in the mirror thinking, "I'm just as guilty as Mike." I was so down on myself.

Sheila would say, "Honey, I'm ready. Let's leave it all. We'll make it."

Did I get rich working for Mike? No doubt about it. But I didn't have no joint account, didn't have no personal access to his money. He was the one who signed our paychecks, and whether it was $2 in my pocket or $2,000,000, I never stopped doing what I do. As far as I was concerned, there wasn't no price he could pay that was what I was worth. I wasn't hung up on that. My health and my time, my loyalty, my friendship, my reputation, my heart, all of that is what I invested into Team Tyson.

In those days, whenever a fight was over, I didn't go to the after-parties, which was customary. I was young, rich, but I didn't go flashing my money around. You know what I did, I flew straight home. I loosened my tie, changed my shoes, and went with Sheila to eat burgers and share a shake at Fat Burgers around the corner.

I had a good life. A beautiful wife. Three wonderful kids. When all this ended, I had a sense of relief. The beast had wore me out. I was tired of chasing Mike all those years. I think he was tired of being chased. He was done with all the training and fighting. He wanted to live his own life, do his own thing, and didn't know any way to do that without crashing the train or getting rid of me.

I just wish he'd told me he wanted off. I would've gone with him. In his mind, I guess, the only way to get rid of me was to make it about business. That way things was less personal, right? He just didn't understand how deep things went with me.

I wonder if he'll ever understand.

Both Gordy and Shorty express gratitude for the opportunities you gave them, for altering their lives and their family's futures in a positive manner. Is that a mutual sentiment?

RORY: Without a doubt. They were essential to the process. Even today, I talk with them on a regular basis. Like Shorty says, it was a beautiful experience, and though we don't share the same DNA, we are brothers. Absolutely. The team still lives, and Mike is a part of that in our hearts and minds. He always will be.

It's funny how people assume I'm mad at Mike. They make negative comments about him as if that shit's supposed to make me feel better. Most times, I stop them in their tracks, because what happened between me and him is between two brothers. When my legal team advised me to take action against him, I refused. I'd rather eat shit off a stick in Times Square than participate in something like that against my brother. Not gonna happen.

We both got our stupid pride. We both blew our wads and made our mistakes.

That's a fact.

What I do know about Mike, though, is he still has that fighting spirit and he never backs down from a challenge. If I were a betting man, I would bet on him now.

PART FIVE

WILL MIKE MAKE PEACE WITH THE PAST?

"Guard your heart above all else
for it determines the course of your life."

Proverbs 4:23

CHAPTER THIRTY-SEVEN

THE MOUSE

R ory Holloway earned close to $30,000,000 in his days at the helm of Team Tyson. Mike earned ten times that amount, and still slid into bankruptcy in 2003. What about Rory's fortune? Where did it go? Here is an attempt to break it down.

He gives the lion's share to the IRS. Minus $12,250,000.

He covers the costs of houses in New York and New Jersey. Minus $5,750,000.

He invests in failed joint-ventures and a stock market that tanked. Minus $5,500,000.

He pays for fancy cars, jewelry, and fine clothes. Minus $3,750,000.

He loans out money to family and friends for household bills, hospital expenses, and business start-up capital that was never paid back. Minus $1,750,000.

He purchases airfare, lodging, and cruises for those close to him, for a decade even treating neighbors from his mother-in-law's own hi-rise. Minus $1,000,000.

Within a year of Team Tyson's dissolution, Rory was back to zero. He liquidated assets and lowered his standard of living another notch each month, accepting the reality that his business and personal relationships with Mike were through. He battled depression and health issues. His weight ballooned. As the public watched Mike decline physically over his last few fights with Shelly Finkel, Rory declined in the seclusion of a Manhattan apartment where he lived with his family.

It seemed that the beast had devoured them all.

In the end, the beast was even larger than Mike Tyson. A verse from the Book of Genesis says, "Sin

is crouching at the door . . . you must subdue and be its master." In what ways, Rory, have you subdued that beast and avoided being consumed by the past?

RORY: If I had seen all this coming, I would've been better prepared. Ain't nobody ever taught me how to handle this kinda money. I didn't have no millionaires or thousandaires or hundredaires in my family. Mike didn't have no exclusivity on being stupid with his money. The way I saw it, I was operating off money that was guaranteed, with millions more to come. These contracts was ironclad. There was a breach clause, but even that required that we get our money. The way Mike gets outta this was if he died, and the team had insurance for that.

My first million, I couldn't give it away fast enough. I got spoiled in the moment. I went out buying four or five cars. I'd come home on a Tuesday and give my wife a 10-carat diamond ring. She was like, "Why you doing this?" I'd say, "Because I can." After a fight, sometimes me and Mike'd take tens of thousands of dollars in our pockets and go on the street corners in Albany, gambling with the old guys. If we lost, we figured we giving to charity. Those cats loved us. We'd pull up in our Bentleys, our Rolls, sharing a taste of that life. I knew most of the Albany cops 'cause I grew up them guys, and they'd keep an eye on our vehicles. They loved us.

One day everything was good. Then the rug got pulled out. Only by the grace of God am I still here. Heart troubles, ulcers, and high-blood pressure. I was feeling down, paralyzed. I was a three-hundred pound hermit.

But I had plenty of time to reflect, right?

One of my regrets is, I was going so fast on the Team Tyson train that I never realized the long-term effect on my kids. Those relationships are a precious thing.

There's still some disconnect with my oldest son, Rory Jr. He grew up living with his mother, a woman I hooked up with before my days with Sheila. Things isn't turbulent or nothing. Rory Jr.'s respectful, intelligent, compassionate, and I love him to death. I can't force my way in, though. He has to let me open that door. We always included him—summers, birthdays, holidays—but he put up that barrier. He says I was selfish, never coming to his ball games, and he's right. I was sacrificing for the team, but I didn't realize I was also sacrificing my relationships. I regret that. I can't get that back. Sheila picked up the slack for all those years, but ain't nobody can take the place of a father.

I look at Michael Paris now. He's like six-foot-five. He has that gene for sports like his father and his uncles. He could've been a helluva basketball player or football player, but I didn't give him an opportunity. I was always moving, 24/7. I wasn't around to take him to Pop Warner games, Little League, high-school football, I didn't do none of that. I never got cussed out by my boys' coaches 'cause I was making too much noise. Paris, he's a smart, responsible kid, but my moving around even affected his schooling. He worked so hard to get back on track, man. So hard. And now he's given us the most beautiful grand-baby in the world. London, she's our pride and joy.

Gloria Nia, she's such a poised young woman. To this day, my daughter comes to me for advice. Since she was little, she given me cards just outta nowhere. She's my girl. I wish I'd been around more in those earlier days, but I never hear Nia or Paris complain or blame me for nothing. I blew my wad, I made some bad decisions handling my money, no real plan, but my kids don't rub that in my face. Many times, me and Sheila were off in Vegas, or Tokyo, wherever, and the kids' grandmother was with them. She played a big part, helping hold things together. They adore their Lela.

Lela's such a giving woman, such a supportive mother-in-law, and so bighearted. She just keeps giving. Her Dominican culture, it really exemplifies what family means. We always ate at the table together, and no one ate till the father sat at the head. Papi was one of these traditional guys, suave, handsome, full of *machismo*. He and Mami never learned English, but you could feel their love, their commitment. Papi was a devoted grandpa. Before he died, he handed over the head of the table to me. That was deep, man. He was so proud of me.

We made due, didn't complain. We family. That's what family does, no shame. I make sure we pay the bills, we got food on the table. We in this together. I don't walk around feeling judged. I walk around feeling love.

Some guys, they lose everything, they go through that public humiliation, and they go throw themselves off the George Washington Bridge. I had my dark moments, for real. I was broke, but I was never broken. I didn't need to hit no bottle or none of that. What I need to numb? No one should be feeling sorry for me. Money comes and goes, but I got my wife, got my kids. It's my relationships that count, and this life I built with my family is priceless.

SHEILA: During that time, it was a big shock. I was like, "Wait a minute, we're being punk'd or something. Not you, Rory, Mike wouldn't do this towards you. I know he's gonna come to you and explain." It just never happened. He pulled the rug out from under us, and it was devastating. I thought, "Mike loves us. This can't be. He knows where we stand with him, not just in the business aspect but as a family." I knew Mike before I met Rory, and he was like a brother.

The friendship Rory and Mike had was really unique, that brotherly relationship, and to see Mike toss that away was sad. I think it was cowardly, it was just very cowardly the way he went about it. There's no excuses for that, because Rory was here for him no matter what. You could see from a mile away what the intentions of Shawnee and Jackie were, and that's the direction Mike still chose to go. I love Mike, I wish him well, but I'm not real happy with him. If I bumped into him, I wonder if I'd have the guts to share my real feelings with him, to ask him why he did what he did.

You know, Rory never bashed Mike. He never sold him out. He had me destroy the sex tapes. We lit it all up. The secrets he knew, he just had so many opportunities to cash in, and he never, ever did.

There were a lot of low moments. I was really concerned about my husband. I knew he wanted to be left alone, but I was there through every bit of it. I had to reassure him many times when we saw that things weren't changing. I said, "Honey, don't worry, we're gonna get through this. We have our family. We have things we can get rid of, and that stuff means nothing. Let's just keep it moving." I know that helped, reminding him of that. We were all there, and I let him know that every day. You can't just get over it, but time can heal all wounds and help ease the pain.

You know, I was raised Catholic by my mom, my dad, but as I got older I kinda felt more connected to the Baptist church. I'm not talking about the type where they're yelling and screaming, because I can't get into that, but I love going to service and hearing the choir. I love the way they tell the story. I'm still Catholic and respect that, but I'm a strong believer in being out in nature, seeing the beauty, feeling connected. I'm like, "This is Him." That is my moment.

With this book, I'm just so glad Rory is telling his story. Years ago, I asked him to just explain himself. People knew who I was married to, and I even stopped going certain places because of all the questions and accusations. It was difficult. I just pray people will read this and give Rory a chance. I really do.

RORY: I hit the Lotto with Sheila. I'm telling you, she is the most remarkable woman in the world. She stood in my corner. She made me snap outta this, and never, ever for one second did she doubt me. She knows me. She never changed, but I seen her shed tears at the way people around us changed, the way they treated us different. That hurt her. Her frustration was never with me, but with these different things we had to deal with. She had the patience to comfort me. She just wanna see me happy.

It's incredible, man. When I'm away from her, I see couples walking by, holding hands, dressed up and going out, and I miss her.

Just last night we was texting each other. Here, I'll read this to you . . .

Rory: *"What's up, boo? How you feeling?"*

Sheila: *"I just took some Alka-Seltzer. Feeling better. We're watching a movie."*

Rory: *"I'm chilling out here with Wisdom, sitting on a bench, smoking stogies. Headed home soon."*

Sheila: *"Sounds perfect for a Friday night. Can't wait to see you."*

I took a picture with my phone and sent it to her.

Sheila: *"Baby, you look good. Keep doing what you doing. We're making a comeback. I know everything you do is for us. I love you so much."*

Rory: *"You make me a true believer that anything is possible."*

Sheila: *"You're my Superman."*

Rory: *"We have something dreams are made of, and you're my Superwoman."*

Sheila: *"Have you been drinking? You're making me watery-eyed. I'm so blessed to have you as my husband, the father of my children, and my only true boo."*

We was texting this stuff all night. That's the kinda relationship we have, and I don't take that for granted.

One thing about my community, black love is an endangered species. The statistics where I come from, it's almost impossible to find a successful marriage. And as Mike's friend and manager, I was surrounded by beautiful woman every day. I was on every continent, all these countries, and not one time did I cheat on my wife. She had her insecurities early on, she got jealous, but we never slept in a different room. We never had time-out from each other. No other women called to tell her what they doing with her man. Sheila lets me know that I'm the man of the house, but she wouldn't never put up with that shit 'cause she got too much respect for herself.

To this day, we have an incredible, intimate, solid marriage. That's success, and I take pride in that.

Sheila, she's so nurturing to our kids. She's just the ultimate mom. She can't stop. My son's in his twenties, and she still going in to clean his room and wash his clothes. I'm like, "When you gonna let him grow up?" Next, she's doing it for our daughter. Our kids're in school, got jobs, and she just wants to help. She's in there rubbing her mom's back, rubbing her feet. She up and down to the store to fetch stuff for her mother. She just never stops.

With the Mike situation, she loved him to death but she knows how wrong he did me. She never sat around and mentioned what we used to have, the million-dollar homes, the cars, the fur coats, the jewelry. It wasn't about material things. It wasn't about that. She went and sold one of her rings when things got tight, and that broke me down, but she wasn't tripping about it.

I love her so much. She was hard as a rock, a gladiator, tougher than any man. She like this perfect female warrior in a movie or something. She didn't waver.

We happy for the memories, we thankful for the fun times, but that stuff in the past ain't what's important. God gives everyone opportunities, and the question is, are you ready? You gonna sleep through it or seize the moment?

Sometimes I get a little stir-crazy, the walls start closing in. What do I do? I come out at night like a little mouse, when everybody else asleep. I get a few minutes to myself. Maybe I just sit and think. Maybe I open my laptop and start brainstorming. My mind, it's always racing, coming up with ideas for the future, ways to help these young guys coming outta high school and college. Sports is in my blood, and even though I'm older now, there's things I can still do, you know. Ways I can apply the lessons that life throws at you.

I know God ain't gonna let me go through more than I can handle. God is good, and I know He got my back.

Listen, Sheila and me, we don't live in the past. We live in the future.

Our best times are still ahead, we believe that.

CHAPTER THIRTY-EIGHT

THE PHOENIX

Cus D'Amato had that demeanor typified in so many boxing movies, the tough old man who dispenses words of wisdom in raspy tones. Think Burgess Meredith as Mickey, the trainer in the first *Rocky* film.

"A certain amount of pain and suffering is good," Cus said, "because it makes a person think they've learned." He added later, from his own experiences with old age, "I believe nature's a lot smarter than anyone thinks. During the course of a man's life, he develops a lot of pleasures and people he cares about. Then nature takes them away one by one . . . preparing you for death . . . I believe a person dies when he no longer wants to live. He finds a convenient disease, just like a fighter when he no longer wants to fight finds a convenient corner to lie down in. It's like boxing. It's all psychological."

You are in your fifties now. Are you looking for a "convenient corner to lie down in," or do you believe your experiences have taught you anything worth sharing?

RORY: I really believe I could step into rookie NFL camps, rookie NBA camps, and teach these guys a story. Every kid's got demons to deal with. Don't tell me that shit ain't true. Every kid who once poor, who once in abject poverty, you hand him a seven-figure check and the demons come out. You got all these zeros going into your bank account, nobody can tell you nothing, and you become your own boss.

Then one day you run out on the court, your knee snaps, or you out on the field and something happens. That's reality. That shit snatched out from under you.

Now we find out what you made of.

It don't take all this insight. Feel the ground rumbling, and you see the train coming at these young athletes—the money, the fame, the temptations. Jameis Winston, quarterback at Florida State, he's this Heisman Trophy winner and high-profile player. What's his dad saying in the news? Says his son needs a full-time handler.

That was me, a handler, been there in that cage.

"Hey, man," I'd say to these athletes, "let me tell you what's gonna happen. Let me speak from my flaws and mistakes." One of them might look at me like, "How you gonna give me a Bible on finance when you didn't even save your own money?"

Good question, right? Well, I can tell you how to save yours, so you don't do what I did wrong. You gotta think ahead. I was thinking this shit ain't never gonna stop, or that I could put it off till another time. No, you gotta be thinking about today, about tomorrow, about your family next week. You gotta be thinking about worst-case scenario at all times. In times of peace, prepare for war.

At the same time, don't let anything monetary define who you are. Listen, one day you could be rich, one day you could be poor. It's all in God's hands at the end of the day. Do you actually need to be rich to make you happy, to define you as a man or woman? No, I was able to survive 'cause money don't define me. Mike didn't do nothing to me. If I had to do it all over . . . Well, I'm secure in who I am. I sleep good at night.

Hopefully, man, I can change something. I loved talking to these kids when I was young. I excelled at it. Maybe that was part of my connection with Mike.

Whether it's the kids in my neighborhood or at Berkshire Farms, my daughter's boyfriend, it ain't about me being cool but about having real conversations with them.

That's my desire, to use ProMax Productions as a vehicle for that. ProMax is a company I'm involved with, and we want it to be the Google of sports, the place where you connect with your favorite athletes, chat with your sports buddies, get all your updates and info, watch exclusive video of LeBron in training, follow an exciting young fighter in the gym, or debate the ref's call in last night's game. It's a company I been dreaming up for years, and it's all coming together. We got a very experienced guy named Robert sitting as CEO, and Andre Prieto's my finance guy.

Andre, man, he just brings this energy. I met him years ago during a business deal. He'd heard about me and figured I was a thief. He started asking me these tough questions about my time with Mike, and he pulled this stuff outta me. He let me get so much off my chest, stuff I didn't wanna burden Sheila with. Andre's the one who convinced me to meet with you about this book. I almost pulled out a coupla times. It's painful dredging up some of this stuff but it's good, man. It's good.

Listen, a number of years ago, my son come home from school one day. He agitated. He says these kids in the hall telling him how his dad is a crook, his dad stole Mike Tyson's money. That's still the word on the streets, and I'll be dealing with that till the day I die. But now my sons and my daughter, they can look at the evidence, hear all the sides, and decide for themselves, not just what some kid in the hallway say. Whether people read this or believe this, that's up to them.

I don't talk about this much, 'cause my spiritual beliefs is personal, but I just waited for God to give me a word, for Him to tell me what to do. I kept saying to myself, "He gonna make it right on my behalf." Somehow, the truth always rises to the top, and I knew no matter how much it seemed like it was buried, it was gonna come out bit by bit.

Am I gonna sit here and tell you I ain't thinking about my company? Absolutely not. I hope this leads to good things. I want ProMax to reach out to these young men and women, to help them develop their careers—boxing, basketball, football, baseball, soccer, all of it. I wanna help with the overall health and wealth of these athletes.

See, I'm an advocate for change, especially in boxing. It's a wonderful sport, and it creates incredible opportunities for these young fighters. A lot of times they're uneducated, not well-spoken, haven't went to school. But they are hardworking people who put their bodies through tremendous stress, both mentally and physically. I wanna see safeguards put in place, insurance, equal pay-structures. The odds are against them right from the beginning, and it's a very small window of opportunity. I wanna teach these cats how to make the most of that opportunity. The risk should be worth the reward. Right now it's the opposite.

My story can help these athletes tremendously. I've seen the pitfalls, the ups and downs. I can tell them not to go down that street. That's the wrong street, man. I been down that one. Team Tyson was a microcosm of what happens when you lose your focus, when you let other things get in the way. It's a cautionary tale, and I thank God that Mike's still alive to talk about it.

In the end, what really makes you rich? When all the money is gone, the fame is gone, the trappings is gone, all you got is your story.

And my story is what makes me rich.

How do you think Mike will react to the things you've shared during this process?

RORY: The glaring truth is here in the open, and you just gotta put the pieces together. It's simple really, we just filling in the blanks. I don't carry no guilt. When everything happened with Team Tyson, I didn't have to turn to no vices, no drugs. I knew a hundred-and-ten percent that I was the best friend I could be to Mike.

Could I have done something better to protect him?

Could I have kept a closer eye on his resources?

Could I have guarded him from the cesspool?

I've asked myself those questions, and I gotta think the answer is yes. I used to beat myself up over that. But never once did I take something from him. That's a no-no. He knows I never did anything intentionally, purposefully, or willfully to harm him. We built a great team, and there is no question that I used him, but I never misused him.

You gotta understand, I have so much admiration for Mike's strength. He showed me compassion. He was a sweet guy, a kind guy, a giving guy. I was mimicking him. He was a good cat. He did what he had to do at the time, I understand that.

Mike's also known for his honesty, right? Well, he cut me off without knowing the truth, just too prideful to go back and find out for himself. Pride can be a good thing, but stupid pride trips you up, and pride triggered by lies is dangerous. Eventually all the lies, all the deceit, it all comes crumbling down. Sometimes it takes longer than others, but it's coming down. Listen, this book gonna liberate Mike, 'cause we sweeping everything from under the rug out into the open. I'm not no thief, no hanger-on, no ball-and-chain.

One thing I refuse to do is to go through somebody else to talk to Mike. Words and messages got twisted when I tried that. I was naive enough to think the truth could be conveyed that way. If Mike and me gonna work things out, it's gonna be with each other. He's the one who called me twenty times a day, since 1982, and he's the one I really need to hear from, my boy, my ace-boom-cool. To this day, I'm at the same place where we used to hang out all those years together. He knows where to find me. He can come to me like a man.

You know, if a friendship rises up again outta these ashes, I'm happy with that. Let the Phoenix rise. But my first priority is my legacy and the truth. Sometimes the truth hurts, but the truth shall set you free.

So what you wanna hear from me, Mike? You want me to say I'm guilty? You want me to stand up and confess. Okay, I'll do that.

I'm guilty . . . of influencing you to take a $73,000,000 signing bonus.

I'm guilty . . . of making you sign a contract for a guaranteed $300,000,000.

I'm guilty . . . of taking ten percent when most managers take thirty-three percent.

I'm guilty . . . of filing a lawsuit against Don King for the money he took from you.

I'm guilty . . . of being overprotective and keeping the drugs away from you.

Like I said, Mike, I'm guilty. But don't charge me for my loyalty, friendship, and do not charge my heart. Don't do that. I wasn't the problem. I was the solution. Even after all we been through, I can look you in the eye and tell you that ain't nobody got the heart for you that I do.

THE SPIDER

May 2014. Dunedin, Florida. Palm fronds are blowing, the sun is sparkling on the Gulf of Mexico, and I am a spider in a corner of the room.

Go with me here. I'll explain in a moment.

The World Wide Web has transformed the way we process information. The strands reach through optic fibers and around satellites, from third-world slums to posh penthouses. Each day, the fabric of the Internet ties together business transactions and social interaction.

When a tasty byte of info comes along and gets stuck in the web, it sends reverberations around the world. News outlets rush in for the kill. Bloggers' fingers start typing. Facebook moms, YouTube kids, and ESPN fanatics jostle for a taste of the latest morsel.

Looking back at the 1990s, it is difficult to fathom how the public got its information. Cellphones were a luxury, available mostly to the rich. The Internet was a functioning system but not yet a global phenomenon. Twitter and tweets were things you heard in a bird sanctuary—and even today, there are a fair number of loony birds tweeting away. All that to say, the news poured through a narrow funnel, and average citizens bathed in that singular stream.

Before the Internet, a sports commentator such as Howard Cosell could build an entire career on his coverage of a star such as Muhammad Ali. The words of one or two journalists could flood millions of readers' minds—yes, people back then read newspapers to get their daily news— and if a story was diluted or polluted, there were few who could refute it. The press told us what to think, and we, the people, had no easy means of talking back.

Imagine if we had a voice in the early 1990s. Imagine if social media could have served as a pressure-release valve during Watts, or the reactions to the O.J. Simpson trial.

Or the demise of Team Tyson.

So let me be the spider here. Let me play Charlotte, if you will, weaving a few final words, pleading for the life of a pig as in the E.B. White classic, *Charlotte's Web*.

During the 1980s and 1990s, a cluster of sportswriters rode Mike Tyson's shoulders to the pinnacle of their profession, and when their little piglet became a hog and wandered off, they were quick to place blame. They raised valid questions, but followed them with assumptions that were often patchwork and contradictory.

So be it. The public hungered for answers, and the media's business is feeding those hungry mouths, whether with junk food or hearty, healthy meals. As Sam Sheridan points out in *A Fighter's Heart*, "The fight fans and writers . . . are always the smartest guys in the room . . . and they form opinions based on misunderstandings and hearsay and 'facts' heard from other writers and commentators. The truth is that they are easily swayed."

Mike still needs help, still needs saving. Despite previous cesspool-wallowings, he deserves every shot at happiness in his marriage and career.

He's "some pig," and I truly wish him well.

As for Mr. Holloway, most boxing fans still believe him to be a lowlife and a leech. That was my own assumption, before I spent a year studying the public record and listening to personal testimony. I weighed the views of Mike Tyson, Robin Givens, Jose Torres, J. Gregory Garrison, and numerous others. Thanks to my father, who instilled in me both an appreciation for sports and for the truth, I was compelled to scour countless newspaper articles, magazines, blogs, college theses, legal documents, and books. I made calls.

For my name to be attached to this project, I had to do my due diligence and be convinced these words were as accurate as possible.

Is Rory blameless? Absolutely not.

Were the accusations against him justified? I no longer believe so.

While journalists and nonfiction authors pride themselves on their objectivity, that very notion is subjective. Who decides which stories are newsworthy? Why do we have both the conservative press and the liberal press? Or a Catholic periodical and an evangelical magazine? Yes, they appeal to different audiences, but even in filtering news for your particular audience, you surrender something of your objectivity.

So I am going to say it. I'll just put it out there . . .

I now call Rory Holloway a friend.

Go ahead, call me Charlotte. If you like, call me by the full name divulged in the book: Charlotte A. Cavatica. Call me what you will, but I have gathered input from all sides, examined it for myself, and come to an informed decision. Rory's testimony matches up with my research. In conclusion, I am convinced he was a flawed yet dedicated team manager, trustworthy to the bitter end.

Whether or not you agree with these conclusions, I thank you for hearing me out. That is more opportunity than Team Tyson was given in their day.

Come to your own conclusions. Blog and announce them to the world.

Weave your own "terrific" viewpoint.

As E.B. White tells us on the final page of his classic, "It is not often that someone comes along who is a true friend and a good writer. Charlotte was both."

I can only hope I live up to that name.

PROFESSIONAL FIGHT RECORD
1985

Date	Opponent	Location	Result	Mgrs./Trainers
Mar.	Hector Mercedes	Albany, NY	TKO/Rd 1	Cayton/D'Amato/ Jacobs/Rooney
April	Trent Singleton	Albany, NY	TKO/Rd 1	Cayton/D'Amato/ Jacobs/Rooney
May	Don Halpern	Albany, NY	KO/Rd 4	Cayton/D'Amato/ Jacobs/Rooney
June	Rick Spain	Atlantic City, NJ	KO/Rd 1	Cayton/D'Amato/ Jacobs/Rooney
July	John Alderson	Atlantic City, NJ	TKO/Rd 1	Cayton/D'Amato/ Jacobs/Rooney
July	Larry Sims	Poughkeepsie, NY	KO/Rd 3	Cayton/D'Amato/ Jacobs/Rooney
Aug.	Lorenzo Canady	Atlantic City, NJ	TKO/Rd 1	Cayton/D'Amato/ Jacobs/Rooney
Sept.	Michael Johnson	Atlantic City, NJ	KO/Rd 1	Cayton/D'Amato/ Jacobs/Rooney
Oct.	Donnie Long	Atlantic City, NJ	KO/Rd 1	Cayton/D'Amato/ Jacobs/Rooney
Oct.	Robert Colay	Atlantic City, NJ	KO/Rd 1	Cayton/D'Amato/ Jacobs/Rooney
Nov.	Sterling Benjamin	Latham, NY	TKO/Rd 1	Cayton/D'Amato/ Jacobs/Rooney
Nov.	Eddie Richardson	Houston, TX	TKO/Rd 1	Cayton/Jacobs/ Rooney
Nov.	Conroy Nelson	Latham, NY	KO/Rd2	Cayton/Jacobs/ Rooney
Dec.	Sammy Scaff	New York, NY	KO/Rd 1	Cayton/Jacobs/ Rooney
Dec.	Mark Young	Latham, NY	KO/Rd 1	Cayton/Jacobs/ Rooney

1986

Date	Opponent	Location	Result	Mgrs./Trainers
Jan.	Dave Jaco	Albany, NY	TKO/Rd 1	Cayton/Jacobs/ Rooney
Jan.	Mike Jamison	Atlantic City, NJ	TKO/Rd 5	Cayton/Jacobs/ Rooney
Feb.	Jesse Ferguson	Troy, NY	TKO/Rd 6	Cayton/Jacobs/ Rooney
March	Steve Zouski	Uniondale, NY	KO/Rd 3	Cayton/Jacobs/ Rooney
May	James Tillis	Glen Falls, TX	Win/Rd 10	Cayton/Jacobs/ Rooney
May	Mitch Green	New York, NY	Win/Rd 10	Cayton/Jacobs/ Rooney
June	Reggie Gross	New York, NY	TKO/Rd 1	Cayton/Jacobs/ Rooney
June	William Hosea	Troy, NY	KO/Rd 1	Cayton/Jacobs/ Rooney
July	Lorenzo Boyd	Swan Lake, NY	KO/Rd 2	Cayton/Jacobs/ Rooney

July	Marvis Frazier	Glen Falls, NY	KO/Rd 1	Cayton/Jacobs/ Rooney
Aug.	José Ribalta	Atlantic City, NJ	TKO/Rd 10	Cayton/Jacobs/ Rooney
Sept.	Alfonzo Ratliff	Las Vegas, NV	KO/Rd 2	Cayton/Jacobs/ Rooney
Nov.	Trevor Berbick	Las Vegas, NV	TKO/Rd 2	Cayton/Jacobs/ Rooney

1987

Date	Opponent	Location	Result	Mgrs./Trainers
March	James Smith	Las Vegas, NV	Win/Rd 12	Cayton/Jacobs/ Rooney
May	Pinklon Thomas	Las Vegas, NV	TKO/Rd 6	Cayton/Jacobs/ Rooney
Aug.	Tony Tucker	Las Vegas, NV	Win/Rd 12	Cayton/Jacobs/ Rooney
Oct.	Tyrell Biggs	Las Vegas, NV	TKO/Rd 7	Cayton/Jacobs/ Rooney

1988

Date	Opponent	Location	Result	Mgrs./Trainers
Jan.	Larry Holmes	Atlantic City, NJ	TKO/Rd 4	Cayton/Jacobs/ Rooney
March	Tony Tubbs	Tokyo, Japan	TKO/Rd 2	Cayton/Jacobs/ Rooney
June	Michael Spinks	Atlantic City, NJ	KO/Rd 1	Cayton/Jacobs/ Rooney

1989

Date	Opponent	Location	Result	Mgrs./Trainers
Feb.	Frank Bruno	Las Vegas, NV	TKO/Rd 5	Holloway/Horne/ Rooney
July	Tony Tucker	Atlantic City, NJ	TKO/Rd 1	Holloway/Horne/ Rooney

1990

Date	Opponent	Location	Result	Mgrs./Trainers
Feb.	Buster Douglas	Tokyo, Japan	Loss/Rd 10	Holloway/Horne/ Snowell/Bright
June	Henry Tillman	Las Vegas, NV	KO/Rd 1	Holloway/Horne/ Snowell/Bright
Dec.	Alex Stewart	Atlantic City, NJ	TKO/Rd 1	Holloway/ Horne/ Giachetti/ Bright

1991

Date	Opponent	Location	Result	Mgrs./Trainers
Feb.	Donovan Ruddock	Las Vegas, NV	TKO/Rd 7	Holloway/ Horne/ McKinley/ Bright
Nov.	Donovan Ruddock	Las Vegas, NV	Win/Rd 12	Holloway/ Horne/ McKinley/ Bright

1995

Date	Opponent	Location	Result	Mgrs./Trainers
June	Peter McNeeley	Las Vegas, NV	Win/Rd 1	Holloway/ Horne/ McKinley/ Bright
Dec.	Buster Mathis, Jr.	Philadelphia, PA	KO/Rd 3	Holloway/ Horne/ McKinley/ Bright

1996

Date	Opponent	Location	Result	Mgrs./Trainers
March	Frank Bruno	Las Vegas, NV	TKO/Rd 3	Holloway/ Horne/ McKinley/ Bright
Sept.	Bruce Seldon	Las Vegas, NV	KO/Rd 1	Holloway/ Horne/ McKinley/ Bright
Nov.	Evander Holyfield	Las Vegas, NV	Loss/Rd 11	Holloway/ Horne/ McKinley/ Bright

1997

Date	Opponent	Location	Result	Mgrs./Trainers
June	Evander Holyfield	Las Vegas, NV	Loss/Rd 3	Holloway/ Horne/ Giachetti

1999

Date	Opponent	Location	Result	Mgrs./Trainers
Oct.	Francois Botha	Las Vegas, NV	KO/Rd 5	Finkel/Brooks
Jan.	Orlin Norris	Las Vegas, NV	NC/Rd 1	Finkel/Brooks

2000

Date	Opponent	Location	Result	Mgrs./Trainers
Jan.	Julius Francis	Manchester, ENG	TKO/Rd 2	Finkel/Brooks
June	Lou Savarese	Glasgow, SCOT	TKO/Rd 1	Finkel/Brooks
Oct.	Andrew Golota	Auburn Hills, MI	NC/Rd 3	Finkel/Shields

2001-2005

Date	Opponent	Location	Result	Mgrs./Trainers
Oct. '01	Brian Nielsen	Copenhagen, DEN	RTD Win/Rd 7	Finkel/Brooks
Jun '02	Lennox Lewis	Memphis, TN	KO Loss/Rd 8	Finkel/Fenech
Feb. '03	Clifford Etienne	Memphis, TN	KO/Rd 1	Finkel/Fenech
July '04	Danny Williams	Louisville, KY	TKO Loss/Rd 4	Finkel/Fenech
Jun '05	Kevin McBride	Washington, DC	TKO Loss/Rd 6	Finkel/Fenech

BIBLIOGRAPHY

Berger, Phil. *Blood Season, Mike Tyson and the World of Boxing.* New York: Four Walls Eight Windows, 1996.

Dundee, Angelo and Sugar, Bert. *My View from the Corner: A Life in Boxing.* New York: McGraw-Hill, 2009.

Evans, Gavin. *Kings of the Ring, The History of Heavyweight Boxing.* London: Orion Publishing Company, 2008.

Garrison, J. Gregory and Roberts, Randy. *Heavy Justice: The Trial of Mike Tyson.* Fayetteville: University of Arkansas Press, 2000.

Givens, Robin. *Grace Will Lead Me Home.* New York: Miramax Books, 2007.

Hauser, Thomas. *Muhammad Ali: His Life and Times.* New York: Simon & Schuster, 1992

Heinz, W.C. and Ward, Nathan (editors). *The Total Sports Illustrated Book of Boxing.* Kingston: Total/Sports Illustrated, 1999.

Heller, Peter. *Bad Intentions: The Mike Tyson Story.* Cambridge: Da Capo Press, 1995.

Hoffer, Richard. *A Savage Business: The Comeback and Comedown of Mike Tyson.* New York: Simon & Schuster, 1998.

Kimball, George and Schulian, John (editors). *At the Fights: American Writers on Boxing.* New York: Library of America, 2012.

Layden, Joe. *The Last Great Fight: The Extraordinary Tale of Two Men and How One Fight Changed Their Lives Forever.* New York: Macmillan, 2007.

O'Connor, Daniel (editor). *Iron Mike: A Mike Tyson Reader.* Cambridge: Da Capo Press, 2002.

Sheridan, Sam. *A Fighter's Heart: One Man's Journey through the World of Fighting.* New York: Grove Press, 2008.

Tyson, Mike and Sloman, Larry. *Undisputed Truth.* New York: Blue Rider Press, 2013.

White, E.B. *Charlotte's Web.* New York: Harper & Brothers, 1952.

APPENDIX

If you would like to explore further:

Upcoming Team Tyson Documentary

Saylors Brothers Entertainment will soon enter the production phase of a film project documenting the untold story of Team Tyson. It will be submitted for consideration at major film festivals and marketed toward international theatrical release.

The Saylors Brothers have an extensive filmography in advertising, documentaries, and sports pieces. They directed and produced Red Bull's TV series, *Game-Breakers*. Their work has been featured in the *Los Angeles Times*, *New York Times*, *Time*, *Variety*, and numerous others. Their 2014 documentary, *Veil of Tears*, highlighted social issues and mistreatment of women in modern India.

Website: SaylorsBrothers.com

ProMax Productions

ProMax Productions, LLC
1221 Brickell Avenue, Suite 900
Miami, FL 33131

Website: ProMaxPro.com
Email: info@ProMax.com

Eric Wilson

Website: WilsonWriter.com
Email: EricWilsonAuthor@gmail.com

Agent: Jonathan Clements
Wheelhouse Literary Agency
jonathan@WheelhouseLiterary.com

Made in the USA
Lexington, KY
03 May 2015